THE ARAB WORLD
AN
ILLUSTRATED
HISTORY

ILLUSTRATED HISTORIES FROM HIPPOCRENE

THE ARAB WORLD

AN ILLUSTRATED HISTORY

KIRK H. SOWELL

Hippocrene Books, Inc.
New York

© 2004 Kirk H. Sowell

ISBN 0-7818-0990-8

For information, address:
   Hippocrene Books, Inc.
   171 Madison Avenue
   New York, NY 10016
   www.hippocrenebooks.com

Cataloging-in-Publication data available from the Library of Congress.

Printed in the United States of America.

To the memory of someone whose life
exemplified verities
that do not change with time:

My late grandmother, Lorene Sowell
(April 19, 1928–September 8, 2003)

She read to me my first book of history when I was six,
and I haven't stopped reading them since.

Contents

Acknowledgments

I would like to thank first and foremost the Center for Middle Eastern Studies at the University of Texas at Austin (my alma mater), and especially the center's graphic artist, Diane Watts, without whose aid the "illustrated" element of this history would have been impossible, or at least vastly more difficult. All of the photos and drawings found in this book were taken from the center's slide collection. The individual photographers to whom I owe credit include Ron Baker, Vincent Cantarino, Martha Diase, Robert Fernea, Christy Gish, Ann Grabhorn-Friday, J. J. Hobbs, J. A. Miller, Christopher Rose, Diane Watts, Caroline Williams, and John A. Williams. The drawings were done by the illustrious Scottish traveler and artist David Roberts (1796–1864). First published in a six-volume series of lithographs on Egypt, Nubia, and the Holy Land, reproductions of his drawings are now sold all over the world.

My editor, Anne Kemper, is another indispensable person who deserves credit for more things than I have space to explain. It was at her initiative that a project like this was first proposed, and her extensive revisions greatly improved upon the original product.

The historical maps I have used with permission of the University of Washington Press. They originally appeared in *A Near East Studies Handbook* by Jere Bacharach, published in 1977. The modern maps were purchased from the United States Government or were taken from the public domain.

Finally, I would like to thank my cousin Jeremy Sowell, who was the only person who read the entire manuscript without getting paid for it. Even after I had been through several revisions, he still managed to find a few errors. Naturally, I alone bear responsibility for any that may remain.

Note on Transliteration

Writing a book containing a large number of names and terms from a language that does not use the Latin script poses the problem of transliteration. Arabic contains a number of letters and sounds not found in the English language, and, moreover, there is no standardized romanization for most names and terms. In general, I have transliterated words in order to approximate as closely as possible their sound in Arabic. Thus I use *Quran* instead of *Koran*, *Shi'a* instead of *Shi'ite* (or *Shia* or *Shiite*), *Muhammad* instead of *Mohammed*, and so on.

I have made a small number of exceptions to this general rule where I felt literalism in transliteration was impeding comprehension. Thus, in Arabic there are certain "sun letters" in which the first consonant is doubled when preceded by the definite article ("al-"), but I have omitted this practice because it is nonsensical if one does not know Arabic. Thus, the name of the greatest of the Abbasid caliphs is spelled *Harun al-Rashid* and not *Harun ar-Rashid*. Likewise, I have used "Sa'ud" prior to 1932 and "Saudi" afterward, even though their roots are spelled the same in Arabic, because the latter term denotes nationality and the former does not. For similar reasons, I have adopted the practice of referring to "the Al-Sa'ud," in order to make clear that I am speaking of the tribe, since there were thousands of people who had "Sa'ud" attached to their name (in Arabic "the Al-Sa'ud" would literally mean "the *the* Sa'ud").

Preface

The events of recent times have demonstrated a greater need for the public to be informed about the Arab world. Both the nature of the modern economy, in particular its dependence on petroleum, and the "consciousness" globalization fostered by advances in communications and transportation have made the Arab world and the West in many ways inseparable. Whether this is positive or negative is beside the point. A greater understanding of the "other" is now an imperative. Whether one is interested in politics, religion, business, economics, or simply has a traveler's curiosity, this book is meant to provide an introduction to that other part of the world.

Today the differentials of wealth, power, and development between the Arab world and the West are vast, and it is a central goal of this book to show that it was not always this way, and to attempt to explain why. For a thousand years after the rise of Islam in the seventh century, a series of Islamic empires, some Arab and others not, were central to the international political and socio-economic order. At the same time, by almost any cultural, economic, intellectual, or political measure, the Arab world was at least the equal, and often the better, of Western civilization. Due to a variety of trends, which took centuries to develop, that relationship changed greatly, and is characterized by tension, conflict, and mutual misunderstanding.

Those readers not familiar with Islam or the Arab world easily can find the vast array of new terms and concepts bewildering. For this reason a glossary of key terms has been placed near the end of the book. Readers are encouraged to reference it regularly when needed.

KIRK H. SOWELL
September 15, 2003

CHAPTER I

The Arabs in Antiquity

In our quest to understand the Arab world, the first questions one must answer are the basic ones: who are the Arabs, and where did they come from? In antiquity there was no single characteristic that could be used to describe them. Language alone would not suffice because many "Arabians" did not speak Arabic. The same is true of religion (most were polytheistic, some Christian, some Jewish), culture (some were Hellenized and/or Romanized), political allegiance (most were independent, some supported Rome, others Persia), or mode of living (some were nomadic, others settled). Since not choosing a definition is not an option open to a writer of history, the geographical definition adopted by Eratosthenes of Cyrene, chief librarian of Ptolemaic Egypt, will suffice for our purposes here:

> The northern side is formed by the above-mentioned [Syrian] desert, the eastern by the Persian Gulf, the western by the Arabian Gulf, and the southern by the great sea that lies outside both gulfs.[1]

Thus, the "Arabs" are those who inhabited the Arabian Peninsula and the border regions of the Levant (modern Syria, Jordan, Lebanon, and part of Iraq).

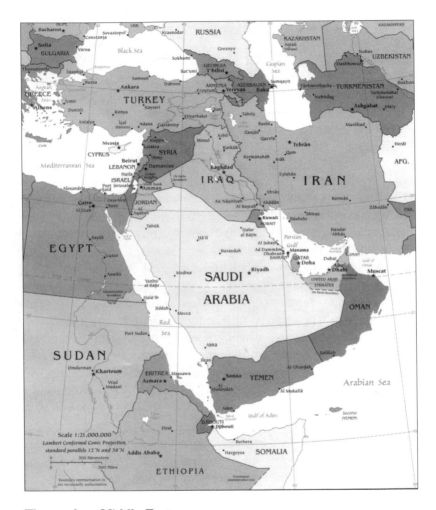

The modern Middle East.

Courtesy of the U.S. Government, Central Intelligence Agency.

Origins in the Ancient Near East

Linguistic anthropology may provide the most accurate method of analyzing the origins of peoples during the transition from the prehistorical to the historical age, as well as assessing their relationship to one another. Since Arabic is a Semitic language, the origin of the Arabs must be figured in relation to other Semites of antiquity.

The oldest civilization in close proximity to Arabia was a region today known as Mesopotamia. The earliest of the Mesopotamian peoples were the Sumerians, located in what is now southern Iraq, whose distinctive culture was fully developed by the late fourth millennium B.C. The next to clearly develop were the Akkadians farther up the Tigris-Euphrates region in central Iraq, around 2400 B.C., and their origin holds the key to that of the Arabs, for Akkadian was the first known written Semitic language. A Mesopotamian script called Cuneiform was the first recognizably Arabian script outside of Arabia proper.[2]

By the first millennium B.C., two distinct categories of Arabian languages can be identified, Southern Arabian and Northern Arabian. It is from the latter that three languages central to much of human history arose: Hebrew, Aramaic, and Arabic. While Hebrew was the language of the ancient Israelites, Aramaic came to prominence during the Persian period (from the mid-sixth century B.C. to Alexander's conquest in 334 B.C.), and remained predominate in the Levant for over a thousand years. Aramaic adopted its script from Phoenician (which is also the base of the Greek script).[3]

During the same time period, Arabic took several forms that have been preserved for us through thousands of inscriptions in northern Arabia. After the Aramaic script of the Levantine Nabataeans became widespread, at some point in the early centuries of the Christian era the Arabs adopted the script for their own language. The adaptation of this script to the sounds of Arabic produced what might be referred to as "Old Arabic," which in turn developed into Classical Arabic, the dominance of which was made comprehensive by its use in the Quran and the subsequent rise of Islam.[4]

The earliest extant physical record of significant permanent settlement in Arabia concerns the land of Dilmun, which comprised what is now Kuwait, Bahrain, Qatar, and the nearby areas of Saudi Arabia. Most of what we know of Dilmun comes from the copious records of ancient Mesopotamia. The evidence indicates a great degree of interaction for the purposes of trade. Aside from being the source of a great many commodities, in particular copper, Dilmun merchants functioned as proto-"import-export" agents between the lands of Mesopotamia and more distant trading areas, such as Africa and the Indus Valley.[5]

The Mesopotamia-Dilmun connection reaches so deep into antiquity that the latter became central to the former's creation story. It is recorded that after the deluge the gods settled Ziusudra, the Sumerian Noah (Assyrian *Utnapishtim*),[6] in Dilmun.[7] In the saga of Enki and Ninhursag, Dilmun is described as previously existing in a paradisiacal state in which the lion and wolf did not kill, pains and diseases did not exist, and people did not grow old.[8] There was also a strong link between Sumerians and Semites generally. Of the twenty-two kings identified in the Sumerian King List for the dynasty of Kish, twelve have names or nicknames of Semitic origin.[9] Mesopotamians and Semites also shared some of the same deities; Inanna, goddess of carnal love for the former, was known as Ishtar among the latter.[10]

Eventually Dilmun entered a period of decline. Its trade-dependent economy was hit hard by a long-term commercial decline of the Indus Valley, the disintegration of Hammurabi's rule in 1750 B.C., and the discovery of alternative sources of copper. With economic weakness came political subservience under the Kassites, who ruled Mesopotamia from 1595–1158 B.C. Kassite documents record the affairs of appointed governors of Dilmun. They complain extensively of problems controlling the inhabitants as well as the effects of material decay and instability. The details of these crises and their resolution remain unknown.[11]

Somewhat more evidence exists for the region that is now Yemen and south-central Saudi Arabia, as there are literally thousands of inscriptions that have survived. Unfortunately, they cannot be dated with any precision until the first century A.D. It appears that from a relatively early date the south Arabian peoples were fragmented into cult communities each ruled over by a king (*mlk*, the same root as in modern Arabic), typically with its own sanctuary.[12] The first people of southern Arabia to make their mark on history were the Sabaeans. They are first mentioned in the Bible, where the Queen of Saba' (Sheba) visits Solomon (I Kings 10).[13] The Sabaeans

4

can be identified primarily by their common devotion to the god Almaqah. They were the "progeny of Almaqah" and were bound together by a common ruler and system of rituals, festivals, and sanctuaries. There are also inscriptions which refer to "Saba' and the union," a larger federation of south Arabian peoples bound together by a common interest in protecting their holy sites, defending against raids, and conducting irrigation projects.[14]

The most oft-mentioned ruler of Saba' was one Karib'il Watar, son of Dhamar'ali. An ancient text ascribes to him the achievement of dominance in southern Arabia for Saba', and control over the southern incense routes. A later text describes his building of fortifications, colonies, and irrigation works.[15]

The earliest inhabitants of the northern Arabian/Syrian desert were practitioners of nomadic pastoralism.[16] Pastoralists make their livelihood through the raising of animals, and can be either settled or nomadic. Given the climate, Arabian pastoralists were forced to resort to nomadism, moving from place to place in search of nourishment. It is among these nomads that we find the earliest contemporary reference to a person called an "Arab." In 853 B.C. an inscription hails the victory of the Assyrians over a coalition that included "Gindibu the Arab," who reportedly had a thousand camels at his disposal.[17] When the Assyrian ruler Tiglath-pileser III (744–727 B.C.) routed Shamsi, "queen of the Arabs," his booty included 1,000 people, 30,000 camels, 20,000 cattle, and 5,000 bags of spices.[18] These quantities illustrate the Arabs' centrality to the aromatics trade at this early date.

The Assyrian ruler Sargon II (721–705 B.C.) seems to have initiated the policy of making Arab tribes satellites of his empire, a practice that would continue from both east and west until the rise of Islam thirteen centuries later. Sargon would select certain tribal chiefs for appointments to official positions that carried both titles and financial rewards. They in turn would have the obligation to both protect the settled lands from nomads, and, after the rise of Rome, to function as a buffer between, and an auxiliary to, the two empires.[19]

Of particular interest during this formative period are the Qaderite Arabs. Qader entered history on the side of an ill-considered Babylonian revolt against Assyrian rule. Apparently one Uaite, the son of the "King of Arabia," was able to throw off Assyrian rule temporarily and convince the Arabs to join him. It was a bitter war, "waged against elusive enemies fighting bravely and vanishing in a dreadful desert 'where parching thirst is at home, and there are not even birds in the sky.'"[20] After the revolt was put down, first Sennacherib (704–681 B.C.) and then Assurbanipal (668–627 B.C.) punished the Qader with extreme severity. The latter boasted that he enslaved so many men and women that they (along with their "donkeys, camels, cattle, and flocks") filled "my whole land, in its entirety . . . as far as it stretches." Assurbanipal seems to have taken great care to round up every head of cattle his army could find, and noted that those that remained "ate the flesh of their children to keep from starving." Rhetorically the Arabs are said to ask: "Why had such a disaster befallen Arabia? It is because we did not abide by the great oaths of Assur, and sinned against the kindness of Assurbanipal, who pleases the heart of Enlil."[21] An enlightened ruler indeed.

Aside from this account, information on the Qaderite Arabs is sketchy, but it appears that the nomadic-pastoralist Qader acted as a buffer/intermediary between Babylon and its main rival at the time, Egypt. Around 400 B.C. there is a pottery inscription in Aramaic near the Egyptian-Arabian borderland referring to the "King of Qader" and his offering to the Arabian goddess Allat.[22]

So we return to the question, from whence did the Arabs come? The most credible theory is that the "proto-Semites" originated in the Levant, and then some settled in Mesopotamia and adopted Sumerian cultural norms and became the Akkadians. Others spread southward and became the Arabians, and others stayed in the area and developed the Canaanite languages, most prominently the Aramaeans (Aramaic speakers) and the Hebrews. The reverse may have occurred also: Semites may have started in Arabia and moved northward; it was not always a desert, after all, and they could have originated in Yemen. All facts considered, this split likely occurred in the early third millennium B.C. at the latest. Since the Semitic languages are not related to the huge Indo-European family of languages (Sanskrit, Hindi, Russian, German, Latin, Greek, etc.), the Semites must have been separate from the speakers of those languages for thousands, perhaps tens of thousands, of years.

The Peoples of South-Central Arabia

As already noted, settled peoples emerged independently of surrounding civilizations in both north and south Arabia by around the beginning of the first millennium B.C. According to early Greek sources, three Arabian peoples are worthy of mention, in addition to the abovementioned Sabaeans; the Minaeans, the Qataban, and the Himyarites.[23] The Minaeans likely flourished between 500 and 100 B.C. They minted no coins (a sign of political ambition), avoided warfare, and focused on commerce. They were mostly identified by others with aromatics; Pliny says that they originated the frankincense trade and led it to his day.[24]

The Qataban enter recorded history for the first time in the abovementioned Sabaean document by Karib'il Watar and appear to have been an ally. Pursuing an expansionist agenda, their influence grew over time, eventually displacing Saba' by the third century B.C.[25] This is apparent from the increasing appearance of Qatabanean inscriptions in what earlier had been Sabaean settlements, as well as some outside literary evidence.[26] In the same area dwelled the Hadramawt, also mentioned by Karib'il Watar as an ally of Saba' who prospered from the fourth to the second centuries. They took advantage of increasing seaborne traffic from Egypt to India, founding ports along the southern coast of the peninsula at Qana and Samhar (located in modern Yemen and Oman, respectively).[27] This change, precipitated by Augustus' decision to incorporate Egypt into the Roman Empire, had the incidental effect of weakening the caravan cities, shifting the balance of power within Arabia from the center to the periphery.[28]

Another tribe, described in one source as "the most numerous,"[29] was the Himyarites, the rise of which was to have a great impact on Arabia thereafter. Its predominance began in the southwestern tip of the peninsula. It expanded with the achievement of a unified monarchy with Saba'. The latter at first seemed the dominant partner, since a Sabaean revival made the temple of Almaqah at Marib important again. This period lasted about one hundred and fifty years beginning in the second century A.D. By the end of the third century the Saba' element of the dynasty had died out, and an empowered Himyar tribe divided the lands of the Qataban with the Hadramawt. Shortly thereafter the Himyarites overpowered the

7

Hadramawt; by A.D. 299, the Himyarite ruler Shammar Yuhar'ish could style himself ruler of Saba', Hadramawt, and the tribe of Yamanat, uniting southern Arabia under a single ruler for the first time.[30]

The Himyar then began enlarging their power, to the point of being able to claim the title of kingship over both central and coastal Arabia. They used the Hujr clan of the tribe of Kinda as a satellite to control the center, and lesser tribes elsewhere, including the area north of the trading city of Mecca. This expansion naturally brought them within the realm of international politics. Byzantium began cultivating Kinda as a satellite, and through its influence with Ethiopia, began to intervene in Arabia itself in order to protect Christian missionaries and communities. Kinda was a key tribe because it controlled the territory containing trade routes linking southern and eastern Arabia with Iraq (itself an old Arabic word for Mesopotamia). The Himyar established formal relations with major cities in Iraq and Persia, and in the fourth century concluded a formal peace treaty with Ethiopia. By the early sixth century, however, Christianity was perceived to be an extension of Byzantine imperial power, and war broke out between the Himyar and Ethiopia. Ethiopia was victorious and successfully installed a Christian king over the Himyar. Around the same time the strength of the Jewish tribes was increasing, and with his death they were able to take power.[31]

Reports of aggressions against Christian communities brought further Ethiopian intervention, again installing a Christian king, Esimiphaeus, a Himyarite by birth, over the tribe. His Christian successor was one Abraha, a slave of a Roman merchant, whose power was sufficiently secure to quell a revolt among the Kinda and orchestrate two campaigns to subdue rebellious elements in central Arabia.[32] One of the latter appears to be the Attack of the Elephant referred to in the Quran (105), which may have taken place the year of Muhammad's birth. The growth of Byzantine and Jewish power increased monotheistic influence in a region that had been overwhelmingly polytheistic.

The final chapter in the story of the Himyar prior to the rise of Islam was that of Persian conquest. By A.D. 559 resentment toward Ethiopian rule became so great that one Sayf ibn Dhi Yazan appealed to Persia for help. The Persian ruler Khosro agreed to send an army in exchange for annual tribute. After Yazan was

8

installed as king he was killed by Ethiopian slaves, and the Persian army returned, this time bringing southern Arabia under formal Persian rule. And so it remained an adjunct of the Persian Empire until the time of Muhammad.[33]

The Arabs of Northern Arabia and Syria

The peoples of central and northern Arabia in the period of middle and late antiquity fall broadly into two groups: those who spoke a north Arabian dialect and remained distinctively Arab, and those who adopted Aramaic or Greek and were acculturated into the empire that held a sphere of influence over them.

Although there are no Arabian literary works that survive from the pre-Islamic period, there are literally thousands of inscriptions in dialects of various kinds scattered throughout this region. One of the more common is the north Arabian dialect Safaitic, spoken by the tribes of Harra in what is now Syria, Jordan, and northern Saudi Arabia.[34] Another is Hismaic, spoken in southeast Jordan and northwest Saudi Arabia.[35] Neither collection contains facts sufficient to reconstruct even an approximate chronology, but both contain tidbits of information about their nomadic lifestyle. The one clear difference between the two is that while the Safaitic-speaking Harra ranged over a larger area, Hisma culture was more closely tied to the settled Nabataeans (see below).[36]

North-central Arabia also gave rise to three prominent oasis-based tribal confederations. One was the oasis of Tayma, which appears to have supported agricultural life as early as the eighth century B.C. Taimani was a northern Arabian dialect, and of the many inscriptions discovered one may be dated clearly to the sixth century B.C.[37] There are also a number of Aramaic inscriptions that suggest a strong interconnectedness with the wider region, since Aramaic was the *lingua franca* of the Middle East during the period of Persian predominance (539–334 B.C.). Many inscriptions refer to wars with neighboring tribes, two of which, notably, are mentioned in the Bible as having descended from Ishmael.[38]

The oasis of Dedan is mentioned in the Bible in connection with the merchandise trade (Isaiah 21:13; Ezekiel 27:20). Dedan was apparently taken over by the "kings of Lihyan" during the Persian

9

period. A Nabataean inscription makes clear that by 24 B.C. at the latest Dedan had been annexed by them. There are indications of Ptolemaic influence on Lihyanite sculpture that suggest interaction with Egypt (r. 305–31 B.C.). Minaean texts (c. 500–100 B.C.) also mention trading with them. These details together give us a rough idea of the geographic scope and duration of Lihyanite commercial influence.[39] It is not clear where the Lihyanites originally came from, but they disappear from the historical record around the beginning of Nabataean control of Dedan and do not reappear until centuries later. Muslim sources name them as a part of the tribal confederation Hudhayl, located in the Hijaz.[40]

A third oasis settlement was that of Duma, which held a strategic position connecting the trade routes of Arabia with southern Syria. There are a number of Assyrian inscriptions between the eighth and fifth centuries that associate them politically and religiously with the Qader. Duma arises again in the historical record centuries later when a Nabataean inscription mentions its annexation.[41]

Thamud was a tribal confederation in northwest Arabia. Sargon II mentions having defeated them and resettling them in Samaria. Later Pliny and Ptolemy mention branches of Thamud as being enrolled in the Roman army.[42] One of them built a temple in which they extolled the Roman emperors Marcus Aurelius and Lucius Aurelius Verus. In the fourth century A.D., units of Thamud are recorded as having served in the Byzantine army in Egypt and Palestine.[43]

The other sphere of northern Arabia during this period was made up of communities described by Greco-Roman writers as Arabs who eventually became assimilated into the Hellenic, Roman, and Iranian worlds, before being re-Arabized after the rise of Islam.[44] The three most important of such groups are the abovementioned Nabataeans of Petra, the Palmyerens, and the Hatrans.[45]

When Eratosthenes of Cyrene traveled the caravan route from Syria, he encountered the Nabataeans, which he described as Arab.[46] It is believed that they came north from Arabia after the decline of the Qader.[47] Their base settlement was at Petra, now located in southern Jordan.[48] The most reliable early source about their origins is considered to be Diodorus Siculus (80–20 B.C.), who describes them as nomadic pastoralists who fit all of the normal descriptions of Bedouin who have recently adapted a settled way of life.[49]

The Nabataean treasury in Petra, located in southern Jordan. Featured in the movie *Indiana Jones and the Last Crusade.*

Strabo, writing much later, describes the Nabataeans as a thoroughly settled people involved in agriculture but maintaining the kind of economic and political egalitarianism typical of the Bedouin.[50] Diodorus had described them as the wealthiest people in the area, having a central role in the transit of frankincense and myrrh between the Roman world and Arabia, and between Egypt and Persia. At their peak the Nabataeans controlled a mini-empire; Negev in the west (southern Israel today), Transjordan in the north (modern Jordan), and cities as much as three hundred miles or so in the south and west into Arabia.[51]

The Nabataeans' prosperity naturally made them an attractive target for outside powers. Strabo describes Petra as maintaining neutral relations between the empires to its east (the Ptolemies) and west (the Seleucids), but a pair of expeditions made Petra into a client kingdom of Rome. The first one did not go well for the Romans, as, after having raided the city, the Nabataean warriors caught them in the middle of the night and massacred the raiding party. A second expedition threatened a siege, and the Nabataeans accepted terms. They also appear to have had rough relations with the Jews to their west. Rome annexed Syria in 63 B.C., bringing the Nabataeans even closer to Roman control. In A.D. 106 Petra was formally annexed and made the provincial capital, and the Romans transferred military units to the region, built a road through Petra to the Red Sea, made Greek the official language,[52] and remade local laws (for example, by abolishing the practice of circumcision).

In addition to losing its independence, Petra went into economic decline. Strabo notes that the previously pacific Nabataeans turned to piracy, though this appears to have backfired when an aggrieved party attacked and ravaged their settlements.[53]

Palmyra, located in what is now Syria, had the mixed geographical fortune of being perfectly placed as both a hub of Levantine commerce and a forward base for imperial armies. In fact, the first written mention of Palmyra comes from an Assyrian commercial contract from the nineteenth century B.C.[54] Yet it does not appear as a substantial place of settlement until the first century B.C. Being much closer to the point of intersection of the relative spheres of power of Rome and Persia than Petra, the city was irresistible. Rome seems to have first raided Palmyra in 41 B.C. when Mark Antony had it plundered. Although attempting to maintain neutrality for a while, by A.D. 20 it had become a full-fledged satrap of the empire. It eventually became thoroughly Romanized with political institutions (a senate, assembly, judges) and cultural borrowings (theater, baths, architecture) to match.[55]

Yet Palmyra's place of prominence in history was only secured after the second Sasanian monarch, Shapur (A.D. 242–270), sent his army deep into the empire, eventually capturing the Emperor Valerian himself. A citizen of Palmyra and Roman senator of Arab descent, Odenathus,[56] rose and led a revolt which not only liberated the eastern empire but actually entered Sasanian territory. He effectively became the vice-regent of Rome in the east, and appears to have had imperial ambitions before the assassination of both himself and his son around 267.[57]

History has remembered his widow Zenobia much more, in part because she was viewed as the proverbial "power behind the throne" all along. Formally acting in the name of her young son Wahballat, she declared her husband and herself to be the rightful holders of imperial authority. Her husband was posthumously named "King of Kings," and she had coins minted suggesting that her son was co-emperor with first Claudius and then Aurelian. Aurelian reacted predictably and launched a full-scale invasion that resulted in her defeat and capture in A.D. 272. Nevertheless, Aurelian credited Zenobia with her husband's success, and the Romans extolled her beauty and spirit.[58]

Less is known about the Hatrans, a settlement located in northern Iraq over which the Romans and Persians competed for control. The presence of about four hundred early Aramaic inscriptions, dating between A.D. 89 and 238, suggests existence within the Persian sphere of influence. Yet by around A.D. 230 a Roman garrison was stationed there. The Persians reacted with fury at this encroachment and, after a long siege, leveled the city in 240. Written evidence exists that suggests that Hatra had been a thriving city with an economy advanced enough to support numerous specialized trades and a religious bureaucracy. Around 160 the ruler took a title that might be translated as "King of Arabia," suggesting some regional ambition.[59]

The region today called Palestine, later to become very important to the Arabs, was previously inhabited by various non-Arab Semitic peoples (including the Hebrews). The term derives from various terms related to the Philistines (themselves likely of Aegean origin[60]), including the Egyptian *Purusati*, the Assyrian *Palastu*, and the Hebrew *Peleshet* (Exodus 14:14; Isaiah 14:29, 31; Joel 3:4).[61] In Greek and Latin usage Palestine became attached to Syria by the terms *Palasistine Syria* or *Syria Palestina*, but did not include Judea, which was to the south. The Roman province of *Arabia Felix*, created in A.D. 105, was attached to Palestine. After A.D. 358 this enlarged province (the south of modern Israel and Jordan) was renamed *Palestina Salutaris* and, again in 400, *Palestina Tertia*, with its capital in Petra. The same year it was divided again into *Palestina Prima* in the middle and *Palestina Secunda* in the north. All three provinces ran east-west in length, rather than north-south, like modern Israel.[62]

Arabia and Ancient World Order

Reflecting on the place of the Arab peoples in the world more broadly, we can see over the centuries how the fortunes of the Arabs and their role in the wider world had been shaped by empires around them, as well as their ability to turn the situation to their benefit. Where there was peace, the Arabian trade routes to the east, which were longer, were less valuable. When there was war, not only did their trade routes become more valuable, but tribes bordering the empires were able to sell themselves out as mercenaries. Pliny wrote:

> The Arabians are, as a whole, the richest peoples in the world, since the greatest wealth of the Romans and the Parthinians remains with them; for they sell what they take from the sea [sc., pearls] and their forests [sc., incense], without buying anything in return.[63]

It is clear that the Arabs affected Rome's geopolitical strategy beyond those areas annexed. When Trajan conquered northern Arabia, he intended not only to control the Levant but also to build a fortified road down the coast to allow for better control of Red Sea shipping.[64] Augustus had also considered further conquest due to the region's reputed wealth.[65] Much earlier, Aelius Gallus invaded Arabia and attacked "Mariba," perhaps the same as the Sabaean Marib, and if so went quite far south indeed.[66]

In the last years leading up to the coming of Islam the two most important Arab tribes were the Ghassanids (Rome) and the Lakhmids (Persia). As time passed each side began to rely progressively more on its Arab auxiliaries.[67] For example, the Treaty of Dara, concluded in A.D. 561, among other things specifically regulated the movements of the respective tribes.[68] This strategy worked well for Rome, for over time Arabia came to be thought of as a relatively safe front for the empire, at least from the Arabs, if not always the Persians.[69] With time, this complacency would cost them dearly.

Arabian Social and Cultural Patterns before Islam

The structure of Arabian society was based around the tribe. The tribe was essentially a free-standing political unit, able to form coalitions with other tribes when a need arose. Normally, however, tribes were fiercely independent. This did not preclude the acceptance of tribute from a settled power, and though client status may connote subordination, as often as not it involved blackmail—settled peoples had to pay a retainer or suffer from Bedouin raiding parties.

Without a formal criminal justice system to keep order, individuals were entirely dependent upon their tribe. A man without a tribe could be killed or enslaved with impunity. Conversely, a man in good tribal standing could count on the protection of his kin, who would retaliate in case of any harm to him.[70] In addition to retaliation, a tribe could take compensation for a loss. As expressed by one poet, "a slain for our slain, a prisoner for each one of us captured, and goods for our goods."[71] Conflict was further lessened by a variety of customs such as intermarriage, the use of mediators, reciprocal gift-giving, or communal festivals that helped promote the common interest in keeping the peace.[72]

The need for tribal solidarity gave rise to a communal life that was at once egalitarian and participatory yet highly intolerant of divisiveness. Tribes were usually led by a council (*majlis*), the chief

A group of Iraqi tribesmen.
Robert Fernea, photographer. CMES.

(*shaikh*) of which would lead by consensus among the leaders of the clans rather than by force. One poet described the system:

Among them are assemblies of fine men, councils from which follow decisive words and deeds . . . when you come to them, you will find them round their tents in session, at which impetuous action is often obviated by their prudent members.[73]

Notice the double emphasis on participatory decision-making and the decisiveness of the conclusion. With tribal unity essential to survival, those who divided the tribe would not be tolerated.[74]

Such a structure arose naturally in a society with low levels of economic development and little division of labor. Conversely, parts of Arabia that were involved in agriculture and trade were more hierarchical with a more complex division of labor.[75]

Law was derived from a variety of sources, but the most important was the *sunna*, or customary practice of the tribe. In tribal heritage the *sunna* would be exemplified by an *imam*, a heroic figure whose life and teachings would establish the law. Beside pre-Islamic poetry, this idea is expressed in the Quran, where God says to Adam: "We have made you an imam before the people" (2:124).[76]

Within a tribe, trials could take place, to be determined by "oath or contest or evidence."[77] One who had committed a crime within the group might be made an outlaw, thus losing the protection of his tribe.[78] Otherwise, aside from retaliation, arbitrators respected for their wisdom might be chosen to judge between kinship groups. They had no instruments of coercion at their disposal, but depended upon their personal stature as well as respect for custom to make their judgments binding.

Although the lack of literary evidence precludes having the kind of detailed knowledge of Arabian legal customs which exists for contemporaneous civilizations, inscriptions do show evidence for civil litigation, a public registry (at Palmyra), deeds to real property, rules of contract law, and official edicts on a variety of subjects.[79]

In addition to the importance of the tribe, the immediate family was also naturally very important. Although the basic structure of Arabian society varied very little, marriage patterns exhibited almost every possibility. Neither strict endogamy (marriage only

17

within one's own tribe) or exogamy was enforced, sometimes the couple stayed with the husband's household and sometimes with that of the wife; sometimes cousin-marriages were preferred, sometimes not. Of course a man might also bypass whatever practice was common and capture a bride, but this did not necessarily bring her shame, as Hatim al-Ta'i relates in this interesting verse:

> They did not give us Tayyites . . . their daughters in marriage, but we wooed them against their will with our swords. And with us captivity brought no abasement to them . . . we commingled them with our noblest women, and they bore us fine sons, of pure descent. How often will you see among us the son of a captive bride, who staunchly thrusts through heroes in the fray.[80]

Descent was usually accounted through the male line, but it appears that matrilineal descent occasionally existed. Monogamy, polygyny, and even polyandry appear; as with "mercenary husbands," men who would temporarily marry women whose husbands were infertile.[81]

Religion also revolved around the tribe. Each tribe would have its own cult, yet as with the Romans, devotion to one god did not require rejection of another. "When you enter a village, swear by its god," a proverb admonished.[82] Moreover, since Arab paganism envisioned no afterlife, devotion to a god was merely intended to ensure success in this life, and, more importantly, act as a unifying factor in the life of the tribe.[83] Magic and divination were important,[84] and besides gods and men there existed a separate order of beings, including jinn, genies, and ghouls.[85] Sacred places and months in which violence was forbidden also had a central role in promoting commercial cooperation.[86]

Monotheism became increasingly influential in the centuries of late antiquity. Although it is not perceived as such today, in antiquity Judaism was often a proselytizing religion, and several Arab tribes had converted to Judaism. Northern Arabia and Aramaic-speaking Syria and Palestine contained many Christian communities which traded with Mecca. Byzantium's ambitions in the region also brought greater Christian influence. Aside from Jews and Christians, there were monotheistic Arabs called hanifs.[87]

The economic sustenance of a tribe would vary from place to place. Most were involved in either agriculture or pastoralism, but some practiced agropastoralism, a combination of both.[88] Hunting was also common, but very often the killing of given animals was prized as much for the status of the kill as the meat.[89]

Many depended on trade. Aromatics, especially frankincense and myrrh, were an important livelihood. International trade was important, but even larger numbers were involved in intra-Arabian trade. It thrived from the interdependent nature of the relationship between the Bedouin and the settled peoples. Nomadic pastoralists could provide settled peoples with meats and milk, and made for a ready supply of auxiliary soldiers when needed. Lacking a division of labor, they needed the products produced by specialized craftsmen.[90] This synergy promoted peace, because markets were cooperative ventures.

Mining was also important, as Arabia was rich in gold, copper, and silver. Around one thousand mines have been found from this time period, and there are records in early Islamic times of the profits the state made from mining.[91]

The rise of Christianity dampened the aromatics trade to some degree, as Christians sought to separate themselves from pagan rituals. Of greater impact were the changing relationships of the great powers, creating a cycle of boom and bust. Arabian merchants were hurt even more by improvements in navigational techniques that allowed Rome to ship goods directly from Egypt to Yemen and beyond.[92]

Despite the thousands of inscriptions that have been found, there was virtually no literary culture in Arabia. Poetry, while central to Arabian culture, was oral and was not written down until after the coming of Islam. Prior to the Quran, only a couple of writings of more than a few sentences have been found.[93]

By the end of the seventh century, the Arabs remained one of the least developed peoples in the Near East and Mediterranean worlds, whether such development is measured according to political, economic, literary, or scientific criteria. With the classical ages of Greece and Rome already a distant memory, their classical age was yet to come.

Notes

1. Robert G. Hoyland, *Arabia and the Arabs: From the Bronze Age to the Coming of Islam* (New York: Routledge, 2001) 3.
2. Ibid., 198.
3. Georges Roux, *Ancient Iraq* (London: Penguin Books, 1992) 273–6.
4. Ibid., 200.
5. Ibid., 15.
6. Ibid., 111.
7. Ibid., 120. See also Hoyland, *Arabia and the Arabs*, 142.
8. Roux, *Ancient Iraq*, 112–3.
9. Ibid., 114. Compare *Kalbum* with *Kalb*, which means "dog."
10. Ibid., 91.
11. Hoyland, *Arabia and the Arabs*, 15–6.
12. Ibid., 36.
13. Ibid., 38.
14. Ibid.
15. Ibid., 39.
16. Ibid., 89–90.
17. Ibid., 59.
18. Ibid., 60.
19. Ibid., 61.
20. Roux, *Ancient Iraq*, 334.
21. Hoyland, *Arabia and the Arabs*, 61–2. All of the quotations from this paragraph come from an Assyrian inscription cited by Hoyland in which Assurbanipal narrarates in the first person (e.g., "threw off my yoke").
22. Ibid., 62–3.
23. Ibid., 40, citing Eratosthenes of Cyrene and Theophrastus of Eresus.
24. Ibid., 40–1.
25. Ibid., 42.
26. Ibid. Strabo mentions the Qataban as being prominent in trade during this time, but not the Sabaeans.
27. Ibid., 43–4.
28. Ibid., 44–5.
29. Ibid., 46.
30. Ibid., 46–7.
31. Ibid., 49–57.
32. Ibid.
33. Ibid., 55–7.
34. Ibid., 64–5.
35. Ibid.
36. Ibid., 65–6.
37. Ibid., 66.
38. Ibid. See also Genesis 25:13–14.
39. Ibid., 66–8.
40. Ibid., 68.
41. Ibid.
42. Ibid., quoting from Pliny.
43. Ibid., 68–9. Muslims came to believe that the Thamud were wiped out in remote antiquity; the Quran describes how they were destroyed after having rejected

the prophet Salih. Given the record, either the Thamud were never completely destroyed or the name was reused over time.

44. Ibid., 69.
45. Ibid. Hoyland includes several other groups of lesser importance; the Idumaeans of southern Palestine, the Ituraeans of Mount Lebanon, the Emesenes of the Orontes region, the Abgarids of Edessa, the Praetavi of Sinjar, and the Characenes of southern Iraq. Although little concrete information is known about these peoples, the Emesenes are mentioned by Roman authors as having obtained Roman citizenship and were considered a loyal ally/satellite.
46. Ibid., 70.
47. Ibid.
48. And easily recognizable to westerners today because of the appearance of their treasury as an ancient temple housing the Holy Grail in the third of the popular Indiana Jones movies. Perhaps needless to say, none of the rest of the set of the movie is found within the actual location. The author, upon visiting the location, was only slightly disappointed to see that the chamber led only to a large, bare, high-ceiling room with two adjacent nondescript rooms of smaller size. Petra is nevertheless magnificent, even without the medieval knight.
49. Ibid.
50. Ibid., 72.
51. Ibid., 72.
52. Although Latin was of course the official language of Rome, Greek remained the dominant language among the educated throughout the eastern Mediterranean after its conquest by Rome.
53. Ibid., 74.
54. Roux, *Ancient Iraq*, 14.
55. Hoyland, *Arabia and the Arabs*, 75.
56. His full name was Odenathus son of Hairan son of Wahballat son of Nasor. Thus his father was Latinized, but his father's immediate ancestors were recognizably Arab.
57. Ibid., 75.
58. Ibid., 75–6.
59. Ibid., 77–8.
60. Roux, *Ancient Iraq*, 266. The Philistines are part of the larger group the Egyptians called the "Sea Peoples," which also include the Hyksos.
61. Bernard Lewis, *Islam in History: Ideas, People, and Events in the Middle East* (Chicago: Open Court, 2001, 2nd ed.) 153.
62. Ibid., 155.
63. Susan P. Mattern, *Rome and the Enemy: Imperial Strategy in the Principate* (Berkeley: University of California Press, 1999) 79.
64. Ibid., 157.
65. Ibid.
66. Ibid., 78.
67. Averil Cameron, *The Mediterranean World in Late Antiquity A.D. 395–600: Routledge History of the Ancient World* (London: Routledge, 1993) 177.
68. Ibid., 112–3.
69. Ibid., 52.
70. Hoyland, *Arabia and the Arabs*, 113.
71. Ibid., 122.
72. Ibid., 114.
73. Ibid., 122, quoting from Zuhayr.

21

74. Ibid., 114.
75. Ibid., 120.
76. Ibid., 121.
77. Ibid., 122.
78. Ibid., 124–6. Although for minor offenses one might be able to make an offering and rejoin the tribe.
79. Ibid., 125–8.
80. Ibid., 128.
81. Ibid., 129–31.
82. Ibid., 139.
83. Ibid., 139–45.
84. Ibid., 150–7.
85. Ibid., 145.
86. Ibid., 157–63.
87. Ibid., 146–50.
88. Ibid., 89–91.
89. Ibid., 91.
90. Ibid., 101.
91. Ibid., 110–1.
92. Ibid., 73.
93. Ibid., 198–228.

CHAPTER II

The Rise of Islam
(A.D. 610–661)

Muhammad, Prophet of Islam

The central character in Arab history is Abu al-Qasim Muhammad ibn Abd Allah ibn Abd al-Muttalib ibn Hasim, prophet of Islam. Muhammad and his immediate successors laid the foundation for virtually everything in which Arabs today, Muslim or not, take pride. Through a combination of steadfast religious vision, strategic brilliance, charismatic personality, and decisive leadership, Muhammad would remake Arabia, and the Arabs, forever.[1]

Muhammad, who was raised as an orphan, was born in approximately A.D. 570 to the clan of Hashim, of the tribe of the Quraysh, guardians of the Ka'aba. According to Muslim tradition, it was at this place that the patriarch Abraham built a cubed sanctuary after a well sprang up, saving the life of his concubine Hagar and their son Ishmael. This sanctuary became known as the Ka'aba, and its centrality to the Arabian pagan cult system allowed Mecca to become a commercial center in the trade network that went between Iraq, Syria, and the Indian Ocean.

As Muhammad matured, he became known as al-amin, the trusted one. This brought him to the attention of a woman named Khadija, who wanted to hire him to operate her caravan, and they eventually married. It was common at the time for pious men to retreat to a secluded area and pray, escaping the worldly concerns of the city. Muhammad himself, now a semi-prosperous merchant,

23

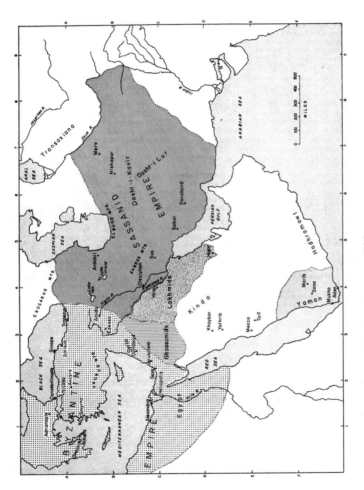

Egypt and southwest Asia, circa A.D. 600.

Courtesy of the University of Washington Press. (Originally appeared in *A Near East Studies Handbook* by Jere Bacharach, 1977.)

took up this practice in adulthood, retreating to a nearby mountain. One night in approximately 610, Muhammad received a visitation from a being named Gabriel who told him that he was to be a messenger from God to others. This worried him greatly, and at first he told only his wife of what had happened.

Later a direct revelation came to him, reassuring Muhammad of his mission, and expounding for him the message of moral behavior and correct worship he would bring to his pagan society:[2]

By the pen, and by that which they write, no madman art thou, . . . By the morning brightness, and by the night when it is still, thy Lord hath not forsaken thee nor doth He hate thee, and the last shall be better than the first, and thy Lord shall give and give unto thee, and thou shalt be satisfied. Hath He not found thee an orphan and sheltered thee, and found thee astray and guided thee, and found thee needy and enriched thee? So for the orphan, oppress him not, and for the beggar, repel him not, and for the bountiful grace of thy Lord, proclaim it!

Soon, not only Khadija but Muhammad's cousin Ali and his friend Abu Bakr became convinced of his mission. Ali was only ten years old, but Abu Bakr was a respected member of the community, the first man of stature to become a *muslim*, one who submits (to God). Another early convert was a merchant named Uthman, a respected member of the powerful clan of Umayya. Within a few years, Muhammad's mission had become public, and one by one, his following in Mecca grew.

It soon became clear to the leaders of the Quraysh that, unlike other cults with which they had dealt, this new religion would not tolerate the polytheistic pantheon that occupied the Ka'aba and over which the Quraysh themselves were guardians. Prior to Muhammad, *allah* had been just one of many gods, the moon god respected as a "high god." Muhammad emphasized that his God was not just a god, or *lah*, but the God, *al-lah*, or Allah. The *sha-hada*, or testimony, became the first basic principle of Islam: "There is no god but God, and Muhammad is the Messenger of God." Muhammad was clearly a threat to their status, and he had to be stopped.

25

The Quraysh began a campaign of persecution against Muhammad's followers, and some were tortured into renouncing Islam. Because he had the protection of the head of his clan, Abu Talib, Muhammad could only be verbally reviled. Nevertheless, Islam expanded in numbers, even taking in members of outside tribes that had come to Mecca to worship at the Ka'aba. The Quraysh came to believe Muhammad was a sorcerer, and told visitors to put wax in their ears if they came near him.

In 617 Muhammad received an important convert. One of the chiefs most vehemently opposed to Muhammad was a man Muslims call Abu Jahl, the Father of Ignorance. His nephew, Umar ibn al-Khattab, one of the greatest warriors of the Quraysh, was also sternly pious in the ways of traditional pagan religion, and a virulent tormentor of Muslims. One day he decided to take matters into his own hands, and, sword in hilt, set off to kill Muhammad. But someone diverted Umar by telling him that his sister Fatima and her husband had secretly become Muslims. He entered their house as they were reading from a manuscript containing a revelation, and demanded to see it. When her husband resisted, Fatima stepped forward and Umar knocked them both down. Seeing his sister bleeding by his own hand, Umar softened and asked to see the manuscript. After reading it, he marveled at its beauty and asked them where he could find Muhammad in order to proclaim his commitment to Islam. He promptly did so, and having had his "road-to-Damascus" experience, returned to his uncle Abu Jahl and declared to him forthrightly that there was no god but God and that Muhammad was his prophet. Abu Jahl screamed: "God curse thee! And may His curse be on the tidings that thou hast brought!"[3]

Becoming more concerned, the Quraysh instituted a boycott on the clan of Hashim and another clan that would not go along. Although a two-year blockade brought both clans to the verge of starvation, neither relented, and the boycott was called off in 619. Yet that same year Muhammad suffered a double loss when his wife Khadija and his protector Abu Talib both died.

From Abu Talib's death Muhammad became increasingly desperate to find a way out of Mecca. After sending out emissaries he was able to obtain an invitation from the tribes of an oasis town to the north called Yathrib, later renamed Medina. Medina was inhabited by five tribes, two Arab, the Aws and the Khazraj, and three

Jewish ones. Unable to solve their internal conflicts, tribal leaders invited Muhammad to come rule as an impartial arbitrator. Muhammad made his Higra, or migration, in 622 and established the "Constitution of Medina," an agreement which outlined Muhammad's role as governor and prohibited any tribe from forming a hostile alliance with outside tribes. Muslims who came with Muhammad became known as the Muhajirun (emigrants), while those already there became known as the Ansar (helpers).

While providing the tribes of the city a means by which to handle their internecine strife, this arrangement also provided Muhammad a base from which to plan his return to Mecca. The Quraysh, though powerful, were vulnerable because their economic vitality depended upon the safety of the trade routes north to Syria, which lay not far from Medina. Lacking the strength to take Mecca directly, Muhammad settled on a strategy of making alliances with key tribes along the coast and raiding Meccan caravans. This was facilitated by sending out reciters to convert outlying tribes to Islam, but even without conversion, tribes could still be allies. This approach brought ample booty to allow him to assemble a network of allied tribes that threatened to strangle the Quraysh. This posed the Quraysh an entirely new difficulty; whereas before Muhammad was merely a poet-sorcerer with an exceptionally wide following, he now headed a military alliance threatening to starve them into submission.

It may have been at this time that Muhammad developed a concept that would be central to Islamic history, that of the *umma*, or Islamic nation. A pivotal moment came when some Muslims raided a caravan during a sacred month. Arabs were scandalized, and many, not just the Quraysh, demanded the booty returned. Muhammad decided that, while violating a sacred month was bad, driving Muslims away from the sacred Ka'aba was worse, and that the cause of Islam took precedence over pagan tribal customs. The *umma* was not merely another tribe that happened to be based upon a religion, but rather an entity representing a cause that superceded tradition, separating Muslims not only from the Quraysh, but all of Arabian pagan culture. Furthermore, whereas tribal bonds had been supreme, now men would be asked to fight their family members in the cause of Islam. Moreover, the *umma* could make treaties with other tribes, just like any political entity,

A drawing of Medina by Sir Richard Burton (1853).
CMES.

but was based upon belief rather than blood, territory, or loyalty to a dynasty.

Having established himself in Medina, Muhammad became engaged in a series of battles that would determine his future. The first was at a place called Badr, where he was met by a Meccan force that had managed to learn of one of his raiding parties. Though outnumbered, the Muslims prevailed and several high-ranking Quraysh were captured. The second battle, the Battle of Uhud, did not go so well. At Uhud, the Quraysh began attacking fields around Medina, which was fortified, hoping to starve the Muslims out. Muhammad took the risk and came out into an open fight even more outnumbered than before, and it almost cost him his life. He was able to escape back to Medina because his attackers thought he was dead, but only after losing a tooth. A third meeting was the Battle of the Trench, so called because the Muslims dug a trench around Medina that would have forced the Meccans to dismount and attack the city on foot. After running out of supplies, the Quraysh had to retreat again.

When Muhammad first entered Medina his relations with the Jewish tribes were good, but they soured with time. They often would make fun of him, because the revelations he gave on figures of the Hebrew Bible—like Abraham, Moses, and Joseph—differed significantly from their versions. Nor, with a few exceptions, did they accept him as a prophet as he expected. As more pagan Arabs became Muslims, Medina became more polarized. Muhammad's battles with the Quraysh also served to heighten tensions. Although the Jews never directly turned against him, they never helped him either, and Muhammad suspected them of leaking his military plans and engaging in negotiations with the Quraysh. After each major battle he forced one tribe to leave, with conditions becoming harsher each time. He forced the first to leave with their possessions, the second to leave without them, and from the third he demanded unconditional surrender, executing the able-bodied men and selling the women and children into slavery.

External conflicts notwithstanding, within Medina itself Muhammad focused on molding a new society. In addition to the abovementioned *shahada*, Muhammad established *salat* (five ritualized prayers a day), *sawm* (fasting during the sacred month of Ramadan), and *zakat* (alms to the poor) as "pillars" of Islam. He laid down rules regarding a variety of legal subjects, including rules of inheritance, marriage, and sexual relations; evidentiary rules for the resolution of disputes; the making of treaties or war with other groups; the status of slaves; and estate administration. Order, justice, and the unity of the believers were his core values. Relations between individuals would be based upon proper principles, the weak would be protected, and the unity of the *umma* would be maintained. Fighting pagans was necessary to achieve his aims, but it was these causes to which Muhammad's mission was primarily directed. One of his most famous sayings was made upon returning from fighting: "We have just returned from the lesser *jihad* (struggle), now we turn to the greater *jihad*."

By 628, with the coalition supporting his enemies in shambles, his blockade of Mecca intact, and his position in Medina unassailable, Muhammad was at last prepared to force a showdown over Mecca, which was for him both his native city and the central focus of his prophetic mission. Having been in Medina for six years, Muhammad set out during the sacred month with a large host on a pilgrimage to the Ka'aba. He met with Meccan leaders at Hudaybiya, outside Mecca, and negotiated a deal. The Muslims would withdraw, but the next year the Quraysh would evacuate Mecca for the Muslims to make the pilgrimage without fear of conflict. There would be a ten-year truce, during which Meccan trade would be unhindered. Quraysh who wanted to join Muhammad would be returned, but Muslims who wished to return to the Quraysh could do so. However, tribal allies were allowed to switch sides. Indeed, tribes began to come over to him, and he completed his control over some of the other major oases in the Hijaz, so the *umma* grew in strength as the Quraysh lost allies. Muhammad also sent an expedition north to Syria to make a show of force to the Byzantines.

The following year, in 630, there was a fight between an ally of the Quraysh and one of Muhammad's own allies, and interpreting this as a violation by the Quraysh, he forced a showdown. Abu Suhayl, now the head of the Quraysh, knew the end had come. Reluctantly, he went to Muhammad and declared his acceptance of Islam, then returned to Mecca and announced that Muhammad would grant a general amnesty if he were allowed to take control of Mecca. Muhammad entered Mecca without resistance.

During, 631, called the Year of Deputations, the power of the *umma* quickly spread throughout Arabia. Most of those in the Hijaz and the central Arabian area of the Najd quickly accepted Islam, or at least Muhammad's leadership. Tribes from the eastern areas of Oman and Bahrain sent representatives to come to terms. The Christians of Yemen were allowed to accept Muhammad's political leadership without giving up Christianity. Muhammad had the least success in the borderlands of Syria and Iraq, and reportedly led an army of 30,000 against them, although without decisive results.

Shortly before his death, Muhammad completed an important step in his campaign against idolatry by making the Ka'aba exclusively Muslim; tribes still pagan were excluded, and the idols and relics of the pagans were destroyed. Shortly thereafter, in the year A.D. 632, or A.H. 10 (*anno Hegirae*, "in the year of Muhammad's Higra"), Muhammad fell ill and died in the arms of his favorite wife, A'isha.

Abu Bakr—Succession and Consolidation of the Umma

The single most fiercely debated issue in early Arab historiography is the question of the succession to Muhammad. The predominant (Sunni) view is that Muhammad did not formally choose a successor, but signaled his preference that Abu Bakr should succeed him by choosing him to lead prayer in his absence while on his deathbed. The alternative view is that Muhammad intended for leadership of the *umma* to be held by his descendants, and, having no male issue, intended that Ali be his successor. Ali was not only Muhammad's cousin; he was married to Muhammad's daughter Fatima. (Those loyal to Ali historically have been called *Shi'a*, also spelled *Shi'ite*.)

It would not have been unusual for Muhammad not to have chosen a successor; Arab leaders usually did not do so,[4] and, although close blood relation to a great leader was an asset, succession was not *per se* dynastic. Yet Muhammad had founded a religious polity unlike any other in Arabia, and with no equivalent to the tribal *majlis* (council) to govern in the interim,[5] the choice

31

of successor was a crisis. Upon their leader's death, Umar hastily called together a Shura Council (*shura* means "consultation"). Abu Bakr first proposed two candidates, Umar and Abu Ubayda. The latter, although respected, lacked the stature to lead, and the former disqualified himself by throwing his support to Abu Bakr, who quickly accepted. Abu Bakr carried the support of the Muhajirun, plus the Aws, one of the two most important clans of Medina, and, perhaps most importantly, the fearsome Umar.[6] Yet the composition of the meeting was very selective, and the pledging of the *bay'*, or oath of loyalty, does not seem to have been entirely consensual. Ali himself and many of his sympathizers were not told of the meeting, and many of the Medinan Ansar did not support Abu Bakr, as suggested by the fact that Umar physically assaulted the chief of the Khazraj afterward.[7]

Ali, like Muhammad, was of the clan of Hashim. Abu Bakr, upon his succession, wisely decided against the use of force and immediately began to isolate the Banu Hashim by consolidating his power through other clans of the Quraysh. Ali eventually decided that he had lost; at a meeting he and Abu Bakr are said to have embraced emotionally, with Ali pledging the most steadfast allegiance. Yet from the same time period there are reports of many verses composed proclaiming that the Banu Hashim had been cheated; the Quraysh as a whole had been given what was rightfully theirs.[8]

The choice of Abu Bakr was wise politically. Most tribes, especially the late-converting among the Quraysh and their allies, viewed their allegiance to Muhammad as lapsing upon his death, just as with any other treaty. Many in Medina supported the leadership of *ahl al-bayt*, or People of the Prophet's House. Yet Umar and Abu Bakr had a vision of an Islamic *umma* that would rule all the Arabs, and they knew that only the Quraysh had the prominence to claim such a position. Moreover, Ali had lived much of his life in Medina, and therefore had little status among the powerful Meccans. Thus, just as only the Quraysh could lead the Arabs, only someone like Abu Bakr could retain the support of both the Quraysh and the Medina faithful. His vision of a polity including all Arabs offered the Quraysh something unexpected; rather than being a threat to their power, Islam could actually be a tool for expanding it. And by supporting the elderly Abu Bakr, Umar helped guarantee his own ascension to power when Abu Bakr died.

Abu Bakr (r. 632–634) took the title of *khalifa*, or caliph, which may mean both successor (to the prophet) and vice-regent (of God).[9] Once his own position was secure, he then had to deal with rebellious tribes. Later generations understandably viewed the rebellions as apostasy. Yet the tribes viewed their treaties with Muhammad as being no different from those with others. Abu Bakr, having assembled a governing coalition which now included the Quraysh, issued a radical new doctrine—the tribes would submit tribute to the *umma* and accept the leadership of the caliph, or he would make war against them. This was indeed radical, because one of Muhammad's more memorable sayings seemed to disallow it: "I was ordered to fight people until they say that there is no god but God. If they say this, they safeguard themselves and their property from me."[10] Moreover, in practice tribute seems to have been based on moral obligation alone,[11] and Muhammad refrained from attacking tribes once they had committed to Islam. Abu Bakr asserted that he would consider Muslims who refused payment as apostates who had forfeited the protection of Islam.[12] The practical effect was to make political allegiance to the head of the Islamic nation, which had always existed, into a religious test, the failure of which constituted apostasy.

With the combined power of the Quraysh and the faithful Muslims of Medina, Abu Bakr was able to quell the rebellions and establish the Islamic community as a unitary state with the right to rule over all Arabs. The actual expansion was largely left to his friend and supporter, Umar ibn al-Khattab.

The Conquests

Although in theory the *umma* was to be governed by *shura*, Abu Bakr did not view the caliphate as an elective office, and appointed Umar as his successor before his death. He likely had two reasons for this, aside from the need to pay back Umar for his unwavering support. One, Umar held the same view as Abu Bakr in regard to the necessity of maintaining the unity of the *umma* and could be relied upon to retain the latter's vision. Two, only Umar had both the strength to suppress any rebellion that might arise among those not committed to the ideals of Islam, as well as a strong reputation

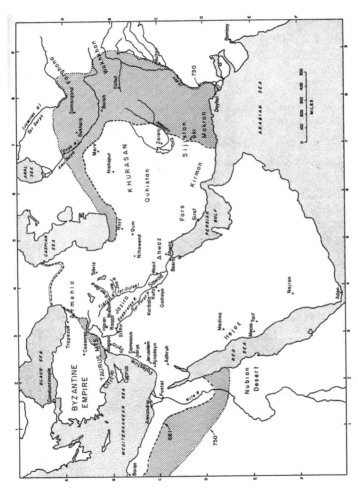

Conquests, Rashidun and Umayyad periods.
Courtesy of the University of Washington Press. (Originally appeared in *A Near East Studies Handbook* by Jere Bacharach, 1977.)

for strict purity that allowed him to retain the respect of those who were.[13]

Once formally in charge—one suspects he was in charge all along—Umar was determined to complete the conquests. Fortuitously, Byzantine control over Syria and Palestine had been seriously weakened by two forces.[14] One, intermittent wars between Byzantium and the Persian Sasanians, especially the widespread destruction of administrative infrastructure during the temporary Sasanian occupation of these areas, left the Byzantines with little reserve military power in the east. Two, the combination of religious fissures and oppressive taxation had turned the subject populations away from their rulers. In addition to Christian doctrinal controversies, the Jews of Palestine had been treated rather harshly and would have had no reason to resist another ruler. In some cases Jews and Christians actually aided the invaders.[15]

The conquests came with amazing ease. The Muslim armies spread out in a three-pronged attack emanating from the Hijaz. One thrust went north toward Byzantium, conquering Palestine and Syria before branching to Egypt. It also invaded Anatolia only to be repulsed. The second went northeast, launched multiple offensives into Sasanian territory and took Iraq and Persia. The third went southeast, conquering what remained independent in the Arabian peninsula, including Oman and Yemen.[16]

Small Muslim forces first began raiding Syria and Palestine under Abu Bakr and then waited for reinforcements. Khalid ibn Walid, who had distinguished himself fighting against Muhammad at the Battle of Uhud, became the greatest general of Islam. He brought his army up the Euphrates via Palmyra and raided Damascus, then turned aside and destroyed a Byzantine army destined to relieve Jerusalem at Ajnadain.[17] Turning back into Syria he blockaded and finally subdued Damascus.[18] The Byzantine Emperor Heraclius later arrived with much larger forces. Khalid first retreated, and then destroyed the main Byzantine army in Syria at the Battle of Yarmuk in 636 after the Arab auxiliaries went over to the Muslim side at a crucial point in the fighting.[19] It is said of both Yarmuk and Al-Qadisiyya (described below) that Khalid used a dust storm to hide his army and regain the initiative.[20] The key to Arab success was skillful use of the desert. As Bernard Lewis summarized their grand strategy,

The mosque of the great general Khalid ibn Walid in Damascus.
Martha Diase, photographer. CMES.

[t]he strategy employed by the Arabs in the great campaigns of conquest was determined by the use of desert-power, on lines strikingly similar to the use of sea-power by modern empires. The desert was familiar and accessible to the Arabs and not to their enemies. They could use it both as a means of communication for supplies and reinforcements, and as a safe retreat in times of emergency. It is no accident that in each of the conquered provinces the Arabs established their main bases in towns on the edge of the desert . . . using existing ones like Damascus when they were suitably placed, creating new ones like Kufa and Basra in Iraq, Fustat in Egypt, [and] Qayrawan in Tunisia where necessary.[21]

Their horses gave them speed, and their camels gave them endurance over long distances,[22] while the desert gave them the ability to simply melt away to fight another day when facing an imposing force.[23]

After Yarmuk the Muslims offered the Syrian towns individual treaties of submission with lower rates of taxation, which they accepted.[24] Whereas in Syria the Byzantines were in a position to attempt a defense, Palestine was simply undefended, and the Muslims were able to conquer it without significant resistance. In 639 the offensive continued into Egypt, for centuries a major supplier of grain to Rome. It was undertaken, some say at his own initiative, by Amr ibn al-As, who had been a merchant there.[25] He took the provincial Roman capital of Alexandria in 642.[26]

At the same time Mu'awiya, a prominent leader of the late-converting clan of Umayya, led the assault deep into Anatolia. Yet with its power-center in Europe still safe, Byzantium was far from defeated, and with the Muslims overextended, Mu'awiya decided that the better part of valor was to wreck as many fortifications as possible and retreat.[27] With the help of the conquered Syrian seagoing merchants, Mu'awiya built a navy and successfully raided Cyprus in 649.[28] The Byzantine fleet was destroyed in 655.[29] Even with the aid of Syrian sailors, this was no small achievement for a people whose only long-distance transportation a few years earlier had been the camel.

From the beginning, Arab chiefs at the Sasanian borderland suddenly found themselves in between two larger belligerents, and some decided to join the *umma*. The Sasanians had recently abolished the subsidized Lakhmid Arab kingdom and replaced it with direct imperial rule. Having been deprived of their pay, Sasanian Arab auxiliaries went over to the Muslims in Iraq as they had in Syria.[30]

Khalid ordered the first thrust into Iraq at Hira in 633, using what was mostly a locally recruited army.[31] The main Sasanian army was destroyed at the Battle of Al-Qadisiyya in 637, where a Persian army estimated at 20,000 was decisively defeated by a much smaller enemy.[32] Shortly thereafter the capital city, Ctesiphon, fell with minimal resistance. By 641 all the Aramaic-speaking areas of the Near East were under Muslim control.[33] Arab tribesmen began migrating into Kufa and Basra in Iraq, adding to the Arab populations of these areas. From these bases the Muslims spread north and east, defeating the last major Sasanian military concentration around the Nahavand region in northern Iran that had also been, along with Iraq, a rich source of agricultural support for the empire. This defeat essentially broke the Sasanian Empire, the last in a long line of non-Muslim Persian empires. Fars was conquered in 650, and Khorasan, the great Persian province on the far side of the empire in the northeast, a year later.[34]

Another campaign swept through Oman and then consolidated Muslim control over Yemen, which had nominally declared allegiance to Muhammad already.[35] Yet a naval offensive against Abyssinia in what is now the northern area of the Sudan ended in failure. With no Arab base from which to work, they would have to wait.[36]

The Organization and Administration of the Early Caliphate

Umar firmly believed in two guiding principles regarding the governance of the Islamic nation—*sabiqa* and *shura*. *Sabiqa* meant "precedence," namely, the preeminence of those who preceded others in adopting Islam. Those who had converted early, when Muhammad's position was tenuous and the reward for conversion was persecution, logically deserved a higher status than those who did not convert until Muhammad had prevailed and conversion brought material benefits. He applied *sabiqa* to *shura* such that the *umma* would be governed based upon consultation between the early companions; those who had by their virtue earned the right to rule the *umma*. Of course Umar would have to listen to anyone with sufficient power to cause him trouble, but he recognized a moral obligation to share power only with those who qualified under *sabiqa*.[37]

Maintaining Muslim unity required enforcing the doctrine that Muhammad was the seal, or the last, of the prophets. This idea, based upon a somewhat opaque Quranic reference, meant that Muhammad could have no successors to his prophetic office. If other prophets were recognized, they might give revelations contrary to the vision of Muhammad's political successors Abu Bakr and Umar. Several had arisen and been declared false, and this stance helped ensure the unity of the *umma*.[38]

There was also the question of the legitimacy of the caliph himself. Although the term *khalifa* (caliph) continued to be used, Umar took the title *amir al-mu'minin*, Commander of the Faithful. This emphasized the military nature of his authority; although Umar had a religious duty to lead the *umma*, he did so in a martial capacity.[39]

The organization of the empire was substantially shaped by the incentives for its expansion. Although core believers viewed the conquests as an expression of *jihad*, the primary goal was not conversion, but the establishment of Muslim rule, and especially for the more materially motivated, the opportunity for plunder. Indeed, for many this war was no different from the many wars which had been waged in the region for three thousand years. The great Khalid ibn Walid himself developed a reputation for raping women on the battlefield and taking baths in wine. He also began hiring poets to proclaim his greatness, and Umar eventually dismissed him.[40]

Umar developed a system to formalize an Arab-Islamic aristocracy that remained the model, with modifications over time, for over a century. Under Muhammad the practice had been established that every *mujahid* (holy warrior) would have a share of the booty in victory, but that a fifth of all spoils were held back for Muhammad, in order to provide for his own family and the needs of the *umma*. He had also said that he had no heirs, and that his widows would be supported by charity. Umar interpreted this to mean that all property administered by Muhammad would accrue to the caliphate, but that his dependent family would receive support from general funds.[41]

There was likewise special provision made under the principle of *sabiqa* for an aristocracy of Islamic virtue, early companions who had suffered with Muhammad.[42] As landowners loyal to Byzantium fled with the conquests, their lands were handed over to the *mujahiddin*.[43] At the edge of the desert, the frontiers were built around garrison towns that functioned as self-sufficient Muslim communities, with religious, taxation, and security functions being the primary municipal responsibilities.[44]

The need for plunder to pay the armies required even further expansion. As the opportunities for booty decreased, this increased both the need to raise more from non-Muslim lands, and to squeeze the portion going to the community, as opposed to the individual soldiers, creating conditions for long-term tension. Muhammad is purported to have said: "The survival of my Community rests on the hoofs of its horses and the points of its lances; as long as they keep from tilling the fields; once they begin to do that they will become as other men."[45] Whether this statement is authentic or was fabricated when it became descriptive, it encapsulates the dilemma that Muslim leaders faced.

This only accentuated the incentive to convert to Islam in order to join in the plunder; thus, "collective entry into Islam, involving obligations of prayer and tax, preceded actual religious conversion."[46] This had started to become the case during Muhammad's lifetime, once the tide had turned in his favor. Conversely, some tribes with only a few or no Muslims were forced by the caliph to join the *umma* at least formally by paying the tax.[47] As the Quran (49:15) states, "The Arabs say, we have adopted faith. Say to them: you do not have faith, rather say, we have become Muslims. For faith has not yet entered your hearts." This dichotomy underlined and accentuated the existence of the Islamic nation as a political entity, not merely a religious faith.

Umar also pursued an agenda of social and religious reformation. He made the *hajj* (pilgrimage to the Mecca) a duty of all Muslims, enforced laws against sexual crimes and drunkenness vigorously, discouraged luxurious living, attempted to make appointments according to the appointee's Islamic virtue rather than his tribal connections, and instituted a lunar calendar.[48]

Uthman, Ali, and the Crisis of Legitimacy

After being struck down by the knife of a Persian slave, Umar appointed from his deathbed a six-member council of early companions, consistent with *sabiqa* and *shura*, to choose the next caliph. In an address two weeks before the attack, Umar had reiterated the principle that the caliphate belonged to the Quraysh generally, not any particular lineage, a swipe at Ali.[49] He nevertheless appointed Ali to the council, along with five others: Uthman ibn Affan, Abd al-Rahman ibn Awf, Sa'd ibn Abi Waqqas, Abd Allah ibn Al-Zubayr, and Talha ibn Ubaydullah. Ali and Uthman emerged as the primary candidates, and after Quraysh leaders made clear that they would defect if Ali were chosen, Uthman won. Only Talha was hostile to Uthman, and he had not returned to Medina in time to take part.[50]

Uthman (r. 644–656) established a system that laid the groundwork for the later Umayyad caliphate (see chapter three). Arabs would stay in the garrison towns and settle on a permanent basis, living apart from others, with the ruling elite being from the Quraysh generally and Uthman's Umayya clan in particular. Yet this engendered a potential problem; because the Sawad, the rich agricultural region of Iraq, attracted so much settlement, emigrants threatened to move the center of power from Mecca and Medina to Iraq, placing the first cities of Islam at the periphery. Uthman thus prohibited the Quraysh from obtaining estates in the Sawad, although they could still do business there.[51] This policy was effective for a time, but it hurt him among the Meccans.

Uthman's practice of favoring his own kin also began to inflame opposition. Uthman's nephew Mu'awiya—previously appointed by Umar—was firmly established in Syria, but his appointee in Egypt was unpopular. Of the two main towns in Iraq, Basra and Kufa, the former accepted his governor reluctantly, but the latter rose in outright opposition. Uthman also had been concerned that there were different versions of the Quranic revelations in circulation, and sensing the potential for crippling disunity, required all to accept a standardized version. Opposition to standardization was generally overcome, but the Kufan reciters refused to accept it. There was also opposition to his financial policies. Uthman reserved the right to expropriate property for the caliphate, as well as levy taxes, whereas the soldiers thought that the lands should have been given to them. In any case no taxes were paid. Ali rallied opposition to Uthman and had solid support in Iraq. [52]

With discontent rising both in the provinces and among the Quraysh, Uthman exacerbated his problems by mistreating prominent members of other tribes, at one point beating a respected member of the Makhzum clan unconscious for criticizing him publicly. Events gathered pace as Talha, still hostile to Uthman, wrote letters inciting revolts against him. To make matters worse, A'isha, Muhammad's most influential widow, turned against Uthman, primarily because she could see that under him the caliphate would forever be denied to her kinsmen. That he had reduced her pension could not have helped. Of the companions, only Zubayr still supported Uthman.[53] Finally, during a riot, supporters of Ali broke into Uthman's home and killed him.[54]

After twenty-four years of waiting, in 656 Ali was acclaimed caliph by his supporters. Yet the five-year period of his reign is generally remembered as a *fitna*, or time of troubles. Ali was supported by most of the rebels who hated Uthman, by the Medinan Ansar, and by the Quran reciters and their followers centered in Kufa. He was immediately challenged by the early companions Zubayr and Talha, and also A'isha. Although the two companions had opposed Uthman, they charged Ali with complicity in his murder because he accepted the support of those directly involved. And as much as she disliked Uthman, A'isha had a visceral hatred for Ali. A victory for Ali, like Uthman, would have meant reserving leadership to descendants of a single lineage.

The two sides soon met at the "Battle of the Camel," so called because A'isha sat in the middle of the battle on a camel as a mascot for the anti-Ali forces. Ali emerged victorious, and he was soon accepted throughout Arabia. Yet the governor of Syria, Mu'awiya, refused to accept Ali on the grounds that the latter refused to give up those who had murdered his kinsman. The two sides met in battle, and at one point Mu'awiya's troops signaled

42

that they wanted to arbitrate the issue, as was the custom in Arabia. Ali accepted, but many of his supporters did not. They insisted that the killing of the impious Uthman was an Islamic duty, and that this compromised Islamic principles with pagan customs. They became known as the Kharijites, "those who go out."[55]

When the arbitration went against him, Ali repudiated the decision, but it was too late. The Kharijites would not rejoin him, and in fact now declared Ali to be a self-serving apostate himself. After that point Ali gradually lost strength, and in 661 he was killed by a Kharijite. Mu'awiya, who originally had not claimed the caliphate for himself, continued to expand his control, and his supporters now declared that he must be the new caliph.[56] The age of the "Rightly Guided Caliphs" was over.

Notes

1. The account of Muhammad's life presented in this chapter assumes what Muslim tradition says about him. The reliability of that tradition is sometimes questioned, as much of it was not written down for two centuries after his death. See Michael Cook, *Muhammad* (New York: Oxford University Press, 1983), as well as Patricia Crone and Michael Cook, *Hagarism: The Making of the Islamic World* (Cambridge: Cambridge University Press, 1977). Yet it is important to understand Muhammad as Muslim tradition presents him; this brief account attempts to summarize that material. For a very detailed but rather dry account of Muhammad's life, see Martin Lings, *Muhammad: His Life Based on the Earliest Sources* (Rochester, Vermont: Inner Traditions International, 1983). For a more concise and readable account, see Karen Armstrong, *Muhammad: A Biography of the Prophet* (New York: HarperCollins Publishers, 1992).
2. Lings, *Muhammad: His Life Based on the Earliest Sources*, 45.
3. Ibid., 85–7.
4. Arthur Goldschmidt, Jr., *A Concise History of the Middle East* (Boulder, Colorado: Westview Press: 1991, 4th ed.) 47.
5. Bernard Lewis, *The Arabs in History* (New York: Oxford University Press: 1993, 6th ed.) 48.
6. Ibid., 35–9.
7. Ibid., 35.
8. Wilfred Madelung, *The Succession to Muhammad: A Study of the Early Caliphate* (Cambridge: Cambridge University Press, 1997) 52–3.
9. Bernard Lewis, *The Middle East: A Brief History of the Last 2,000 Years* (New York: Touchstone, 1995) 54.
10. Madelung, *Succession to Muhammad*, 48.
11. Ibid.
12. Ibid., 49.
13. Ibid., 55–6.

43

14. Cameron, *Late Antiquity*, 186–191.
15. Lewis, *Middle East*, 57–8.
16. Marshall G.S. Hodgson, *The Venture of Islam: Conscience and History of a World Civilization; The Classical Age of Islam* (Chicago: University of Chicago Press, 1974) 202. Hereinafter referred to as Hodgson I.
17. Lewis, *Arabs in History*, 51–2.
18. Ibid., 52.
19. Hodgson I, 200.
20. Goldschmidt, *Concise History of the Middle East*, 49–51.
21. Lewis, *Arabs in History*, 54.
22. Goldschmidt, *Concise History of the Middle East*, 49–50.
23. Roux, *Ancient Iraq*, 334.
24. Hodgson I, 201.
25. Madelung, *Succession to Muhammad*, 61–2.
26. Hodgson I, 203.
27. Ibid., 203.
28. Ibid., 204–5.
29. Ibid., 203.
30. Ibid., 199.
31. Lewis, *Arabs in History*, 52.
32. Ibid., 52; see also Hodgson I, 203.
33. Hodgson I, 201.
34. Ibid., 204.
35. Ibid., 202–6.
36. Ibid., 204.
37. Madelung, *Succession to Muhammad*, 62.
38. Hodgson I, 197–8.
39. Ibid., 207.
40. Goldschmidt, *Concise History of the Middle East*, 51.
41. Madelung, *Succession to Muhammad*, 63.
42. G.E. von Grunebaum, *Classical Islam: A History 600–1258* (New York: Barnes & Noble Books, 1970) 56. See also Hodgson I, 211.
43. Hodgson I, 207–8.
44. Ibid., 209.
45. Von Grunebaum, *Classical Islam*, 57.
46. Ibid., 51.
47. Hodgson I, 198.
48. Ibid., 211.
49. Madelung, *Succession to Muhammad*, 68.
50. Ibid., 70–1.
51. Hodgson I, 212.
52. Madelung, *Succession to Muhammad*, 96; see also Hodgson I, 213.
53. Ibid., 104–5.
54. Hodgson I, 214.
55. Lewis, *Arabs in History*, 63.
56. Ibid., 63–4.

CHAPTER III

From Arab Empire to Islamic Caliphate: The Umayyads and Abbasids

(661–945)

The Umayyads and the Rule of the Arab Aristocracy

After the death of Ali, Mu'awiya ibn Abi Sufyan, the governor of Syria, was well-positioned to take the caliphate. In addition to ruling the most economically important province in the empire, he exercised direct control of the largest part of the army. He further had the custom-sanctified right to avenge the killing of his kinsman, and having been appointed by Umar, he was able to stand above the succession controversies of the reigns of Uthman and Ali.[1]

Domestically, Mu'awiya (r. 661–680) left the Byzantine and Persian administrative structures intact, being sure not to give his largely non-Muslim subjects any incentive to revolt. In the former Sasanian lands of Iraq and Persia he was fortunate to face an opposition divided along tribal lines.[2] He appointed his half-brother Ziyad ibn Abihi (d. 673) ruler in the east. Ziyad was noted for the perfection of his Arabic and the efficiency of his newly organized state police. At his accession speech, Ziyad is reported to have begun thus:[3]

You allow kinship to prevail and put religion second; you excuse and hide your transgressors and tear down the orders which Islam has sanctified for your protection. Take care not to creep about in the night; I will kill every

The entrance to an Umayyad mosque in Damascus.
Martha Diase, photographer. CMES.

man found on the streets after dark. Take care not to appeal to your kin; I will cut off the tongue of every man who raises that call . . . I rule you with the omnipotence of God and maintain you with God's wealth; I demand obedience from you, and you can demand uprightness from me . . . I will not fail in three things: I will at all times be there for every man to speak with me, I will always pay your pensions punctually and I will not send you into the field for too long a time or too far away. Do not be carried away by your hatred and anger against me, it would go ill with you. I see many heads rolling; let each man see that his own head stays upon his shoulders!

Whether these were Ziyad's precise words or words composed later to describe the tenor of his rule, they illustrate the nature of Umayyad governance. He forthrightly proclaims the Islamic legitimacy of the government, but makes clear that if the Quran in one hand were not enough, having the sword in the other would be. The Umayyads would combine the egalitarian leadership style of the Arabian shaikh with the majestic rule of the Persian King of Kings. The reference to the paying of pensions refers to the fact that Arabs had fought with the promise of receiving pensions from the lands that they conquered. Finally, the injunction against kinship loyalty hid the fact that one clan, the Umayya, was ruling over all others.

Shortly after coming to power, Mu'awiya faced a challenge from Hujr ibn Adi, a supporter of Ali. He acted decisively, arresting Adi and having him executed; there would be no consultation with those who opposed his rule. Once subjects accepted his rule, however, he seems to have been respectful of their dignity; ruling in the name of Islam, he represented the unity of the *umma*.[4]

The Umayyad social structure was based upon a mixed religious and ethnic hierarchy. The highest level included pure Arabs. The next level included Muslims of mixed parentage. Below them were non-Arab converts to Islam, the *muwali*, or adopted clients of an Arab tribe. In pre-Islamic times a man without a tribe could be adopted by another tribe for protection, and this practice was continued in this modified form. At the lowest level were the non-Muslim monotheistic subject peoples, the *dhimmi*, mainly

Christians and Jews, which formed their own self-enclosed communities. Polytheists or pagans had no place in the social order; their choice was conversion or death.[5]

This social hierarchy determined the structure and division of political and economic power. Because only pure Arabs could rule, Maslama, a successful military commander and the half-Arab son of a caliph, could hold important positions, but could not become caliph. The *muwali* were further disabled economically, for they often had to pay the same tribute taxes, or *jizya*, paid by the *dhimmi*. Mu'awiya actually (and accurately, as it turned out) viewed the *muwali* as a threat, saying, "I dread that they will ambush the Arabs and [take] the power. I have decided to kill part of them, and to spare another part to run the market and construct the roads."[6] As for the *dhimmi*, their obligation was to pay tribute. Otherwise they managed their affairs themselves.

The administration was divided into five departments: military, taxation, correspondence, registry, and posts.[7] Aside from the *jizya*, the treasury depended on a tithe of 2.5 percent, or *ushur*, on Muslims, and the *kharaj*, or land tax, on everyone.[8] Through legal, tax, and irrigation reforms both local industry and trade were expanded.[9]

Militarily, Mu'awiya continued the pressure on Byzantium in Anatolia, but his only permanent conquest was in Armenia. He attempted the first sustained siege of Constantinople, and he was the first to fail ignominiously.[10]

Mu'awiya's son Yazid (r. 680–683) succeeded to the caliphate upon his father's death. The offensive in Anatolia having collapsed just before his accession, he first began by fortifying that border.[11] This border corresponds roughly to the modern Syria-Turkey border, and thus the limit of the Arab world. Islam would later spread well to the north of Syria and Iraq, but the process of Arabization would not.

Yazid faced two major revolts based on separate causes. One was yet another revolt in Iraq by partisans of Ali, this time led by Hussein ibn Ali, the grandson of Muhammad (through his daughter Fatima). After being first encouraged and then abandoned by supporters from Kufa, Hussein and his outnumbered army were massacred. His "martyrdom" at Karbala is remembered as a holy day by Shi'a Muslims (called *ashura*) to this day. The second was in the Hijaz, led by Abdullah ibn al-Zubayr, a companion of the prophet. That revolt was still alive when Yazid died.[12]

Revolts expanded against Umayyad rule on both fronts. As Yazid left no clear successor, Al-Zubayr was able to consolidate his position to some degree by declaring himself caliph and appointing his own followers in the various provinces. Yet even in the Arabian peninsula he was unable to maintain control because of the continued vitality of the Kharijites who had given Uthman and Ali so much trouble. Engaging in guerilla warfare, the Kharijites controlled the largest amount of territory, but they could not overpower the garrison towns and so were unsuccessful in Iraq and Persia. The Kufan Shi'a, meanwhile, put forward another of Ali's sons, Muhammad ibn al-Hanafiya, as caliph. A Shi'a leader, al-Mukhtar ibn Abu Ubayd al-Thaqafi, advocated a social as well as political change—the *muwali* would be given equality of status, radically changing Islamic society.[13]

For the time being, it was not to be. A cousin of Mu'awiya, Marwan, was able to consolidate control of the military and the tribal factions of Syria, take back Egypt, and overpower Iraq as Mu'awiya had done. The garrison towns continued resisting the Kharijites under his leadership. He also took Mecca in 692, ending al-Zubayr's regime. Thus ended a struggle in which four forces fought for control—al-Zubayr, the Umayyad Marwan, the Shi'a, and the Kharijites—with the triumph of Umayya yet again.[14]

Marwan's son, Abd al-Malik (r. 691/692–705), ascended to the throne and continued the rule of a line called the Marwanids. During the years of internal struggle and consolidation under Abd al-Malik and his son and successor al-Walid (r. 705–715), the Umayyad caliphate entered a period of renewed expansion and confidence. Reacting to a challenge by the Byzantine Emperor Justinian II, Abd al-Malik launched a cultural and religious counteroffensive. Greek had remained the language of administration, but Abd al Malik replaced it with Arabic. Many of his administrators still would be Christians, but now they had to learn Arabic, and this accentuated the trend toward Arabization and Islamization. Whereas until his time the Umayyads had used Byzantine coins, which bore the emperor's face, a new coinage was issued. After some experimentation with more Islamic symbols, the practice of using Quranic inscriptions rather than pictures began.[15] These trends contributed to the development of calligraphy, the uniquely Islamic practice of using the Arabic script as an art form.

Abd al-Malik secured his legacy by staking Islam's claim to Jerusalem more firmly. Jerusalem was still an overwhelmingly Christian city. Mt. Moriah, the site of the Jewish temple, had been cleared by Mu'awiya but then abandoned, suggesting plans laid but unfulfilled. In 691 Abd al-Malik appropriated the mount and built the Dome of the Rock upon it, and adjacent to it he built the al-Aqsa Mosque. This decision probably was the result of a need to affirm Islam's standing in the face of the Byzantine challenge to an empire that ruled a predominantly Christian land. The new monuments contained a number of calligraphic declarations aimed at Christians, including this verse from Quran 112: "God is one, eternal. He neither begets nor is he begotten. Neither is there any like unto him." This may have also had an internal purpose—since in 691 Mecca was still in the hands of the Umayyads' rivals, Jerusalem provided them with a holy city to rival Mecca in case the latter could not be retaken.[16] From that time onward Jerusalem, previously known by its Roman name Aelia, has been called Al-Quds, the Holy City.[17]

Marwan and Abd al-Malik also directed another series of conquests, some more successful than others. Another siege was made against Constantinople, and with its defeat they again were pushed back to Syria. The conquest of North Africa was completed, as the Byzantines gave little resistance, and the drive continued into Spain. The native Berber tribes of the area, not wanting to become a subject people, converted to Islam. In the east, the caliphate expanded its hold into Sind in the Indus Valley.[18]

Al-Walid's brother and successor, Sulayman (r. 715–717), further destabilized the empire's Syria-Iraq core by allowing governors to play tribes against one another. His support among the pious was also weak; Sulayman was known for his hedonism and sadism. He enjoyed watching prisoners being hacked to death with dull swords.[19]

Fortunately for the Umayyads, Sulayman "saw the light" before his death and designated his popular and pious cousin Umar ibn Abd al-Aziz (r. 717–720) his successor. Umar II, as he became known, accomplished much to restore unity to the empire during his short reign. He had a strong following among the pious in the

The Dome of the Rock in Jerusalem.
CMES.

The Church of the
Holy Sepulchre
in Jerusalem.
CMES.

Hijaz, and he attempted a rapprochement with the Shi'a by discouraging attacks on Ali at Friday sermons. He ended the Berber tribute of children, emphasized the equality of all provinces, reduced taxes, fought corruption, and decentralized the administration. Alone among the Umayyads, he won at least partial support from the Shi'a and the Kharijites.[20]

Umar II also adopted a policy of promoting conversion to Islam. Previously conversion had not been encouraged as it reduced tax revenues. He further tightened the disabilities imposed upon non-Muslims; for example, Christians and Jews could not ride horses, only mules, and were forced to wear special marks on their clothing. He is the only Umayyad ruler later recognized by Muslim historians as a true caliph; the others were called "kings,"[21] a derogatory term denoting despotism rather than enlightened rule. For similar reasons, Christians remembered him as a persecutor.[22]

Although the Umayyads would rule for thirty years after the death of Umar II, the six remaining Umayyad rulers at best managed to preserve the status quo. Never again was their Arab aristocracy able to manage the internal divisions of the Islamic empire over which they ruled, and these divisions in turn inhibited further conquest. Sulayman's brother, Yazid II (r. 720–724), inherited this improved situation after Umar's short reign. Yazid was less than devout, "given to women and song," but he avoided all-out revolt. He was faced with a significant uprising from the Qahtan tribe in Iraq and put it down, increasing the grip of an opposing tribe, the Qays, in the east. This did nothing to solve the underlying problems.[23]

Yazid was succeeded by the more devout Hisham (r. 724–743). Hisham's solution to disunity was to expand the bureaucracy and enforce a tighter grip on the provinces. Placing greater distance between himself and local leaders, Hisham set the absolutist example that the Abbasids later would follow. At this time, however, the Abbasi family, descended from Muhammad's uncle al-Abbas, was merely one of the more successful opposition groups. Hisham transferred Khalid al-Qasri, who as governor of Mecca had been unpopular with the pious, to Iraq, where in 737 he arrested many opposition leaders and had them burned alive. Yet the Abbasids survived the repression, and Hisham also faced widespread Kharijite revolts. Hisham's rule was long and steady but failed to provide the Umayyads with a more stable basis of legitimacy.[24]

The seven years following Hisham's death represented the Umayyads' last gasp. He was succeeded by his nephew al-Walid II in 743, who was assassinated after only about a year in power. Al-Walid was quickly followed by Yazid III, a Marwanid with some support from the pious, but he was killed before he was able to institute reforms that might have saved the regime. He was also the last Umayyad caliph with any real power. After the death of Walid II a Marwanid general, Marwan ibn Muhammad, the most prominent of the military leaders fighting the Byzantines, took the foreground to avenge al-Walid's death with the support of the Qays tribe. Later called Marwan II, his disciplined and well-led army suppressed Kharijite revolts in both Arabia and Iraq, as well as a major Shi'a movement in Iraq led by a descendant of Abu Talib, Ali's father.[25]

Marwan II had less success with the Abbasids. In addition to Shi'a sentiment, the Abbasids drew support from the *muwali*, in particular the Persian gentry, and the pious. This latter group was given voice by a new group, the *ulama*, or the scholars of Islam (see chapter four). Abu Muslim, a freed slave of the Abbasid imam Ibrahim, created a coalition of discontents, raising black banners as a symbol of mourning for all the pious Muslims who had been killed by the Umayyads. Marwan II had Ibrahim killed, but he seems to have underestimated the movement. Abu Muslim added Ibrahim to the list of martyrs, and by 748 represented the only major opposition group Marwan's troops had not suppressed. Two years later, the main element of Marwan's army was defeated in Iraq, and the Abbasids took power.[26]

The Abbasids and the "Golden Age" of Islam

Abu al-Abbas (r. 750–754), also known as al-Saffah ("the blood-shedder"), was head of the Abbasi family at the time of their victory and he became the first caliph of the new empire. Like many successful revolutionaries, al-Saffah immediately faced what might be called the Dilemma of the Successful Revolutionary—as revolutions often are brought about by a coalition of forces with different goals and interests, and as revolutionaries tend to be uncompromising (otherwise they would not be revolutionaries), the successful revolutionary must decide which elements of the coalition

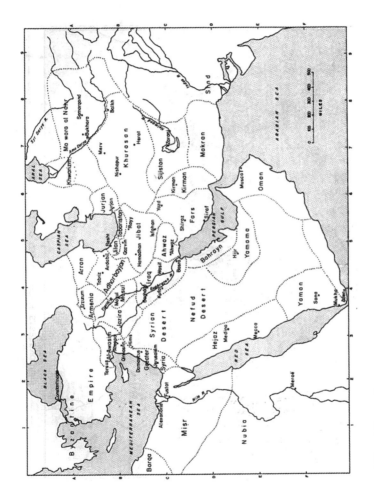

Abbasid provinces.

Courtesy of the University of Washington Press. (Originally appeared in *A Near East Studies Handbook* by Jere Bacharach, 1977.)

are necessary for stable rule, and which have to get the axe, so to speak.[27]

One of the first to get the axe, and not merely as a manner of speaking, was the architect of the Abbasid victory, Abu Muslim himself.[28] As a practical matter, Abbasid power rested upon the mixed Arab and Persian gentry of Iraq and Persia and their military units, so this core had to be maintained above all else.[29] Al-Saffah's brother al-Mansur (r. 754–775) set the foundations for stable Abbasid rule. In 762 he moved the capital to Iraq, near the Tigris River, and this new capital was called *medinat al-salaam*, or the City of Peace. [30] In time it became known by the name of a local village—Baghdad.[31] Al-Mansur then moved to stabilize his coalition. Aside from the non-Arab gentry, Abbasid support had rested on two mutually antagonistic elements, the Shi'a and the piety-minded Sunnis represented by the *ulama*; one or the other had to go. Al-Mansur began systematically assassinating prominent Shi'a, and he repressed a Shi'a revolt at Mecca. He then faced down the *ulama* and forced them to choose between resistance and death or acquiescence and indirect influence without effective power. They chose the latter.[32] He eventually succeeded in consolidating some control over the entire empire except the western provinces (see chapter five).

The economic center of the empire also shifted from Syria to Iraq. Syria had played a central role in Mediterranean commerce both before Islam and under the Umayyads, but the Abbasids allowed Syrian irrigation to collapse and instead invested in rejuvenating the agriculturally rich Sawad region of Iraq. Baghdad's location also had been determined on the basis of its commercial accessibility, and stable rule allowed the state to depend on taxes from merchants. It also became the cultural hub of the empire, and the commercial, administrative, and cultural centralization further isolated Syria.[33]

Al-Mansur was able to manage a peaceful succession to al-Mahdi (r. 775–785). Al-Mahdi made no attempt to recover the western provinces, but renewed the offensive in the north against the Byzantines in Anatolia. His raids had little effect, but al-Mahdi did better domestically. He successfully repressed an Umayyad revival in Egypt and a Shi'a revolt in the Hijaz, and promoted a rapprochement with the *ulama* who just recently had been brought to support the regime at sword point. Not only did he make an effort to promote Islamic unity in his speeches, albeit under Abbasid absolutism, he found common cause with the *ulama* in fighting a theological threat—Manicheanism.

Manicheanism was an ascetic, otherworldly Gnostic religion of Persian origin, founded in the third century A.D. It lacked the formal structures that might have allowed for organized opposition to Islam, but this very characteristic made it hard to root out. The *ulama* viewed Manicheanism as a dagger aimed at the heart of Islam. Based around a transcendental view of the body and viewing temporal life as distasteful, it promoted detachment from society. Although the religion had little appeal to peasants, many government officials were considered secret Manicheans, and their numbers were growing. Since it was not monotheistic, the *ulama* were able to demand that unrepentant Manicheans be executed, and al-Mahdi garnered their support by doing so. By the end of his reign, not only had the *ulama* become more supportive of Abbasid rule, but even many Shi'a and Kharijites had moved from active opposition to passive acquiescence.[34]

The reign of al-Mahdi's son, Harun al-Rashid (r. 786–809), has come to be viewed as the height of Abbasid power and splendor, evoking the "Golden Age" of Islam. He maintained a long period of peace and stability, and used it to improve the administration and promote cultural development. Poets, musicians, and scholars received official support. He believed that the caliph held the dual roles of Muhammad himself in leading prayers as head of the religious community and commanding the *jihad*. Harun thus established a pattern: one year he would lead the pilgrimage to Mecca, the next an attack against the Byzantines.[35] The extent of formal Abbasid rule under Harun included Arabia, Persia, the Levant, Egypt, North Africa to Tunisia, central Asia up to the Aral and Caspian seas, and significant distances into Anatolia.[36]

It was during this time that the "dynasty of viziers," the Persian Barmakids, previously a family of Buddhist priests, reached its pinnacle. Over successive reigns they held the position of vizier, a chief administrator with enormous power. A Barmakid had been a close advisor of al-Saffah, and Yahya ibn Khalid al-Barmaki had been in charge of Harun's affairs when he was young. Harun grew up close to Yahya's son Ja'far, who became chief advisor, and his other son al-Fadl became head of the administration. Yet when

Harun noticed supplicants becoming accustomed to seeking out the Barmakids, he grew jealous. One night he had his friend Ja'far beheaded and both al-Fadl and his father imprisoned, and both soon died.[37] Harun himself died six years later in 809. Ironically, the caliph most associated with the Golden Age of Islam died not prosecuting a *jihad* against infidels, but in suppressing a rebellion by the Muslim Kharijites.[38]

A gentle decline of Abbasid power began after Harun's death with a less than gentle struggle between his sons for power. Prior to his death, Harun had appointed two of his sons as heirs: al-Amin in Baghdad and al-Ma'mun in Egypt. It is not clear why he did this, as it was sure to lead to war, and it did. Unsatisfied with Egypt, al-Ma'mun marched on Iraq. Because much of al-Ma'mun's support was Persian, the population of Baghdad rallied around al-Amin, allowing him to put up a fight before losing.[39]

Al-Ma'mun (r. 813–833) enjoyed a continuation of the economic expansion that had accelerated under his father, and he was able to suppress those revolts that arose through his Persian-led military. His efforts focused on religious reconciliation, consensual and otherwise. After suppressing a Shi'a revolt in Kufa, al-Ma'mun attempted to co-opt them by appointing one of their leaders, Ali al-Rida', as his own heir to the caliphate. This incited rebellion among the Sunni population, so al-Rida' managed to die in a timely manner, giving al-Ma'mun breathing space in Iraq. Sections of the *ulama* who specialized in collecting traditions of the prophet had become very divisive, especially in their hostility toward the Shi'a. Al-Ma'mun aggravated the problem by forcing judges, *ulama*, and officials to take what today would be considered a "loyalty oath" rejecting certain doctrines. In doing so he relied upon a faction called the Mu'atezila—ideological "shock troops"—whose theology was based on deductive reasoning from the Quran rather than the mass collection and recitation of prophetic traditions. This may have served the caliphate's short term need for stability, but the Mu'atezilas were opposed with particular vengeance to the popular doctrine that the Quran, unlike the rest of the world, was uncreated, but had existed forever with God. Al-Ma'mun required all public appointees to reject the doctrine, but in doing so he alienated large segments of the population, most of whom were hostile to the Mu'atezila.[40]

Loss of Sunni Arab support increased the dependence of the caliphate on non-Arab troops. One of the Persian generals, Tahir, set up a military government around Baghdad. It was essentially a state within a state, and Tahir's son succeeded him without opposition. Al-Ma'mun put down a Shi'a uprising in the Hijaz, but soon faced another within his own family that championed an alternative caliph who would rule with the support of Arabs rather than Persians. He was able to retain power, but the attempt itself indicated the growing legitimacy crisis.[41]

His brother al-Mu'tasim (r. 833–842) inherited both the Persian-Arab conflict and the Mu'atezila controversy, both of which turned the population of Iraq against the caliphate. In order to deal with the former problem, al-Mu'tasim found a "solution" that would haunt the Arab world for centuries. In order to end his dependence on the Persian military, he developed a self-perpetuating and self-governing elite military guard made of slaves of Central Asian Turkic origin, supervised only by the caliph himself. He created an alternative capital in nearby Samarra, regaining some independence. Al-Mu'tasim also initiated another offensive against the Byzantines in Anatolia and planned a joint land-naval siege of Constantinople. The attack was called off when the fleet was destroyed in a storm, and in retreat the army lost all ground gained during his reign.[42]

Al-Mu'tasim was succeeded by his son al-Wathiq (r. 842–847) and then by al-Mutawakkil (r. 847–861), who instituted major changes. He reversed the religious policy of his predecessors, placing the previously persecuted *ulama* in charge of religious affairs. He also returned to vigorous persecution of the Shi'a and the formerly favored Mu'atezila. Yet he seems not to have taken the responsibilities of governance too seriously. His lifestyle was not merely extravagant, which would have been standard, but ludicrous; he once threw a "Yellow Party" at which everything had to be yellow—the clothes worn, food and drink consumed, the water in the fountains, even the girls had to be blond.[43]

Al-Mutawakkil met his end at the hands of his Turkic guards, who installed his son in his place.[44] In a decade four caliphs were installed or removed at the whims of their military commanders. The next Abbasid with any effective power was al-Muwaffaq (r. 870–891), a leader of exceptional talent who was able to restore some order

58

while governing in the name of his brother, al-Mu'tamid, who was the titular caliph. Yet he was forced to allow the Turkic military ruler of Egypt, Ahmad ibn Tulun, to establish his own dynasty, the Tulunids. He also had to accept the establishment of a Shi'a Zaydi state to the north of Iraq near the Caspian.[45] Turning east, al-Muwaffaq faced an attempt by his governor in western Iran, Ya'qub ibn al-Saffar, to seize power. Al-Muwaffaq managed to save Iraq but lost Iran (which had been under formal Abbasid rule through the Tahirids). Then in the south al-Muwaffaq had to deal with a rebellion of African slaves that had arisen just before the time of his own accession. These African slaves, called the Zanj, established a state in southern Iraq that al-Muwaffaq was not able to suppress for fourteen years, until 883.[46]

After this whirlwind of retrenchment and consolidation al-Muwaffaq's son al-Mu'atadid (r. 891–902) and grandson al-Muktafi (r. 902–908) managed to oversee a tenuous but real reassertion of caliphal control over the military. The capital was returned to Baghdad in 892 from Samarra.[47]

Yet even this "revival" of caliphal authority was essentially limited to Iraq. Since the beginning of the Abbasid caliphate a variety of trends had tended to pull the empire apart. One, as we have seen repeatedly, was religious factionalism. Although Kharijite forces weakened over time, they did not dissipate entirely, and Shi'a sentiment remained resistant to the vision of the Sunni *ulama*. Two, the sheer size of the empire and the nature of communications at the time made tight control impractical. Stretching from Spain to India horizontally and from Arabia to Anatolia vertically, the empire could not be controlled by the administrative apparatus in Baghdad. Three, the nature of the caliphate's federal structure— tax money only went one way, from the provinces to Baghdad— provided another impetus for regionalization. When a governor like Tulun in Egypt withheld taxes and promised to spend the money at home, this served to strengthen his position.[48]

Having lost all territory west of the Sinai and east of Iraq, Baghdad lost control of much of the "central periphery" as well, including Arabia. Two apparently separate Shi'a groups, both called Qarmatians, arose. One gained both peasant and Bedouin support in the borderlands between Iraq and Syria, but in a last gasp of strength, the Abbasids put them down. The other group established itself in eastern Arabia and Bahrain, and could not be suppressed. There also was a successful Shi'a movement in the Hijaz.[49] In 897, Zaydi Shi'a came to power in Yemen, and in 905 the heads of a tribal confederation called the Hamdanids established an independent state in Syria and northern Iraq with its capital in Mosul. Sensing weakness, the Byzantines went on the offensive, even to the point of almost reconquering Syria. A Persian military coterie, the Ziyarids, had become independent and in 928 took control of not only Persia but eastern Iraq. Meanwhile, the Abbasids had managed to regain Egypt from the Tulunids in 906, but around 937 the new governor, Muhammad ibn Tughj, later called al-Ikhshid, declared independence. He next went to the aid of Syria against the Byzantines, and thereafter ruled Syria himself.[50]

After the death of al-Muktafi in 908 the caliphate was on life support. A child, al-Muqtadir (r. 908–932), was put on the throne. His reign was known for its profligacy, and it pushed the treasury into bankruptcy. For fourteen years following his death, four successive caliphs were installed by military factions. In 945 the Buyids, the dominant faction among the Persian Shi'a Ziyarids, completed the conquest of the heartland of Iraq, subduing Baghdad. Formal Abbasid rule would last until the Mongol invasion in 1258, but the age of Arab caliphal leadership was over.[51]

Notes

1. Lewis, *Middle East*, 64.
2. Von Grunebaum, *Classical Islam*, 70.
3. Ibid., 70–1.
4. Hodgson I, 218.
5. Lewis, *Middle East*, 65–6.
6. Nazih N. Ayubi, *Over-stating the Arab State: Politics and Society in the Middle East* (London: I.B. Tauris, 1995) 61, quoting Ibn Abd Rabbih in Tayyib Tizini, *Mashru' ru'ya jadida li al-firk al-'arabi* [A Project for a New Perspective Towards Arab Thought] (Damascus: Dar Dimashq, 1981).
7. Ibid., 61.
8. Von Grunebaum, *Classical Islam*, 73.
9. Ayubi, *Over-stating the Arab State*, 61.
10. Hodgson I, 219.
11. Ibid.
12. Ibid., 219–21.
13. Ibid., 222.

14. Ibid., 223.
15. Michael Angold, *Byzantium: A Bridge from Antiquity to the Middle Ages* (New York: St. Martin's Press, 2001) 66–9. For a more in-depth discussion of the use of coins as medieval propaganda, and comparisons between the Umayyads and later Islamic empires in their use of writing, see Irene A. Bierman, *Writing Signs: The Fatimid Public Text* (Berkeley: University of California Press, 1998).
16. Lewis, *Middle East*, 67–9.
17. Ibid., 70.
18. Hodgson I, 226.
19. Ibid., 267–8.
20. Ibid., 268–9.
21. Lewis, *Middle East*, 71.
22. Hodgson I, 269.
23. Ibid., 271.
24. Ibid.
25. Ibid., 272–3.
26. Ibid., 273–4.
27. Lewis, *Middle East*, 76–7. This proposition was inspired by a passage of Lewis', although he uses the phrase "dilemma of power," and states the issue somewhat differently. The formulation given here is my own, and is thus not in quotes. Henry Kissinger frames the issue as the "iron law of revolutions": "the more extensive the eradication of existing authority, the more its successors must rely on naked power to establish themselves." See Henry A. Kissinger, *Diplomacy* (New York: Simon & Schuster, 1994) 655. This "iron law" is demonstrated over and over again in Arab history.
28. Ibid.
29. Ibid.
30. Von Grunebaum, *Classical Islam*, 86.
31. Lewis, *Middle East*, 77.
32. Hodgson I, 284–5.
33. Ibid., 286–7.
34. Ibid., 289–91.
35. Ibid., 291–4.
36. Ibid., 294.
37. Ibid., 295.
38. Ibid., 300.
39. Ibid.
40. Ibid., 480.
41. Ibid., 475.
42. Ibid., 482.
43. Ibid., 485.
44. Ibid., 485–6. See also Von Grunebaum, *Classical Islam*, 98.
45. Ibid., 486–7.
46. Ibid.
47. Ibid., 488.
48. Ibid., 490.
49. Ibid., 490–491.
50. Ibid., 494–495. See also Philip K. Hitti, *History of the Arabs* (New York: Palgrave, 2002, 10th ed.) 455–6.
51. Ibid.

The mosque courtyard in the Nasr Citadel in Cairo.
Christopher Rose, photographer. CMES.

CHAPTER IV

Islam, Law, and the State

The Islamic Concept of the State

More than merely rulers of a new empire, the Umayyads and Abbasids as well as their subjects also were the creators of a new civilization. The lands that they had conquered—Arabia, Syria, Iraq, Persia, and North Africa from Egypt to Morocco—previously had been the home of two ancient civilizations. To the east, there was an Irano-Semitic tradition stretching back to ancient Mesopotamia. When Islam appeared, the culture of the Persian Sasanian Empire was sustained by a Zoroastrian priestly hierarchy and an ancient Iranian literary tradition.[1] The west was dominated by a civilization that was Greek and Roman in its political structure and Christian in religion, with all three major elements contributing to its culture and intellectual traditions. The eastern Mediterranean was ruled by Byzantium, an heir to the Roman Empire, which emphasized the supreme religious authority of the emperor.

At first, the caliphs had been content to leave the provincial structures intact as long as the Christian population paid taxes and respected Muslim rule. With the reign of Abd al-Malik, however, the first Muslim-Christian "culture war" broke out as the Umayyads responded to Byzantine propaganda aimed at their subjects. This threat, combined with the desire to prevent Muslim conquerors from assimilating into the non-Muslim cultures they ruled, spurred Muslims to further develop their own political, legal, intellectual,

63

The Roman ruins of Volubilis in Morocco.

Ron Baker, photographer. CMES.

and literary identity. While taking much from prior civilizations, they formed a unique Islamic civilization that set them apart from their forebears. Religious legal scholars, collectively referred to as the *ulama*, held a special place in this civilization.

Perhaps the most important element of the new civilization was Islamic law, or the *shari'a* ("the way"). Law is as essential to Islam as theology is to Christianity, or as philosophy was to the civilization of the ancient Greeks. Many Quranic and prophetic statements refer explicitly to matters of law. From the beginning, the injunctions of Islam had been viewed as both legal and moral obligations among the faithful. While members of protected religions (i.e. non-Muslim monotheists), or *dhimmi*, were exempt, their status itself was regulated by law. Just as Muhammad made no distinction between his roles as prophet, governor, and military leader while ruling Medina, Muslims made no distinction between the institutions of religion and state.

Indeed, Islam had no institutional structure comparable to the ecclesiastical institutions of Christendom. The state itself thus came to fulfill both its normal role and that of a religious institution, and this required the creation of sub-state communities for monotheistic non-Muslims. This notion of the state as an agent of religion has been exemplified, for example, in the application of the death penalty for apostasy from Islam, just as states execute people for treason. While considered barbaric by many today, this practice follows logically from the geopolitical nature of the *umma*. Converting from Islam was not merely a change of religion, but a form of treason.[2]

Islamic political theory was based around the model established, or thought to have been established, by Muhammad while he ruled in Medina. The caliph performed Muhammad's political function as head of the *umma*. As the caliph was only a successor to Muhammad in his political role, not his prophetic one, he could not introduce religious innovations. Instead, it was his duty to enforce the *shari'a*. It was the duty of the *ulama* to say what God's law constituted. The Islamic state was thus made up of an executive branch consisting of the caliph and his functionaries, and a judicial branch made up of the *ulama*, but no legislative branch, since the law had already been given and merely needed to be interpreted. These concepts are sometimes referred to in

65

Arabic collectively by the phrase *din wa dawla*—religion and political state.

There were differing views on the extent of caliphal power. Most *ulama* took the view that the caliph was more a servant of the *shari'a* than a ruler of the *umma*, a first among equals. In this capacity, he was to consult closely with the *ulama*, and then simply implement the law as given to him.

In contrast, the High Caliphal view emphasized the preeminence of the caliph, "the Shadow of God on earth."[3] Islamic empires adopted a view of monarchial rule, without adopting dynastic kingship *per se*, similar to that which was widespread elsewhere prior to modern times. It was understood that the power of the ruler had to be absolute, for only an absolute ruler could maintain order and prevent the strong from abusing the weak. Having absolute power, he could listen with open-mindedness and magnanimity to the petitions of his subjects. No one would think that such petitions posed a threat to his rule, since granting them was an act of pure grace on his part. Thus, whereas in the modern mind monarchy often connotes tyranny and repression, to the premodern mind it represented security and justice.[4]

Under either view, caliphal authority did not mean that there were no limits on the ruler. To the contrary, the ruler was bound by the *shari'a* to the same extent as everyone else. Yet, as Bernard Lewis put it, "this is a duty of the sovereign, not a right of the subject."[5] Indeed, the concept of a subject having rights that might be enforced against the ruler did not arrive in the Arab world until relatively recently. The very idea of "liberty" as it appears in Anglo-American political theory simply did not exist. Both Western and Islamic thought contained the concept of tyranny, but in Western ideology the opposite of tyranny was liberty, while in Islam the opposite of tyranny was justice.[6] Since no legal mechanism for enforcing the *shari'a* against the ruler ever was developed, those who believed that a ruler had become too impious had to remove him by force.

The influence of Byzantine concepts of religion and state may be inferred. Byzantium's unity of religious, political, and military authority was a model with which early Muslims had extensive contact, not only in the lands they conquered but also through Byzantium's struggle for control over Arabia in the decades before

Islam. Religious and political identity thus came to be fused in the Arabian mind.[7] A complementary theory that has been proposed is that after the conquest of Persia, ancient Iranian ideals of autocratic, religious rule permeated the Muslim ruling ideology.[8] Both traditions were no doubt important influences.

What became the orthodox Muslim view, which has prevailed into modern times, is expressed in a statement purporting to come from Muhammad himself:

> Islam (or religion) and government are twin brothers. One cannot thrive without the other. Islam is the foundation, and government the guardian. What has no foundation, collapses; what has no guardian, perishes.[9]

The "Heirs of the Prophet"

There is an adage that while the caliph was the successor to Muhammad in his political role, the *ulama* collectively were the "heirs of the Prophet"[10] in his religious role, as it was their function to study the divine law and to declare it to others. Although there is no formal clergy in Islam, the *ulama* came to be the closest analogy existing for the positions of both theologians and ministers in Christianity. Given the Islamic conception of the state, the *ulama* took over much of the role of a judiciary as well.

The judicial infrastructure began to take shape under the Umayyads. In order to handle judicial cases, the ruler would appoint a *qadi*—a judge—to make decisions on questions of law. The position itself was not an Islamic one. The *qadi*, rather, was a state judicial official who could rely on any materials available in order to come to a just decision. Initially, *qadi*s relied upon the legal precedents of the provinces in which they sat, which usually meant applying Byzantine or Sasanian practice. In order to bring judicial practice in line with Islam, a *mujtahid*, or legal scholar, could engage in *ijtihad*, or independent legal reasoning, and give an opinion on a specific question. When acting in this capacity a *mujtahid* is called a *mufti*, and the legal opinion that he renders is called a *fatwa*. In order to be a *mujtahid* a man needed to be recognized as having a proficient understanding of Islamic principles,

67

but a fatwa was not considered binding, as there were—as in most of the Muslim world today—no systematic criteria for who could become a *mujtahid*.[11] (The most prominent exception today is modern Iran, in which a hierarchy of religious scholars has developed such that a fatwa can be binding).

Parallel to, but independent from, the growth of the state's judicial apparatus was the development of the *shari'a* itself through the efforts of Muslim scholars, primarily from Iraq, Syria, and Arabia. Their goal was to take scattered principles and opinions and fashion them into a formal system of legal thought which then could be implemented by the caliph and his mandarins as well as by *qadis*. The first prominent legal scholars were Malik ibn Anas (c. 715–795) and Abu Hanifa (699–767), and their systems of thought have survived in schools of law named after them (Maliki and Hanafi) to this day. Coming later were al-Shafi'i (767–820) and Ahmad ibn Hanbal (750–855), whose schools of law also survive.[12]

The diversity of legal opinion, combined with the non-binding nature of the individual fatwa, might have led to a great deal of uncertainty. However, the concept of binding precedent existed collectively in the concept of *taqlid* ("tradition"). In terms of Islamic law, *taqlid* meant that the law's traditional understanding had to be maintained. By the tenth century this was facilitated by the closing of the gates of *ijtihad*—an end to the use of independent legal reasoning. Scholars still could give fatwas, but, at least in theory, they had to be based upon the *shari'a* as it developed during the early centuries of Islam, rather than advancing new legal concepts. Furthermore, the rulers of a given province would usually adopt a specific school of law and make it mandatory. This also served to increase the predictability of the law.

The idea that innovative legal reasoning was not permissible naturally has given rise to a high degree of rigidity in Islamic law, but scholars have found ways to ameliorate its severity. One is through the use of a *hiyal* ("means"), a legal device by which an inconvenient principle can be managed. *Hiyal*s came to be used in many contexts, but nowhere more often than in commercial transactions. For example, if A wished to borrow money from B, A would give B a book in exchange for the amount needed, and later would buy the book back from B for the amount that originally changed hands, plus an extra amount. This marginal increase in effect would constitute the payment of interest on a loan without technically violating the Quranic ban on usury. In other cases, it might be easier to simply interpret an old principle in a new way without explicitly saying so, and this is usually what has been done.

In recent centuries there have been increased calls for reopening the gates of *ijtihad*. After all, the Quran was revealed by God and the Sunna by His prophet, but the *shari'a* was formed by men. Although this idea might seem to be a means of promoting modernization, the reality is often to the contrary. The most influential advocates of *ijtihad* in recent centuries have been fundamentalist reformers who wanted to abolish the traditions of the societies in which they lived and reestablish pure Islam by going back to the roots. Others have sought a reopening as a means of moving closer to Western norms of legal thought.

The Essentials of Islamic Law

Islamic law has four sources: the Quran, the Sunna, analogy, and consensus, collectively known as *usul al-fiqh*, or tools of understanding (*fiqh* refers to the application of human understanding to practical problems). The Quran, as we have seen, is a collection of verses or recitations believed to have been revealed to Muhammad and collected into a single volume some years after his death. It contains passages on a variety of legal subjects, mostly dealing with inheritance, family law, and criminal punishment. Yet alone they are far from sufficient to establish a legal system.

The Sunna, or *sunat al-nabi*, the "way of the Prophet," includes reports, or *hadith*, regarding things Muhammad said, did, or passively approved by allowing them to take place in his presence. (The term *Sunni Muslim* is derived from *Sunna*.) The earliest extant reference to the Sunna is from a letter written by a Kharijite leader to Caliph Abd al-Malik (c. 695), an example of the opposition citing legal authority against a ruler.[13]

There was, however, a documentation problem. In Islam's early years there were many people alive who could give firsthand testimony to Muhammad's life and teachings. After the death of his companions, such testimony had to be relayed indirectly, and there was increasing concern as time passed about the accuracy of the hadith. In addition to the fallibility of human memory, the political environment provided a powerful incentive to fabrication.

There thus arose a group called *ahl al-hadith*, which we may call "hadith specialists."[14] These hadith specialists, acting independently of any central authority, gathered reports about Muhammad. Over time they gathered thousands of hadith with various degrees of trustworthiness. At first there appears to have been an attitude that the Sunna was the living tradition of the community, valid even if not clearly traced to Muhammad. There is even a hadith in which Muhammad is purported to say precisely this![15] Yet when it became clear that this loose approach encouraged fabrication for personal ends, specialists developed a system of authentication. In order for a hadith to be accepted, it had to be accompanied by a chain, or *isnad*, of reporters, each of whom had to be a trustworthy individual. Thus a typical hadith with *isnad* would be: "I heard A say that B said that C said that D said that he was at the mosque when he heard the messenger of God say X, Y, and Z." If the four persons cited all were known to be of reputable character, the hadith was accepted.[16]

The third source of Islamic law is *qiyas*, or analogy. Al-Shafi'i was especially known for his emphasis on this tool. If no Quranic or prophetic precedent could be found for a given situation, then the mufti could find something analogous. Thus, since wine is prohibited in the Quran, later scholars also could prohibit substances that had a similar effect, such as opium. What constitutes a proper analogy of course is subjective; to take the present example, it is disputed among *ulama* today whether substances such as opium are prohibited. Nevertheless, the use of analogy provided increased flexibility in dealing with new issues, and it is widely, but not universally, accepted. The Hanbali school, for example, is known for its preference of "'a weak hadith over a strong analogy.'"[17] Hanbal and others thought that the use of analogy brought human reasoning into the formation of divine law. Their critics responded that those who said they rejected human reasoning were using it anyway without saying so.

The fourth source of Islamic law is *ijma'*, or consensus. This principle is based upon a convenient hadith in which Muhammad says that "my community will never agree upon an error." Although consensus provides for a basis for decision where even analogy is not helpful, there is no consensus on consensus itself. What percentage of agreement is required? Who makes up the consensus? (The *ulama* is the usual answer.) Can a decision reached by consensus be changed by consensus?[18] The concept of *ijma'* was essentially developed as a catch-all principle. When the Quran, the Sunna, and analogy fail to provide an answer, you do what you can agree on.

Eventually it became clear that the *shari'a*, even when expanded in scope by the use of analogy or consensus, could not cover many mundane aspects of human life towards which legal norms are usually directed. Thus developed the concept of *qanun*, a term that means "law," but unlike *shari'a*, it was admittedly a man-made law. During the twentieth century it became common for Arab states to adopt codes based upon Western models for certain subjects, such as investment or environmental regulation. Such codes are referred to as *qanun*.

To summarize: the Quran, the Sunna, analogy (*qiyas*), and consensus (*ijma'*) are the four *usul al-fiqh*, or tools to understanding. Whereas *shari'a* is the substantive law itself, *fiqh* is the application of human understanding to these principles in order to solve problems. A *mujtahid*, acting as a mufti, uses the *usul al-fiqh* to establish a legal opinion (fatwa) that guides state agents in the straight path. In the view of the *ulama*, the caliph is merely a chief administrator of the *shari'a*, a first among equals.

From these constituent elements—the sources of Islamic law, the special role of the *ulama* in their interpretation, and the role of the ruler in their implementation—developed a concept of the state thought to be faithful to that established by Muhammad. It remained the undisputed model in the Arab world until the modern period brought very different ideas about the state and society from the West.

Notes

1. Hodgson I, 280–358. Hodgson discusses his theories regarding the influence of pre-Islamic Persia throughout the work, but these pages are the most relevant to the present chapter.
2. See Lewis, *Islam in History*, 261–322.

71

3. Hodgson I, 280.
4. Ibid., 281.
5. Lewis, *Islam in History*, 352.
6. Ibid., 323–36.
7. Robert G. Hoyland, "The Rise of Islam," in *The Oxford History of Byzantium*, Cyril Mango, ed. (New York: Oxford University Press, 2002) 124.
8. Hodgson, *supra* note 1.
9. Lewis, *Middle East*, 149.
10. Hodgson I, 349.
11. Ibid., 338, 345–8.
12. Ibid., 318–32.
13. Joseph Schact, *An Introduction to Islamic Law* (New York: Oxford University Press, 1982) 18.
14. Bernard G. Weiss, *The Spirit of Islamic Law* (Athens, Georgia: University of Georgia Press, 1998) 12. The term "hadith specialist" is his.
15. Hodgson I, 315–38.
16. Ibid.
17. Ibid., 338.
18. Ibid., 330.

CHAPTER V

The Arab West: North Africa, Sicily, and Spain

The Conquest and Arabization of the West

During the time of the Umayyads, Arab armies swept westward from Egypt. Completing an Arab version of "Manifest Destiny," they encountered little resistance from Byzantine North Africa. The native Berber tribes decided that it was better to rule than be ruled, converted to Islam, and joined in the raids of Spain and Sicily. This brought all of northwest Africa, or the Maghrib[1] (modern Tunisia, Algeria, Morocco, and Mauritania), under Muslim rule.[2]

In 670 the Umayyads established a garrison town at Qayrawan, in Ifriqiya (modern Tunisia).[3] It was used both as a base for military operations and as an administrative center of the caliphate, replacing Byzantine Carthage. As their armies raced toward the Atlantic and crossed the straits into Spain, all of North Africa was claimed first by the Umayyads and then, after 750, by the Abbasids. Although the caliphs now ruled a vast expanse, their success in suppressing Kharijite and Shi'a revolts in the Levant and Arabia simply shifted the problem to the Maghrib. Kharijite merchants, preachers and refugees brought with them their violently anti-authoritarian version of Islam, and it appealed to the Berbers more than the Umayyad version. It is also suggested that Kharijite preachers resembled the "holy men" of traditional Berber culture.[4] Whatever the attraction, Kharijites established a large number of

73

The Mediterranean Basin.

Courtesy of The General Libraries, The University of Texas at Austin.

small Islamic states from Libya westward, and in fact probably controlled more territory than the caliph.[5]

In addition to the Kharijites, the Shi'a prince Idris ibn Abdallah, fleeing from a failed revolt in the Hijaz, also came west to establish a state (c. 786). He established his state in Morocco, and the Idrisid state was ruled from Fez.[6]

In 800 Caliph Harun al-Rashid decided make the best of a lost cause and granted his governor, Ibrahim ibn al-Aghlab, independent rule over Ifriqiya in exchange for tribute denoting formal Abbasid sovereignty. This allowed the caliph at least to get some revenue out of a province he could not control, and al-Aghlab must have believed that retaining Abbasid sovereignty would strengthen him among those sympathetic to the ideal of Islamic unity. Qayrawan was becoming a center of Islamic legal and philosophical thought in the west, and the pretense of Abbasid sanction might well have been helpful in a hostile environment. Ruling for just over a century (800–909), the Aghlabs failed in their repeated attempts to suppress the Kharijite Berbers, but while in power they built mosques and irrigation systems, patronized the *ulama*, and, most significantly, conquered Sicily.[7]

A Moroccan village in the Atlas Mountains.
Ron Baker, photographer. CMES.

75

A water wheel in Meknes, Morocco, used for irrigation.

Ron Baker, photographer. CMES.

Unfortunately for the Aghlabs, around 899 a Shi'a leader from Syria, Ubayd Allah, fled from the Abbasids and made it to Ifriqiya, where he promptly instigated an uprising. Ubayd had broken with the Qarmatian Shi'a and declared himself the imam, the spiritual leader of Muslims. His followers became known as the Fatimids (he presumably having descended from Muhammad through Fatima). Although Ubayd was himself arrested for a time, the Fatimids maintained sufficient momentum to overthrow the Aghlabs in 909. Ubayd took the messianic name Mahdi as his regal name, founded a new capital called Mahdiya, and set up a counter-caliphate to the Abbasids by assuming the title "Commander of the Faithful" (*amir al-mu'minin*).[8]

Despite having little support from the population, the Fatimids consolidated their rule. Building a powerful navy and controlling the seas, they began an aggressive move to conquer all of the Maghrib. The Fatimids faced numerous Berber revolts, one of which was almost successful (c. 940), and not only faced these down but overcame all the other small states, including the Shi'a Idrisid state still ruling in Morocco. Having expanded their rule to the Atlantic but having no attachment to the region itself, the Fatimids began preparing for a move to Egypt. Beginning with extensive missionary work to promote Shi'a Islam there, the caliph al-Mu'izz and his general, the master tactician Jawhar, successfully invaded Egypt in 969, and moved the capital there in 972. They left the Zirids, Berbers converted to Fatimid Shiism, in charge of Ifriqiya. The Fatimids thus were able to launch the only genuine attempt to unite the Muslim world under a Shi'a dynasty in place of the Sunni Abbasids (see chapter six). After the Fatimids had decamped to Egypt, this left the Maghrib in its previous condition, ruled by small Islamic states and numerous independent tribes.[9]

Arab Sicily

Throughout history Sicily has been viewed as the key to naval supremacy in the Mediterranean Sea as well as a base for any invasion of North Africa or Italy from either. In the middle of the first millennium B.C., Greeks and Phoenicians established trading colonies there, and Rome's intense struggle in the third century B.C.

to overcome them in Sicily paved the way for imperial control of the Mediterranean. Likewise, Byzantium's conquest of Sicily in A.D. 535 was central to Justinian's plan to reunify the Roman empire.[10]

The Arabs were keenly aware of the island's strategic importance, and Mu'awiya was the first caliph to begin raiding the island (c. 670). Later attempts were launched from North Africa, and the nearby island of Pantelleria was seized around 700. In 740 Habib ibn Abi Ubayda made the first serious attempt at conquest. He besieged the Greek city of Syracuse and exacted tribute, but was forced to withdraw to face Berber revolts. Another attempt in 752 ended inconclusively. [11]

In 825 the Arabs had a stroke of luck. A Byzantine admiral named Euphemius, having done something to incur the emperor's wrath, rebelled to avoid arrest and seized the island himself. When Byzantine forces retook the island Euphemius defected to the Aghlabid ruler of Tunisia, Ziyadatallah, and encouraged him to invade Sicily. Ziyadatallah took this advice, landing in 827. The Aghlabids took Palermo in 831, which would be the capital for the remainder of Arab rule in Sicily. After some setbacks they were saved by a band of Muslims coming from Spain. One by one they took the island's major cities, including Messina and Syracuse, until in 896 the Byzantines signed a peace treaty surrendering Sicily. At the same time, the invaders expanded their raids to the mainland, threatened Naples and Rome, and even forced the Vatican to pay tribute for two years.[12]

Three Muslim dynasties ruled over Sicily. The Aghlabids completed the conquest but were overthrown by the Fatimids in 909. Aghlabid rule thus lasted a mere thirteen years. When the Fatimids moved the capital of their dynasty to Egypt in 972, this weakened their control over their governor, al-Hasan ibn Ali al-Kalbi. He founded what became the Kalbid dynasty. The Kalbids, formally acknowledging Fatimid sovereignty, maintained real control in Sicily until the time of European attempts to retake it in the eleventh century.[13]

Byzantium began a concerted effort to retake the island under Basil II (r. 976–1025), who began the offensive near the end of his reign. It ended in failure around 1041, but during the same period a civil war began between Sicilian and Tunisian Muslims. This led to an interlude during which the island became politically fragmented, with provinces ruled by local princes. Five years before a relative would begin a much more famous invasion of England, the Norman ruler Count Roger I took Messina in 1061, where the Byzantines were still just hanging on. He went on to take Palermo in 1072 and quickly thereafter subdued the rest of the island.[14]

By the time of the Norman invasion, however, both Islam and Arab culture had become deeply rooted in Sicily, and the island was interwoven into the larger Arab-Islamic civilization which was flourishing across the Mediterranean. A Muslim traveler in Sicily around 970 noted that he had never seen a city with as many mosques as Palermo, and still people had to wait in line to pray.[15] The survival of Arabic words and place names in modern Sicily reflects this cultural influence. Arab colonization also brought a new agriculture to the island including oranges, sugarcane, and cotton. Roger II (r. 1130–1154) relied heavily on Arabs for military campaigns, administration, and architecture, keeping Arabic as an official language. Although perhaps more reflective of the status of Arabic in the wider Mediterranean world, the language's staying power was such that Roger's grandson William II (r. 1166–1189) was able to read and write it.[16]

A Muslim traveler arriving—actually, shipwrecked—at Messina in 1184, over a hundred years after the Norman conquest, noted that the Arab-Muslim presence was still very strong in Sicily. This tourist, Ibn Jubayr, recorded that many of the Christian women wore veils in the Arab fashion,[17] and that the Normans were still using Arab coinage with dates based on the *hijra*.[18] Mosques seem to have been much less prominent, but Muslims still made the call to prayer and went to the mosque, although the traditional Friday sermon or *khutba* was prohibited due to its political implications.[19] Yet conversion was becoming common as the Normans reversed the Muslim strategy; Muslims were allowed to practice their religion, but because advancement in society was predicated on becoming Christian, many converted over time.

However, near the end of his reign William II began to feel insecure and increased the persecution of Muslims, and Muslim leaders were forced to convert in order to preserve their status. Well into the reign of Frederick II (r. 1198–1250) Arab culture survived; Frederick himself was the patron of a translation effort that showed the knowledge of Arabic was still present among the elite. Eventually,

79

through a combination of conversion and emigration, Islam died out in Sicily around the beginning of the fourteenth century.[20]

Islamic Spain—The Splendor of Al-Andalus

By the time that the Arabs were settling across most of the Near East and North Africa in the latter part of the seventh century, Christian Spain, ruled by the Visigoths, was in a "weak and deplorable state."[21] A small class of landowners owned almost everything, with the vast majority of the population comprising serfs, slaves, and bandits, the latter of which controlled the countryside. The first half of the century had seen an intense campaign of persecution against the province's important Jewish population. Any promise of change would have been welcomed.[22] A new age was dawning, and Muslims would make Spain, which they called al-Andalus, one of the crown jewels of the Muslim world.

In 710 a Berber chief named Tarif initiated a raid from North Africa into Spain with the help of a scheming Visigoth notable named Julian. This encouraged the Umayyad governor of the region, Musa ibn Nusayr, to send a larger force, mostly Berber, the next year under a Berber named Tariq ibn Ziyad. They landed at a place renamed Jabal ("the mountain of") Tariq (Gibraltar). Tariq defeated the Visigoth army and took the important cities of Córdoba and Toledo. In 712 Musa himself came over with a larger Arab force estimated at 10,000 and took Seville and Mérida. By 718 the Arabs had taken most of the Iberian Peninsula and crossed the Pyrenees mountains into what is now France. They were checked at the Battle of Poitiers by Charles Martel in 732; this marked the high tide of Arab conquest in Europe.[23]

The Arabs remained dominant in Spain as in Africa, but in 741 the Berbers staged a general revolt. The heritage of Islamic Spain thus might have been more Berber than Arab, except that in 742 the Umayyad caliph sent a large Syrian army (with a significant Egyptian contingent) to maintain control. The wisdom of this decision might be called into question, as the Umayyads were barely fending off the Abbasid-led revolutionaries at the time, but it proved decisive in Spain. The new migrants set themselves up as estate-holders and more thoroughly Arabized the region.[24]

The inner courtyard of Alcazar in Seville, Spain.
Caroline Williams, photographer. CMES.

After the Abbasid victory a fleeing Umayyad prince, Abd al-Rahman, fled to Spain in 755. With the help of the Syrian Arabs, who by this time were well established, Abd al-Rahman was able to take power from a governor who had recognized the Abbasid caliphate and seize Córdoba in 756. Abd al-Rahman became the founder of what is usually referred to as the Second Umayyad Caliphate (r. 756–1031), although it would be some time before it formally declared itself as such.[25]

Maintaining stability was not easy. Berber immigration continued while Arab immigration stalled, and the former soon dominated the countryside, although Arabs ran the cities. An even larger portion of the population, of course, was Spanish/Latin and Christian. Yet over the next six decades the Umayyads were able to bring unity. Abd al-Rahman II (r. 822–852) introduced a centralized administration along the lines formed by the Abbasids in the core Arab lands. This development culminated in the formal declaration by the amir Abd al-Rahman III (r. 929–961) of the caliphate.[26] The reign of Abd al-Rahman III coincided with the rise of the Shi'a Fatimid counter-caliphate based in Tunisia, and the decline of the Abbasid caliphate in Baghdad. This confluence produced the anomaly of three contemporaneous Arab-Islamic caliphates, all formally claiming the right to rule all Muslims.

Al-Hakam II (r. 961–976) succeeded Abd al-Rahman III and continued his policies of centralization. His vizier al-Mansur was the effective ruler, and his death during the reign of al-Hakam's successor, Hisham II (r. 976–1009, 1011–1013), brought about a reaction against the regime that ended the caliphate.[27]

Despite their long rule, the primary achievements of the Spanish Umayyad caliphate lay outside the realm of the political. The destruction of the landowning elite and the creation of a new class of small landholders brought about a revival of Spanish agriculture and overall economic activity.[28] The Arabs brought a more scientific approach to agriculture, and the products they introduced included cotton and sugar, which through Christian Spain were brought to the western hemisphere. They developed numerous industries, including paper-making, sugar-refinement, pottery, and textiles. The latter, especially wool and silk, was extremely important, and there were reportedly 13,000 weavers at Córdoba alone. Their products were traded all over the Mediterranean, including

Byzantium, and from Mediterranean merchants to India and central Asia.[29]

The stability of the state was maintained in part by its broad tolerance of its Christian and Jewish subjects. Many Christians worked for the government and at times even bishops served as diplomats of the caliph. The state was as repressive as it needed to be to hold on to power, but only so. The caliphs and their ministers were patrons of the literary arts, and three languages flourished—Arabic, Hebrew, and the Latin vernacular that would become Spanish.

Arabic naturally held the place of prominence and was widely studied by even non-Muslims. In the middle of the ninth century the Archbishop of Seville had the Bible translated into Arabic, not for evangelism, but for his own parishioners. A famous statement by Alvaro, a Christian at Córdoba, mirrors the frustrations of contemporary Arab teachers frustrated that their students prefer English or French to their native language:[30]

> Many of my co-religionists read the poetry and tales of the Arabs, study the writings of Muhammadan theologians and philosophers, not in order to refute them, but to learn how to express themselves in Arabic with greater correctness and elegance. Where can one find today a layman who reads the Latin commentaries on the Holy Scriptures? Who among them studies the Gospels, the Prophets, the Apostles? All the young Christians noted for their gifts know only the language and literature of the Arabs, read and study with zeal Arabic books, building up great libraries of them at enormous cost and loudly proclaiming everywhere that this literature is worthy of admiration. Among thousands of us there is hardly one who can write a passable Latin letter to a friend, but innumerable are those who can express themselves in Arabic and compose poetry in that language with greater art than the Arabs themselves.

More than anything, this revealing statement demonstrates the attractive power of the Arab-Islamic cultural model at the time.

The Andalusian taste in high culture was not limited to literature. Ziryab, a Persian musician fleeing from the court of Harun al-Rashid, was taken in by the Umayyads and introduced a variety

83

of elements of oriental civilization from music to clothing to the eating of asparagus. The Umayyads developed a distinctive Islamic style of art and architecture, and played a significant role in the transmission of the intellectual heritage of the classical world into Europe (see chapter seven).[31]

The Almoravids, the Almohads, La Reconquista, and 1492

Following the transfer of the Fatimid caliphate from Tunisia to Egypt in 969, and its growing focus on conquering the *Mashriq*, North Africa returned to a state of political fragmentation, with towns or Berber tribes controlling relatively small areas around them. Yet independent of any central authority, Islam itself had become well entrenched and began spreading southward into pagan Africa.

Ibn Yasin was the leader of a group of armed enthusiasts that spread northward from as far south as the Senegal River. After recruiting Berber allies, he set up a strict Islamic state first in the far west of the Sahara and then over much of the Maghrib (c. 1056). At this North African outpost of Islamic civilization he imported Maliki legal scholars to implement the *shari'a* properly. Their basic concept was that of the *ribat*, or outpost of *jihad*, and they became known as the Murabits, or, as they are usually called by Western writers, the Almoravids.[32]

The collapse of the Spanish Umayyad Caliphate in the eleventh century created an opening for Almoravid expansion into Spain. The Spanish princes, with help from the Franks, became reener-gized and began what became known as *La Reconquista*—the Christian retaking of Spain. This revival achieved its first major success by taking Toledo in 1085, shocking the Muslims into an awareness that something had to be done. The Almoravids crossed into Spain in 1090, and the Muslim city-state rulers recognized that they had no alternative but to accept their rule or be ousted entirely by the Spanish.[33]

Although the Almoravids brought temporary respite to Spanish Muslims, dissatisfaction with Almoravid legalism engendered a reaction in their Maghrib base. Typical of many with an intense

The courtyard of Alcazar in Seville.
Caroline Williams, photographer. CMES.

An Almoravid mosque in Marrakesh, Morocco.
Caroline Williams, photographer. CMES.

commitment to the *shari'a*, the Almoravids had been very intolerant of the mystical Sufi orders. Ibn Tumart, a reformer who mixed philosophical speculation and Shi'a sentiment with a *shari'a* emphasis as strict as the Almoravids, began his own movement. He declared himself the Mahdi, an imam-like figure with apocalyptic overtones, and proclaimed his followers, the Almohads, to be the true monotheists.[34]

Ibn Tumart himself died in 1130 after retiring to the mountains, but the chief of the Berber tribal bloc that was the core of his support, Abd al-Mu'min, was declared the *khalifa* to the Mahdi and began waging war against the Almoravids. After a twenty-year struggle ending around 1147, the Almohads had taken virtually all Almoravid territory in North Africa and southern Spain. In addition to shoring up Muslim rule in Spain, the Almohads extended their rule east from Tunisia to Tripoli (modern Libya), and prevented a Christian takeover of that region following the Kalbid loss of Sicily.[35]

Yet even the Almohads were not enough to save al-Andalus. The Muslims won their last major victory in 1195 at Alarcos. The Christian victory in 1212 at Las Navas de Tolosa, and the conquests of Córdoba in 1236 and Seville in 1248, effectively sealed the fate of Muslim Spain. By the end of the century the Spanish had retaken all of the Iberian Peninsula except for the province of Grenada, whose Alhambra palace retains a historic mystique for its luxury and splendor. Although Grenada remained a thriving center of agriculture and trade, as well as high culture, there was never any real hope of expansion again. On January 2, 1492, Grenada fell to the Spanish. Through conversion or migration, Muslims disappeared from the Iberian Peninsula, and Arabic died out. Arab Spain would be no more.[36]

Porte de Elvira in Granada, from the eleventh century.

Vincent Cantarino, photographer. CMES.

The walls of Alhambra.
Caroline Williams, photographer. CMES.

Notes

1. *Maghrib* is also the Arabic term for the modern nation-state of Morocco, but when used in transliteration it refers to all four regions. This may be contrasted with the *Mashriq*, referring to all the Arab world east of Tunisia.
2. Hitti, *History of the Arabs*, 213–4.
3. Fred M. Donner, "Muhammad and the Caliphate: Political History of the Islamic Empire up to the Mongol Conquest," in *The Oxford History of Islam*, John Esposito, ed. (New York: Oxford University Press, 1999) 35.
4. Ibid.
5. Ibid., 35–6.
6. Ibid.
7. Ibid.
8. Marshall G.S. Hodgson, *The Venture of Islam: Conscience and History of a World Civilization; The Expansion of Islam in the Middle Periods* (Chicago: University of Chicago Press, 1974) 21–4. Hereinafter referred to as Hodgson II.
9. Ibid.
10. Angold, *Byzantium*, 147.
11. Lewis, *Arabs in History*, 126–7.
12. Ibid., 127–8.
13. Ibid.
14. Ibid. See also Angold, *Byzantium*, 148.
15. Angold, *Byzantium*, 147.
16. Ibid., 153–61; Lewis, *Arabs in History*, 129–30.
17. Angold, *Byzantium*, 162.
18. Lewis, *Arabs in History*, 130.
19. Angold, *Byzantium*, 162.
20. Lewis, *Arabs in History*, 130–1.
21. Ibid.
22. Ibid.
23. Ibid.
24. Ibid., 132.
25. Ibid., 133.
26. Ibid., 135.
27. Ibid., 136.
28. Ibid., 132.
29. Ibid., 138.
30. Ibid., 134.
31. Ibid., 135, 139.
32. Hodgson II, 268–9.
33. Ibid., 269; Lewis, *Arabs in History*, 136–7.
34. Ibid.
35. Ibid., 269–70.
36. Ibid.

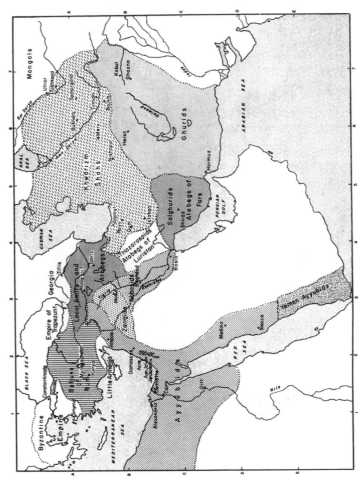

Egypt and southwest Asia, late twelfth century.

Courtesy of the University of Washington Press. (Originally appeared in *A Near East Studies Handbook* by Jere Bacharach, 1977.)

CHAPTER VI

Arab Sunset, Turkish Dawn:
The Struggle for International Islam
(945–1517)

The final collapse of Abbasid power in the face of the Persian Buyids in 945 should have shocked no one. Succession struggles, economic decline, popular alienation, and an ongoing crisis of religious legitimacy were all internal points of weakness that left the Abbasids vulnerable to two separate challenges: the reassertion of historical Persian dominance in the Levant, and the migrations of central Asian peoples into the region.

Despite the constant revolts that the Umayyids and Abbasids faced, the ideal of Islamic unity under a universal caliphate remained strong. Yet this was undercut by two crosscurrents, one religious and one ethnic. First, after three centuries of failure, Shi'a dynasties were able to reach a degree of power parity with the Sunnis for a time. Unable to translate this power into popular religious conversion, Shi'a power proved ephemeral.

Second, the struggle for leadership within Islam up to this point had largely been between the Quraysh aristocracy and then the Abbasid family, and those loyal to the descendants of Muhammad, the Shi'a, also members of the Quraysh. Yet between the middle of the tenth century, with the rise of Persian and Turkic military elites, and the extension of Ottoman control in the Arab world in the sixteenth, most Arabs lived under Turkish or Persian rule. Within this context the world witnessed the birth of an international Islamic social order stretching from Spain to India, in many ways richer than that existing during the previous "Golden Age" of Islam.

The Buyids: The Reawakening of Persia

However insecure Abbasid power may have been before, the Buyids made the caliphate into a mere formality in 945. Due to the strength of the ideal of unity, they did not abolish it, but took the traditional (and pagan) Persian title of *shahansha*, or "King of Kings."[1] Literally held captive as a symbol of Islamic unity, the caliphs were kept in their place; one was blinded, another was reduced to begging in the streets, and all were kept without means of independent support.[2]

The Buyid Empire (r. 932–1062) included almost all of modern Iran and a large section of the eastern Arab world including most of Iraq and all of modern Kuwait. The main capital was the Persian city of Isfahan, while Baghdad essentially was the provincial capital of Iraq. The Buyids were Shi'a and were the religious successors of Abu Muslim and the Shi'a element that originally had put the Abbasids in power two centuries earlier. However, unlike the Fatimids in Egypt, they were not religiously driven. They made no attempt to press for conversion of Sunni Muslims or the spread of Shiism internationally. They even patronized Sunni as well as Shi'a *ulama*.

Instead, the Buyids' primary concern was economic development. They promoted trade, and, dependent on Iraq, they were hurt when trade began to shift toward Egypt. They continued the *iqta'* system of land grants to soldiers, which had begun under the Abbasids. The Buyid system allowed for holders to both collect taxes and sometimes to pass on the land to their heirs. This melded well with the military style of government, as it allowed the Buyids to pay their troops with minimal drain on the treasury.

The *iqta'* system, however, should not be compared to European feudalism.[3] The landowner had no formal authority over peasants, and the government could revoke the grant or exchange it for another at will. Owners also could request to exchange their land for another grant once the original had become unprofitable. This reduced the incentive for long-term agricultural investment and encouraged owners to squeeze a plot for all it was worth and then exchange it, furthering the economic decline of Iraq.[4]

The Buyids' difficulties were increased by having to fight on two fronts, one in Syria and Iraq against the Fatimids and another in central Asia against the rising Turks. It was the latter that would eventually destroy them. Control in Iraq was difficult to maintain because they had little support from the largely Sunni Arab population. Viewed from below, the Buyids represented a foreign culture, believing in a heretical religion and holding power through Persian and Turkic troops. Yet it is notable that there was no Arab resistance movement, no serious uprising to restore the Abbasid caliph to power, although support did exist for the Turkic opposition, which championed Sunni Islam.[5]

The Buyids lived uneasily side-by-side with the Hamdanids (r. 905–1004), who governed most of Syria from Mosul. The Hamdanids were Arab nomads who gave up Kharijism for Shiism. Despite their nomadic origin, they gained a reputation for being patrons of the arts.[6] They, like the Buyids, were in time swept away in the Turkic tide.

The Fatimids: The Shi'a Counter-Caliphate

In chapter five we saw how the Shi'a Fatimids first rose to power in Tunisia, and then spread their control over the rest of North Africa to the Atlantic Ocean. Of the many Islamic states and dynasties of this time period, two aspects of the Fatimids' ideology made them exceptional. One, whereas the major powers across the Arab world recognized the formal suzerainty of the Abbasid caliph in Baghdad, the Fatimids forthrightly rejected his authority. A second difference, relating to the first, was that whereas most dynasties were content to control a province or two, the Fatimids challenged the Sunni caliph for leadership of the entire *umma*. This latter point distinguished them from the Shi'a Buyids; the Fatimids were zealous evangelists who sent missionaries across the Arab world and beyond to spread their version of Shi'a Islam.

The Fatimids, therefore, were hardly content to rule from Tunisia. In 969, after several attempts, the Fatimid General Jawhar took Egypt from the Tulunids, who had ruled under formal Abbasid suzerainty. Naturally, in order to rule as a Shi'a caliph one needed to be descended from Muhammad. The Fatimid caliph Mu'izz, when confronted by *ulama* on the point, reportedly drew his sword and said, "Here's my pedigree!" He then began throwing gold coins at the crowd and said, "And here's my proof!"[7]

Up until this time Egypt had not played a significant role in the Muslim world. Not only did it contain neither a holy city, as Arabia and Palestine did, nor an imperial capital, as Syria and Iraq had, but when the Fatimids came to power much of the population was still Christian, and Muslims would not be a majority for centuries. Yet under the Fatimids it became the base of a Shi'a caliphate that, at its greatest extent, ran from Morocco to Egypt, north into Syria, around the coast of Arabia, controlling the Hijaz (and thus Mecca and Medina), Yemen, and even the Sind region in the Indian subcontinent.

Three characteristics seem central to Fatimid success. First, Egypt had always been an agricultural powerhouse in the Mediterranean, and they were careful to maintain it as such. Second, having established themselves as the primary naval power in the western Mediterranean, the Fatimids dominated their foes on the sea. This facilitated the production and export of fabrics and luxury crafts, preexisting industries which the Fatimids promoted. Third, by sending missionaries across the Muslim world, they gained the support of Shi'a Muslims living under other rulers, especially in Iraq and Iran.[8]

Just as the Abbasids had founded a new city to mark the beginning of their caliphate, the Fatimids founded a city near Fustat, called *Al-Qahira*, or Cairo. They also founded al-Azhar Mosque, partially in order to promote learning, and the institution into which it developed, al-Azhar University, became the most prestigious Islamic academic institution in the world.[9] Despite their zeal abroad, they were broadly tolerant at home of Sunnis and *dhimmi* alike. Their ability to maintain power must be partially attributed to the fact that the non-Shi'a population was divided between these two groups.

Al-Mu'izz was succeeded by another successful Fatimid, Caliph al-Aziz (r. 975–996). Unfortunately for the Fatimids, he was succeeded by al-Hakim (r. 996–1021), a bizarre but significant individual. At one point he ordered that all businesses stay open at night, forcing everyone to sleep during the day, because he preferred the night and because he wanted to show that his security could prevent any crime. He also operated a kind of lottery, in which some individuals would be gratuitously given great sums, while others would be killed for no reason. This was supposed to parallel divine providence. He was intensely pious, and at times took it to extremes. He lived simply and rode on a donkey when going out, and he was brutally violent in dealing with privileged persons whom he suspected of having abused their position in society. He ordered all vineyards in Egypt to be destroyed (most rulers allowed them to non-Muslims), and prohibited women from leaving their homes.[10]

More dangerously for the state, he began sympathizing with Sunnism and angered many by appointing a Sunni chief *qadi*. If that were not bad enough, he encouraged violence against the upper class, warning all of a coming apocalypse. Then one day, having destabilized the regime, he walked off into the desert, never to be seen again.

After his death, the Fatimids began returning confiscated property and restoring order. Yet al-Hakim's following was such that, whether he taught them so or not before his disappearance, many believed him to be an incarnation of God. They fled to Syria, where some Shi'a peasants were won over to their cause. The sect of al-Hakim survives to this day through the Druze in Lebanon, Syria, and Israel, and they await the time when he will return and rule in righteousness.

Al-Hakim's grandson al-Mustansir (r. 1036–1094),[11] managed well enough for the first few decades of his long rule. In 1058 Baghdad and part of Iraq came under Fatimid control, although this was primarily due to internal divisions in Baghdad. Yet within four years different factions within the military were fighting over control in Egypt, and the caliphate was only saved when an able general, Badr al-Jamali, returned from Syria to restore stable Fatimid power. He succeeded in 1074, but this was the end of Fatimid international ambition. During this time Sicily was taken by the Normans and Syria, in Badr's absence, was undefended against a Seljuk conquest. When al-Mustansir died in 1094, the Shi'a of Iran repudiated the Fatimids, and the Shi'a of Arabia and the Indian subcontinent did likewise after the death of the last effective Fatimid ruler, al-Amir (1101–1130). Fatimid power in Egypt itself then continued to decline until it was eliminated completely by Saladin in 1171.

The Mosque of Al-Hakim in Cairo, from the Fatimid period.
Caroline Williams, photographer. CMES.

The Seljuks and the Rise of the Turkic Military Class

Perhaps the most significant trend to hit the Eurasian landmass in the latter part of the first millennium and for several centuries afterward was the migration of nomadic warriors and their populations from central Asia into settled lands as far apart as China, Russia, the Indian subcontinent, Persia, and the eastern Arab world. The Ghaznavids became the first Turkic empire by overthrowing the power of the Persian Samanids (c. 819–999) and taking control of much of Persia and the Indian subcontinent. The Ghaznavids maintained Farsi as the language of administration, further increasing its status relative to Arabic.

More significantly for the Arab world, after the complete collapse of the Samanids in Persia, a group of tribesmen called "Seljuk" moved into the area. By 1040 the Seljuks had consolidated their strength and taken up the cause of Sunni Islam. At this time the Abbasid caliphate was still in the midst of the "Shi'a Century," controlled by the Buyids in Iraq and pressured by the Fatimids almost everywhere else. The Sunni Seljuks offered themselves as the champions of Islamic unity, and the Baghdad caliphate (for that is all it was) accepted. The takeover was complete in 1055.

Under the new arrangement, Toghril Beg, the head Seljuk, became the "caliphal lieutenant" over the Islamic *umma*. While keeping the Abbasids under tight control, the Seljuks emphasized their "special relationship" with the caliph. Yet the Turkic warriors who gave the Seljuks power were hard to manage. They continued on through Iraq and into Syria and Anatolia, attacking almost everyone along the way. The Seljuks were concerned that the tribesmen would disrupt the settled economies of the Levant, and so herded them northward into Anatolia, encouraging them to attack non-Muslims there rather than their Muslim subjects in Syria. This actually worked, and the Byzantines suffered a major military reverse in 1071 at Manzikert.[12]

The apex of Seljuk power came under MalikShah (r. 1073–1092) and his vizier, Nizam al-Mulk, who had also served under Malik-Shah's father Alp-Arslan (r. 1063–1072). In the tradition of the Barmakids, Nizam al-Mulk was a Sunni Persian who had trained under the Ghaznavids. His administration was run largely by other Persians, producing a strange anomaly; a titular Arab caliph sat on top of an empire ruled by Turkic military chiefs and administered by Persian mandarins with an Arab subject population.

Holding most of the effective power under MalikShah, Nizam al-Mulk pushed a reform agenda. His central goals were to restore the centralized bureaucratic structure of previous times, revive the agricultural prosperity of the Iraqi Sawad, and increase control over the military through the *barid*, an information service based upon frequent exchange of messages (*barid* is the modern Arabic term for the mail). He largely failed. This was partly because the Sawad could not be restored for ecological reasons, and partly because of the additional harm caused by the pastoral economy of the tribesmen. In addition, the Seljuk system was so thoroughly military in nature that local commanders could not be administratively controlled.[13] He was more successful in the arena of military expansion. He not only wrestled Syria away from the Fatimids, he managed to conquer the Hijaz and Yemen as well. Thus, even if for only a few decades, the Seljuks restored the old caliphal empire in all the important areas of the Arab world east of the Nile.[14]

After the death of Nizam al-Mulk, the mainstay of Seljuk power, the tribal solidarity of the Turkic chiefs, could not be maintained under the luxuries of power and the temptations to factionalism. MalikShah's son Muhammad Tapir (r. 1104–1118) maintained some power, but after his death the central authority was limited to parts of Persia. Nevertheless, the historical legacies of the Seljuks in the Arab world and beyond loom large. Sunni rule was returned to the Arab world, and, the Seljuks having essentially adopted the Iranian heritage, Persian culture and learning were given much more prestige. Perhaps most importantly, the vision of Islamic unity gave way to extreme fragmentation, with Turkic amirs in some cases only ruling over an individual city. Formally representing the Abbasid caliph, they were functionally independent, with pure military power providing real legitimacy.[15]

The Latin States, the Zengids, and the Ayyubids

It was the weakness in the heart of the Arab world following the collapse of the Seljuks that allowed the European offensives remembered as the "Crusades" to take significant plots of land along the eastern Mediterranean. While the Crusaders probably pillaged and plundered as many Christian as Muslim cities and villages, for many this period has come to symbolize the medieval conflict between Islam and Christianity.

Although the crusades were meant as a reaction to the Muslim conquest of Palestine, the immediate catalyst was the advance of Turkic tribes through Anatolia. The Battle of Manzikert in 1071 had opened the Anatolian buffer zone between the heartlands of Byzantium and the Islamic world, and the Byzantines had decided that they had no choice but to ask for the aid of their doctrinal rivals in Western Europe. Since Constantine's founding of Constantinople in 330, Christianity had been increasingly divided between western and eastern churches. Doctrinal disagreements predated Constantine, but time and political divisions gradually widened them. Yet these were desperate times, and Pope Urban II responded by calling upon Western Christendom to liberate the holy land from the Muslims.

The Crusaders, mostly Franks, responded enthusiastically and cascaded across Europe, through Anatolia and down the Syrian coast. The first of seven crusades took Jerusalem, which was guarded by only a thousand Fatimid troops, in 1099.[16] These offensives pillaged towns of all sizes along the way, including, ironically, Constantinople itself. Upon taking Jerusalem the Franks engaged in the indiscriminate killing of its inhabitants, Muslim, Jewish, and Christian. The Byzantines were allowed to take back Anatolia, but the Crusaders rejected their leadership and established four separate states in Syria and Palestine: Jerusalem, Antioch, Tripoli, and Edessa (present-day Ruha).[17]

The Muslim reaction to the crusades was initially quite subdued. None of the most commercially important cities of the Arab world—Baghdad, Cairo, Aleppo, and Mosul—had been taken. The Crusaders controlled significant territory only in the extreme north near Anatolia and in the south near Egypt.[18] In the Levant, Muslims were too divided to react, and the Fatimid state in Egypt did not wish to upset its economic relations with European trading partners. By this time, the Mediterranean was dominated by Italian sailors and merchants. Although the Franks provided the force on land, they benefited from the support of Italian-dominated seaports along the coast and were sustained over time by the Italian fleets.[19]

The old city of Jerusalem.
CMES.

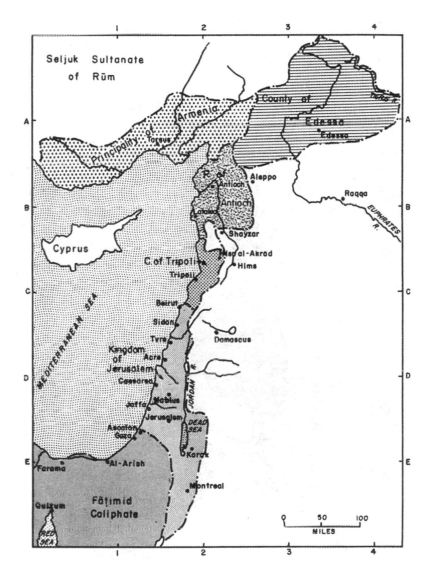

Crusading States, circa 1130.

Courtesy of the University of Washington Press. (Originally appeared in *A Near East Studies Handbook* by Jere Bacharach, 1977.)

Two new dynasties allowed Muslims to regain their position. The first was that of the Zengids (r. 1127–1222), founded by Zengi, the son of a Turkic slave officer under the Seljuks.[20] The Zengid dynasty was able to take control of most of Syria and northern Iraq, including Mosul. Zengi recaptured the Latin state of Edessa in 1144 but died two years later.[21] His son Nur al-Din established himself in Damascus and sent his best general, a Kurdish officer named Shirkuh, to save Egypt from an invasion by the Franks. Shirkuh and his nephew Salah al-Din ibn Ayyub (Saladin) not only defeated the Franks but deftly took control of Egypt. As the last Fatimid caliph lay dying, Saladin replaced his name in the Friday sermon with that of the Abbasid caliph, symbolizing a return to Sunni rule in 1171. Although a Kurd among largely Turkic legions, Saladin was able to consolidate his rule, engage in an effective diplomacy with Muslim states in the lands formerly held by the Fatimids, and retake Jerusalem in 1187. He was respected by the Christians as a man of chivalry, unlike King Richard ("the Lion-Hearted") of England, who retook Acre in a joint offensive with the Franks and massacred the inhabitants even though they had surrendered on condition that they could be ransomed (negotiations were reportedly taking too long). By his death in 1193, Saladin had reduced the Crusaders to limited areas along the coast. First his brother, al-Adil (d. 1218), and then his nephew, al-Kamil (d. 1238), held the Ayyubids together in Egypt. The dynasty persisted until 1250 before being terminated by the Mamluks.[22]

The Mongols, the Mamluks, and the Abbasids' Last Stand

In the first three centuries after the Persian takeover of the Baghdad caliphate in 945, the main struggle in the Arab world was between a dynasty based in Egypt attempting to reestablish Islamic unity through Shi'a dominance and a variety of dynasties, mostly Persian or Turkic, attempting to simply hold power over as much of the Levant and Arabia as they could. The next three centuries before the beginning of the Ottoman age would be almost a reenactment but with different actors; a Turkic sultanate based in Egypt would attempt to reestablish Islamic unity through Sunni dominance, while another central Asian people, the Mongols,

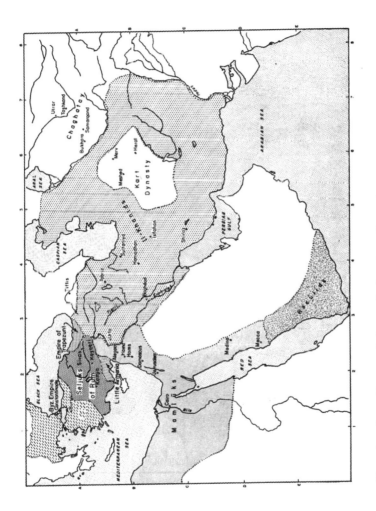

Egypt and southwest Asia, early fourteenth century.

Courtesy of the University of Washington Press. (Originally appeared in *A Near East Studies Handbook* by Jere Bacharach, 1977.)

would attempt to conquer the Arab world just as they had already engulfed much of Eurasia.

The close of the period of Seljuk dominance in the Near East corresponded to a brief but real reassertion of Abbasid power. The Caliph al-Nasir (r. 1180–1225) used the residual prestige of the caliphate to reorganize a military force and regain control of Iraq. Through an alliance with the Persian Khwarezm-Shah Ala al-Din Tekish (r. 1172–1200), he was able to launch a campaign in western Persia and eliminate the last Seljuk ruler in 1194. Al-Nasir and Tekish afterward came into conflict, but al-Nasir was able to keep control not only in Iraq but also in part of southwestern Persia. Al-Nasir maintained himself through a system of alliances with minor rulers, none powerful enough to remove him but collectively strong enough to keep the region free from an outside power.[23]

Al-Nasir also developed a symbiotic relationship with the influential mystic Umar Suhravardi (1145–1234), leader of the dominant Sufi order in the region. Suhravardi propagated a fusion of *shari'a* legalism and Islamic mysticism which posited the caliph as not only the enforcer of the *shari'a* but also chief patron of Sufi organizations. He also managed to get himself certified as a legal authority in all four of the schools of law—Hanafi, Shafi'i, Maliki, and Hanbali. That he was able to maintain the support of all four while also being considered head of the Sufi orders despite the latent conflict between them is a testimony to his political skill.[24]

Tekish's son Muhammad (r. 1200–1220) dreamed of restoring Khwarezm-Shah rule to all the lands ruled by the Seljuks. To this end he completed the conquest of Persia to the Oxus region and then turned against al-Nasir. He intended to attack Baghdad in 1217, but was forced to call off the offensive due to the weather. He never would get another chance. On his eastern border the Mongols were gathering their strength. Muhammad defied them and was crushed in 1220.[25]

The origin of the Arab world's experience with the Mongols might be measured from the ascension of Genghis Khan to the head of the vast nomadic empire in 1206. This empire, stretching from China to Eastern Europe south to India and Persia, was split into separate khanates. His great-grandson Hulegu ruled the dynasty that became known as the Il-Khans based in Persia. The Mongol method was to offer urban areas amnesty if they would submit to Mongol rule, and to kill every man, woman, and child in sight if they refused. Ever pragmatic, they did allow artisans to survive to serve the state. The latter was the destiny of Baghdad. While the local rulers of Persia mostly accepted Mongol rule without a fight, the Abbasids were too proud to surrender. In 1258 Hulegu's warriors descended on Baghdad, overwhelmed the caliph's army, and easily subdued the walled city. Every member of the Abbasid family that could be found was killed, and Iraq became part of the Mongol empire.[26] Yet just as the Mongols were bringing the five-century Abbasid caliphate to an end, a new Sunni power was rising in the Arab world.[27]

Although the memory of Saladin has remained strong in the Muslim world to this day, the dynasty he founded would not last long. In 1250 the Mamluks ("owned ones"), a slave caste of central Asian origin, took control and for nearly three centuries maintained a self-perpetuating warrior-slave elite based in Egypt. It became one of the marvels of Islamic history.[28]

When the Ayyubid sultan died in 1250, his son and heir was away from the capital. The sultan's widow, Shajar al-Durr, attempted to conceal his death and rule in his name until her son could return. When he did return, the dominant Mamluk faction sensed he favored another Mamluk faction and decided to take power. They killed him and set Shajar al-Durr herself on the throne. Within a few months, however, the Mamluk commander married Shajar, and Mamluk rule officially began.[29]

It was not long before the Mamluks had the chance to prove themselves the champions of Islam. Having overwhelmed all resistance in Iraq, the Mongol hordes next had their eye on Egypt. The Mamluks met them at Ayn Jalut south of Damascus in 1260 and handed the Mongols their first defeat, evicting them from Syria in the process. The victorious general Baybars I (r. 1260–1277) then came to power through the assassination of the Mamluk Sultan al-Muzaffar Sayf al-Din Qutuz.[30]

The Mamluk sultanate was not a dynasty but had a more violent system of succession, although an outside observer might be forgiven for not thinking it to be a system at all, but more a merit-based thugocracy than a sultanate. When a sultan died, his son would succeed him in a caretaker capacity. The major factions would then fight for control, and the victor would be the new ruler. This

The Cairo Khayrbak Mosque, from the Mamluk era.
John A. Williams, photographer. CMES.

Tombs from the Mamluk period in Cairo.
Caroline Williams, photographer. CMES.

system, remarks one historian, "should have been the worst government in history; oddly enough, it worked for more than 250 years."[31]

The Mamluks maintained themselves as a slave class, even as
they taxed subject populations to ruin. New "recruits" to the slave
system were taken from not only the Mamluks' own ancestral
homeland, the central Asian steppes, but also from among Circas-
sians around the eastern Black Sea area, Kurds from east Anatolia,
sub-Saharan Africans, as well as from inhabitants of islands in the
Mediterranean. Basically, anyone but an Arab could become part
of the ruling elite through the world's most meritocratic slave
system. Boys were usually taken around the ages of ten to twelve
and kept in dormitories where they lived under a strict system of
military discipline, learning a variety of military skills. Academic
study stressed the learning of Islam and Arabic. After graduating
from training, the Mamluk would maintain camaraderie with his
fellows and loyalty to a master who brought them up, and their fortunes would rise and fall with his.[32]

The Mosque of Ayed Bey in Cairo, Mamluk period.
Drawing by David Roberts. CMES.

Not content to rule Egypt and Syria, Baybars aspired to wider leadership. He took in a survivor of the Abbasi family after the Mongol conquest, and so claimed that the caliphate now rested with the Mamluks. It was also during his reign that the Mamluks gained suzerainty over the Hijaz and the holy cities. Baybars showed diplomatic skill by reaching out to Christian princes in the Mediterranean in order to expand trade. He also formed an alliance with the now Muslim "Golden Horde" of Russia against the closer Il-Khanid threat based in Iran.[33] Having established a firm foundation, the Mamluks remained the primary power in the Arab world until their defeat at the hands of another central Asian people, the Ottoman Turks, in 1517.

Notes

1. Albert Hourani, *A History of the Arab Peoples* (New York: Warner Books, 1992) 38.
2. Goldschmidt, *Concise History of the Middle East*, 83.
3. Von Grunebaum, *Classical Islam*, 145.
4. Hodgson II, 101–2.
5. Von Grunebaum, *Classical Islam*, 145–6.
6. Hodgson II, 36–7.
7. Goldschmidt, *Concise History of the Middle East*, 81.
8. Hodgson II, 21–3.
9. Ibid., 23.
10. Ibid., 26–7.
11. This appears to be the second-longest reign in Egypt's exceptionally long civilized history, after Pharaoh Pepi II Neferkare of the Old Kingdom (r. 2294–2200 B.C.). Jaromir Malek, "The Old Kingdom," in *The Oxford History of Ancient Egypt*, Ian Shaw, ed. (New York: Oxford University Press, 2000) 116.
12. Ibid., 43–4.
13. Ibid., 44–5.
14. Ibid., 45.
15. Ibid., 52–3; see also Goldschmidt, *Concise History of the Middle East*, 87.
16. Goldschmidt, *Concise History of the Middle East*, 88.
17. Ibid., 89.
18. Ibid. See also Hodgson II, 265.
19. Hodgson II, 264–6.
20. Ibid.
21. Ibid.
22. Von Grunebaum, *Classical Islam*, 67–9.
23. Hodgson II, 279–80.
24. Ibid., 280–3.
25. Ibid., 285.
26. Ibid.
27. Ibid., 286–92.
28. Goldschmidt, *Concise History of the Middle East*, 93.
29. Ibid., 114–5.
30. Hodgson II, 417; see also Goldschmidt, *Concise History of the Middle East*, 115.
31. Goldschmidt, *Concise History of the Middle East*, 115.
32. Ibid., 115–7.
33. Ibid.

CHAPTER VII

Society, Culture, and the
Life of the Mind
(661–1517)

The Development of Arab Societies

In the early years of Arab-Muslim rule over what is now the Arab world, the underlying societies were for a long time not Arab. From the eighth century onward, the use of Arabic as the official language and the consolidation of a huge trade area in which Arabic could be used as a *lingua franca* encouraged the Arabization, if not always the Islamization, of the populations living under Muslim rule. Even beyond the area in which Arabic was used, the effect of political fragmentation at the time was very different from what it is today. Although at any given time the Muslim world was usually ruled by several regional powers and a multitude of local ones, there were no borders in the modern sense. Muslims felt themselves to belong to the Muslim world as a whole, not the dynasty that ruled their province. This meant that a merchant, poet, preacher, or legal scholar could get up and move from Iraq to Egypt and not feel like a foreigner. There was also a good deal of mobility between Persia and the Arab lands, and after the rise of the Ottoman Turks in the fourteenth century, many intellectuals simply migrated north to the new locus of Islamic power.[1]

Both tribal life and the relationship between tribes and settled areas did not change radically after the coming of Islam, although many tribes moved out of the peninsula and settled in other parts of what is now the Arab world, especially Iraq and Syria. Kinship remained the primary source of individual identity, although Islam took over this role vis-à-vis non-Muslims. Arrangements were often made with other tribes, or else forced on them by the government, for the sharing of land or water. As in earlier times, tribal structures became more hierarchical where tribes became more settled. Nomadic tribal leadership remained relatively egalitarian, while in settled areas increased complexity brought by the economic division of labor caused relationships between individuals to be more stratified. Men had the primary responsibility for herding flocks and were solely responsible for relations with the outside world. Women were primarily responsible for domestic work and raising children, although they often helped with the flocks, and even more so with agriculture in semi-pastoral tribes.[2]

Cities became more important in Arab society. Islam was a religion of the city, a place where its scholars and institutions predominated. The coming of empire, with both its wealth and its administrative apparatus, gave urban areas greater centrality. In terms of activity but not necessarily geography, there were two main centers of city life. One was the religious complex, dominated by a mosque and sometimes extended buildings, which served as a place of study and prayer. The other was the *suq*, or commercial market, a lively center of activity that remains the lifeblood of urban areas to this day. If the political apparatus was significant, such as in Cairo, it would be set apart as a guarded city within a city or—especially in the case of a capital like Baghdad—sometimes set outside the city with its own defensive arrangements. Residential areas would be found around the city, with different quarters housing peoples grouped by some common identity, usually kinship but also religion or ethnicity. Poorer quarters were located farthest from the center, near the city walls or outside them. The walls themselves were an important element of a city's defense before the age of the cannon, and a waste of time and materials afterward.[3]

Merchants came to dominate the economic life of the cities. Rulers cared only that they paid taxes, and absent oppressive taxation, there was little conflict between them. Merchant-dominated "free cities" did not develop similar to those in early modern Europe, as power resided with the military. The mantra "city air breathes free" would not have made much sense. Common trade commodities included textiles, glass, porcelain, gold, slaves, and spices.

A Morrocan girl carrying bread to a neighborhood oven to be baked.
Robert Fernea, photographer. CMES.

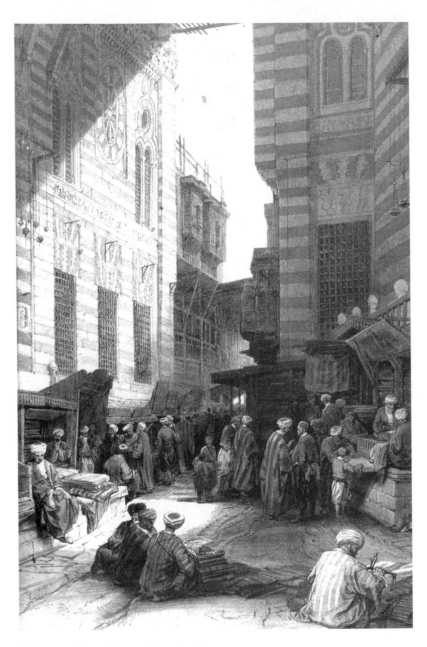

Silk merchants in an Egyptian bazaar.

Drawing by David Roberts. CMES.

Coppersmiths in an Egyptian bazaar.
Drawing by David Roberts. CMES.

The trade routes ran through the Red Sea and Egypt, and from there to the Mediterranean or other parts of the Arab world.[4] Since the maintenance of these routes required stability, merchants and rulers developed a symbiotic relationship whereby the latter provided stability and the former wealth. In addition to being trade hubs, cities were also centers of manufacturing. Staples, including processed foods, textiles, and metalwork, were made for the local market, while finer goods were made for long-distance trade.[5]

Commercial concerns took two primary forms. One was the partnership, similar to that which exists elsewhere. The other was the *mudaraba*, a business form taken from the Italian *commenda*, in which investors contribute goods, labor, or capital to a business and then receive a share of profits or losses from the outcome.[6] There was no credit system in the modern sense, but the Islamic prohibition on usury could be circumvented through a *mudaraba*. This is a major way Islamic banks function; the depositor gives over money to the bank, which can then invest it in business ventures. The bank and the depositor/investor then share the profits or losses.

115

There was little social mobility between classes. In addition to the ruling and military classes, the merchants and the *ulama* were the most powerful segments of society. Sons of merchants usually became merchants, and the same was true of *ulama*. Those with wealth could give money to a *waqf*, a pious foundation given in perpetuity for some specific purpose. A *waqf* might fund charities, mosques, or schools, or it might be administered by a family for its benefit, to be given to charity if the line died out.[7]

Family life naturally continued to be at the center of Arab society, and much of Islamic law was designed to deal with family-related issues. Islamic law allows a man up to four wives, but he has a legal obligation to support them. Therefore, polygamy has never been commonplace, especially in urban areas where large houses are expensive. Men were allowed to have sexual relations with only legal wives and slaves; otherwise illicit relations by either gender were in theory, and often in practice, severely punished.

There exists a perception that women in the Arab world have been universally veiled or secluded from public life. This has usually not been the case, either during earlier times or today, but practices have varied by region and often by family. Broadly speaking, during this time period women from the more affluent families were most likely to be veiled or secluded. The home of a family affluent enough to have a large house might be divided into two parts, one for the women and men of the family, and another into which male visitors could enter.

Rules of family law were also important in the spread of Islam. A Muslim man could marry a non-Muslim woman, but not vice versa, and the children would have to be raised Muslim. As already noted, the political system provided natural incentives for Christians to covert to Islam, but a Muslim who converts to another religion, even a monotheistic one, is given the death penalty. Thus conversion is one-way. These factors combined to create a "Ratchet Effect" whereby, once Muslim rule became established, the society would eventually become Muslim unless the territory was retaken.

Slavery held an important and, in many ways, unusual position in the Muslim world. Much of the Arab world from the late ninth century until early modern times was ruled by powers employing self-perpetuating slave armies, and in the case of the Mamluks, a slave government. Otherwise male slaves were used for hard labor, while female slaves were kept as domestic help and as concubines.

116

Slavery was expressly sanctioned in Islamic law, but was in many ways ameliorated by it. Manumission was considered a pious act, and the law provided slaves with some degree of protection from abuse. Moreover, the enslavement of Muslims was prohibited, and the same protection was given to monotheists who accepted Muslim rule. Thus, a Christian city that surrendered on terms could not be subject to enslavement.

Yet the great irony of Islamic slavery was that these very protections resulted in the creation of an intercontinental slave trade wider in scope than anything the world had ever seen. As the borders of Islamic rule grew, slaves had to be taken from ever farther distances. The Ottoman conquest of the Balkans and the conversion of central Asian tribes caused Africa to become an even more important source of supply. This intercontinental African slave trade was, of course, later taken up by Europeans.

Development of the Sciences

The Abbasid period also saw the blossoming of "Islamic science"—the incorporation of philosophical and scientific works from previous civilizations and their development over time. The Abbasids took a great interest in intellectual endeavors and were particularly interested in the sciences. While Muslims viewed the *shari'a* as replacing all other systems of legal and social norms, in the realm of science, their attitude was very different. The attitude which took root early and persisted over time was expressed by the great thirteenth-century thinker, Ibn Khaldun:[8]

> The intellectual sciences are natural to man, inasmuch as he is a thinking being. They are not restricted to any particular religious group. They are studied by the people of all religious groups who are all equally qualified to learn them and to do research in them. They have existed (and been known) to the human species since civilization had its beginnings in the world.

The new intellectual age first began to blossom under Harun al-Rashid, but the process accelerated under his son al-Ma'mun.

117

Al-Ma'mun founded an institute for translation and study called the "House of Wisdom," which began large-scale translations from Greek and Syriac in particular. Islamic science also got a boost from the conquest of Alexandria. After the Greek conquest, it had replaced Athens as the intellectual center of the eastern Mediterranean and had incorporated the achievements of both Greek and Mesopotamian thinkers. Muslims in turn incorporated both.

One of the earliest achievements was *Kitab al-Jabr wa al-Muqabalah* (Book of Compulsion and Comparison) by the mathematician al-Khwarizmi (c. 780–850). This book laid the foundation for the development of mathematics for centuries.[9] Its influence, and that of its author, is shown by the English terms "Algebra" (from *al-jabr*) and "Algorithm" (actually a corruption of al-Khwarizmi's name).

Building on the work of al-Khwarizmi, Abu Bakr Muhammad al-Karaji (c. 1000) broke new ground in the application of regular arithmetic to algebra. Qusta ibn Luqa al-Ba'labakki (d. 912) translated the first seven volumes of Diophantus' *Arithmetica* into Arabic, giving it the title *The Art of Algebra*. The Persian Umar al-Khayyam (d. 1131) achieved a number of advances in geometry, including the theory for equations of degree equal to or less than three, which is often wrongly attributed to René Descartes (d. 1650). Sharaf al-Din al-Tusi (c. 1200) built upon al-Khayyam's work, applying algebra to geometry, and was responsible for the development of the concept of the maximum of an algebraic expression, often wrongly attributed to another French mathematician, François Viète (d. 1603). Mathematicians also made progress in trigonometry, and al-Tusi actually appears to have written the first treatise on trigonometry not linked to astronomy, a milestone for mathematics as an independent discipline.[10]

It was also under al-Ma'mun that the Abbasids instituted a program of astronomical observations in Baghdad and Damascus. Thabit ibn Qurra (c. 836–901), although not a Muslim, worked with the Baghdad group, and appears to be the first to have produced a mathematic analysis of motion. Al-Battani (c. 858–929) from Syria is noted for his meticulous observations and appears to be the first to have deduced the possibility of an annular eclipse of the sun.[11]

The fact that for much of history mathematics was the handmaiden of astronomy underlines the importance of the latter. It was certainly important for Muslims both practically and theoretically. Around the turn of the millennium, Muslim astronomers began making significant technical strides that improved the technology used in observational instruments. The scientist al-Biruni (d. 1048) exemplified the world of science in the Middle East at the time. A Persian who produced the vast majority of his work in Arabic, al-Biruni also knew Sanskrit and was able to integrate Indian astronomy into the Muslim corpus. He produced approximately 150 works on fields as diverse as astronomy, mineralogy, and pharmacology. The contributions of Indian trigonometry were especially important to the progress in Islamic astronomy during this period.[12]

Al-Biruni also contributed to making a clear distinction between metaphysical philosophy and what are now known as the hard sciences. In correspondence with Ibn Sina (980–1037), al-Biruni challenged the illustrious philosopher on the relevance of Aristotelian philosophy to science. Whereas both Europeans and Muslims had always viewed philosophy as a science, al-Biruni argued that philosophical theories did not constitute valid evidence for real sciences such as astronomy.[13]

While Islam and its *lingua franca*, Arabic, might in some regards be said to have played only a facilitating role in medieval science, some efforts in astronomy and mathematics were specifically Islamic. Much of this was due to Muslim dependence on a lunar calendar, which regulated both the times of day for prayer and the beginning of the holy month of Ramadan, for which visibility of the moon was important. Finding the direction of the *qibla*, the orientation toward the Ka'aba in Mecca, was a special problem. For those nearby in Arabia, it was sufficient to know the astronomical alignment of the Ka'aba. For locations farther away, using the same alignment would mean praying in the wrong direction, so Muslim astronomers used science to find a better answer.[14]

The Way of the Mystics

The orthodox Islamic model that coalesced during the early centuries was based upon a framework of legal analysis founded upon divine revelation, either directly through the Quran and prophetic

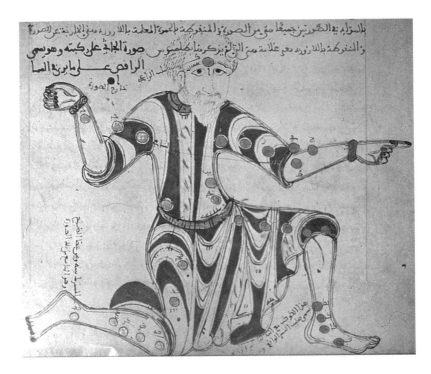

"The Dancer."

CMES.

statements given a similar status, or indirectly through the prophetic model exemplified in the Sunna. Both the substantive body of knowledge contained in the *shari'a* and the concept of complete dependence upon revelation came to be supplemented—some would say challenged—by two developments: a form of Islamic mysticism referred to as Sufism, and the continued development of philosophical thought as a mode of analysis independent from revelation.

The emphasis of the *ulama* on the expression of Islam through law provided Muslims with rules by which they should live their lives and structure their public affairs. Islamic legalism alone, however, left many unsatisfied, desiring deeper meaning in religion. This gap was filled by Sufism, or Islamic mysticism. Sufis sought to become close to God through meditation and varying forms of asceticism and otherworldliness. A Sufi order was called *al-tariqa*, or "the way." The term has the same formal meaning in Arabic as the word for Islamic law, *shari'a*. Yet whereas the *shari'a* pointed to an external way of serving God, the Sufi orders sought an internal way.[15]

Sufism was sometimes viewed with skepticism, especially by the *ulama*, but many Sufis viewed it as a supplement to, rather than a substitute for, the *shari'a*. They pointed to verses from the Quran or Sunna which have a mystical bent: "And when My servant asks thee concerning Me, surely I am nigh. I answer the prayer of the supplicant when he calls on Me, so they should hear my call and believe in Me that they may walk in the right way (Quran 2:186)."[16] In other words, although obedience to the *shari'a* is important, the core of Islam is becoming close to God first, and then right living will follow.

Al-Junayd (d. 910) was a Sufi intellectual based in Baghdad. He helped fill the void after the fall of the Mu'atezila philosophy, and promoted the concept of *fana*, or annihilation, in which one would simply have one's consciousness lost in God. This would be reached through a type of trancelike meditation.[17]

Perhaps the greatest Arab Sufi to express his spirituality through poetry was Ibn al-Farid (d. 1235). He would compose verses while in a state of ecstatic meditation, and one of his more well-known poems was called "Ode to Wine," in which he used intoxication as a metaphor for union with God. In one verse he

121

states, "Joyless in this world is he that lives sober, and he that dies not drunk will miss the path of wisdom."[18] It is no wonder that many regarded Sufis warily.

Although al-Junayd was careful to keep his mysticism within the bounds of the *shari'a*, there grew up a branch of Sufism based upon the rejection of the letter of the law, and for some the substance as well, in favor of complete dependence on God. This was in part based upon a rather ambiguous verse in the Quran (5:54) about one who "turns from his religion" but who "struggle[s] in the path of God," not fearing the reproach of any person. At times they would openly engage in outrageous conduct to show their independence from society. Perhaps the most extreme form of Sufism is represented by the Persian Sufi al-Hallaj (d. 922), who claimed that his *fana* caused him to achieve such oneness with God that he was God. Al-Hallaj was burned to death.[19]

Philosophy and Metaphysics

Muslim intellectuals also relished the philosophical works of earlier peoples, in particular the Greeks. Harun al-Rashid's vizier was instrumental in promoting the translation of Greek philosophical works, and al-Ma'mun would likely have held his own as a poet and scholar even had he not been caliph. Some Greek works are known only from Arabic translations.[20]

Acting as more than mere transmitters of knowledge, Muslim scholars began developing their own systems. Al-Kindi (795–866) is reported to have written some three hundred works, and developed a dialectical system under which all Quranic teachings could be deduced from logic. Al-Razi (c. 900) controversially took this thinking a step further and argued that revelation itself, including the Quran, was superfluous for this precise reason (understandably, he did not have a wide following). [21]

While mystics sought an Islamic alternative to a life based upon legal observance, Muslim philosophers sought an alternative means of knowing truth through human reason. The Mu'atezila taught that there was a place for reason in Islam independent of revelation, due to the many points on which revelation might be ambiguous. In the mid-ninth century the Mu'atezila lost favor due to their insistence on the doctrine of the created nature of the Quran and the independent nature of human actions. Abu al-Hasan al-Ash'ari (c. 873–935) became the founder of a new philosophical approach which retained the Mu'atezila belief in the independent role of reason, but rejected their position on the nature of the Quran and attempted to draw a middle course between absolute free will and absolute predestination.[22]

The greatest of Muslim theologians was al-Ghazali (1058–1111). Al-Ghazali was appointed under the Seljuks as head of the state academy in Baghdad. Becoming dissatisfied with a life of legal scholarship, al-Ghazali gave up his post and began traveling the Muslim world, embracing Sufism. It was al-Ghazali who first introduced Sufism into mainstream legal thinking, showing many that the *shari'a* of the *ulama* and the *tariqa* of the Sufi orders were compatible. Writing in both Arabic and Persian, he is equally known for his contributions to Islamic philosophy. His *Incoherence of the Philosophers* was a blistering attack on many aspects of the dominant thinking of his day. In particular he attacked them for their denial of the omniscience of God and of bodily resurrection.[23]

Islamic Spain played an especially important role in medieval philosophy, acting as a bridge between Europe and the lands of Islam. The caliphal advisor Ibn Tufayl (d. circa 1185) forcefully advocated the independent role of reason. In his book *Letters of the Life of Ibn Yaqzan*, he describes a man born on an island in the Indian Ocean. Although completely isolated all of his life from human contact, through reason he was able to discover the truth revealed in Islam, as well as much else in the physical world.[24]

More famous was the Córdoba native Ibn Rushd (1126–1198), known as Averroes in the West. First introduced to the caliph by Ibn Tufayl, Ibn Rushd was known as the preeminent scholar of Aristotle, and building on the earlier work by al-Kindi, he developed a complex system on the harmony of Aristotelian philosophy and Islam. He wrote a response to al-Ghazali titled *Incoherence of the Incoherence* and achieved a huge following among European intellectuals such that they came to be divided into "pro-Averroists" and "anti-Averroists."[25]

Another thinker who influenced Europe greatly was Ibn Sina (980–1037), or Avicenna. Although a Persian from Bukhara (modern Uzbekistan), Ibn Sina wrote in Arabic and was well known all the way to Spain. His most influential works, which became standard medical texts in Europe for centuries, were *The Canon of Medicine* and *The Book of Healing.*[26]

The rationalist school engendered a backlash, however. Ibn Hazm (994–1064) was a writer of extreme erudition who completely rejected all forms of reasoning including deduction, analogy, or opinion, arguing that only divine revelation, sense experience, and intuition were reliable.[27] He was followed by Ibn Taymiya (1263–1328), who savaged Ibn Rushd and others for their dependence on human reason. He went further than al-Ghazali in attacking philosophy, including logic, which al-Ghazali had supported. Ibn Taymiya is especially important because the Wahhabi ideology supported by the modern state of Saudi Arabia descends from his thinking.[28]

Ibn Khaldun (1332–1406), along with his near-contemporary Niccolò Machiavelli (1469–1527), might be regarded as the forefather of modern political science, having developed a theory explaining the rise and fall of states. His thesis was that the founders of great dynasties were able to succeed because of group feeling, or tribal unity. Once in power, however, rulers become corrupt with luxury and begin to fight with one another over shares of power. This brings about a state of weakness that can then be exploited by opponents with greater unity of purpose and identity.[29] Unlike Aristotelian science, which was almost entirely wiped away by the scientific revolution, Ibn Khaldun's arguments can still be debated and defended in terms recognizable by modern political theorists.

Language and Literature

Prior to Islam, Arabic had developed a great deal as a poetic medium, but had never been a true literary language. This changed radically afterward. The Quran itself repeatedly refers to the importance of a people having a "book"—the Jews had a book, the *torah*, the Christians had the *ingil*, or gospel, and Muslims had an Arabic recitation, or *qur'an*. Christians and Jews were thus called *ahl al-kitab*, "People of the Book," and were in turn respected for having a book from God, and chastised for ignoring

124

it. To this religious impulse was added the record-keeping needs of an expanding administration.

Yet the place of poetry, or *shir'*, in the world after Islam was hotly debated. Most Arabian poetry had centered on the glorification of the tribe and its deities, erotic love stories, and wine—all impious themes. At a minimum it was decided that poetry had to be studied and recorded because it provided the best lexical tool to understanding Arabic as used by Muhammad's contemporaries, and thus was necessary for understanding the Quran and hadith. Beyond this, the *ulama* were on the whole antagonistic to it.[30]

At the same time, the Umayyads created a climate in which the old themes could prosper. The Hijaz was flooded with booty after the conquests, fostering an expansion of erotic love poetry and riotous living, with Mecca itself being known for its abundance of dancing girls. Throughout the empire poets developed a literary culture, or *adab*, which played a role similar to modern pop culture, in which wine and eroticism were two of the main themes.

Politically, the *adibs* (men of literature) were at the opposite end of the spectrum from the *ulama*. Although not rejecting the *shari'a*, the *adibs* were enthusiastic supporters of caliphal absolutism. This may be attributed partly to self-interest, given the dependence of many upon the caliph for employment. Yet to a large extent it can also be attributed to an issue of principle; they genuinely admired the Persian literary tradition and its Mazdaen absolutism, and wanted to have an equivalent.[31]

The foundations of literary Arabic had become well developed in the centuries immediately after the rise of Islam, and this was built upon in the middle periods. More complex lexical aids were developed, as dictionaries contained both word meanings and examples of their use in classical texts. Reference works similar to the modern encyclopedia, discussing various regions, persons, or specific places listed according to time period or region, were produced.[32]

Arabic literature developed a distinctive genre called the *muqama*, which was essentially a short play including two or more individuals, with a narrator telling the story with a wide variety of contexts. Although the point may be entertainment or information, they often contain a moral the author wants to get across.[33]

125

In addition to the *muqama*, the essay also became very well developed, as did the fiction genre. Humor and parody were very popular and could be used to make fun of serious topics. Bernard Lewis provides this example of a parody of bureaucratic language:

Two Muslim galleys were lost at sea with all hands, and the secretary reported this, on behalf of his master, to the prince. He wrote: 'In the name of Allah the Merciful and the Compassionate. Be it known to the Prince—God strengthen him—that two galleys, I mean two ships, foundered, that is sank, because of the turbulence of the sea, that is, the force of the waves, and all within them expired, that is, perished.' The prince of Aleppo replied to his lieutenant: 'Your letter has come, that is, arrived, and we understood it, that is to say, we read it. Chastise your clerk, that is, hit him, and replace him, that is, get rid of him, since he is dim-witted, that is, stupid. Farewell, that is to say, the letter is finished.'[34]

More generally, it might be said of Arabs that language takes a much larger pride of place for them than for many others. More than any other characteristic it defines their identity. The use of proper Arabic has always been a point of immense significance in how one is perceived in society. Prior to Islam creating poetry was the Arabs' "national pastime," so to speak, and in recent times authoritarian regimes have allowed Arab novelists to take a far greater place within society than they otherwise would. With few recognized, legal fora through which writers could express themselves, fiction writers have acquired a special role in expressing dissenting ideas.[35]

Notes

1. Norman Itzkowitz, *Ottoman Empire and Islamic Tradition* (Chicago: University of Chicago Press, 1972) 21.
2. Hourani, *History of the Arab Peoples*, 101–8.
3. Ibid., 122–5.
4. Ibid., 111–2.

5. Ibid., 112.
6. Ibid.
7. Ibid., 115.
8. Ahmad Dallal, "Science, Medicine, and Technology: The Making of a Scientific Culture," in *The Oxford History of Islam*, John Esposito, ed. (New York: Oxford University Press, 1999) 157.
9. Ibid., 184–5.
10. Ibid., 185–90.
11. Ibid., 164–6.
12. Ibid., 166–8. Note that the "Arabic numerals" which Westerners use were actually invented in India, but were transmitted to the West through the Arabs, thus the misnomer.
13. Ibid., 169–70.
14. Ibid., 177–9.
15. Frederick Mathewson Denny, *An Introduction to Islam*, 2nd ed. (New York: Macmillan, 1994) 231.
16. Ibid., 220–2.
17. Ibid., 232.
18. Ibid., 229.
19. Ibid., 236–7.
20. Majid Fakhry, "Philosophy and Theology: From the Eighth Century c.e. to the Present," in *The Oxford History of Islam*, John Esposito, ed. (New York: Oxford University Press, 1999) 271–2.
21. Ibid., 272–3.
22. Ibid., 280–1.
23. Ibid., 283–4.
24. Ibid., 285–6.
25. Ibid., 286–9. See also Friedrich Heer, *The Medieval World: Europe 1100–1350* (New York: Welcome Rain, 1998) 190–212.
26. Hitti, *History of the Arabs*, 367–8.
27. Fakhry, "Philosophy and Theology," in Esposito, ed., 289–90.
28. Ibid.
29. Ibid., 291.
30. Hodgson I, 453, 461.
31. Hodgson I, 444–57.
32. Lewis, *Middle East*, 264.
33. Ibid., 258.
34. Ibid., 259.
35. The best known writer in the modern Arab world is Naguib Mafouz, an Egyptian who won the Nobel Prize for Literature in 1988.

CHAPTER VIII

The Ottoman Age
(1517–1798)

The Ottoman Empire (1301–1924) was principally a central Asian and European phenomenon. The forebears of the Ottoman Turks themselves came from the vast stretches of central Asia. Having established themselves in Anatolia, primarily a part of the Greek world until that time, their main focus was on leading the *jihad* into Europe. Yet the Arab provinces of their empire were integral to the whole. Egypt and Syria would become important economically, as they had been for previous empires. For the Ottoman sultans, claiming the mantle of the Prophet Muhammad by maintaining suzerainty over the holy cities of Mecca and Medina was essential to their status. The North African provinces held strategic importance in the ongoing struggle against the European powers. And, like every holder of the caliphate since the seventh century, they wanted to hold on to Iraq, often struggling with their Persian adversaries there.

For the Arabs themselves, life under Ottoman rule was hardly a time of dynamic change. Even worse than bystanders to history, they were for the largest part simply unaware of the great changes taking place in early modern Europe. Parts of the Arab world also occupied margins of independence from Ottoman rule. The Ottomans never took Morocco, and they never seriously attempted to control the Arabian Peninsula in its entirety.

The World of the Ottoman Empire

The Ottoman Empire had its origins in the movement of Turkic peoples into Anatolia that began under the Seljuks. After the defeat of the Byzantines at the Battle of Manzikert in 1071, the way was open for the Turkic *ghazis* (holy warriors) to expand the borders of Islam farther westward. By the late thirteenth century, Byzantium essentially had given up Anatolia.

The *ghazi* principality closest to Byzantine lands was the Emirate of Osman in western Anatolia. Osman (d. circa 1326) managed to lead his warriors to victory over a large Byzantine army at Baphaeon in 1301. Through this victory Osman raised himself above the other amirs and established his leadership over a number of other principalities, and his followers became known as the Ottomans. Osman's son Orhan continued the campaign, and he was instrumental in creating the embryonic Ottoman state, minting his first coins in 1327.[1] Orhan's son Suleyman established the Ottomans in Europe, taking the key coastal fortress at Gallipoli near Constantinople.[2]

The Balkans at the time were deeply fragmented, both politically and religiously. Before conquering small states, the Ottomans developed a strategy of requesting submission in return for refraining from the traditional pillage.[3] The protection of peasants against mistreatment by local elites was a hallmark of Ottoman policy, and combined with the suppression of Catholicism, this ensured the popularity of the new rulers among the East Orthodox population.[4] Their main weakness lay in their lack of naval power.[5]

In 1444 Sultan Murad II abdicated in favor of his twelve-year-old son Mehmed in order to live a quieter life. Byzantium decided to seize the advantage and organized a coalition to drive the Ottomans from Europe. When it became clear that young Mehmed, later known as Mehmed the Conqueror, was not up to the challenge, Murad returned to the sultanate and defeated his Balkan enemies decisively near the Black Sea coast in Bulgaria. The Ottoman Janissaries (elite military units) successfully adopted European gunpowder weapons, both firearms and cannons, and were set to conquer the world.[6]

When Murad II died, Mehmed was almost twenty, and he now was ready to rule. On May 29, 1453, his cannons finally achieved

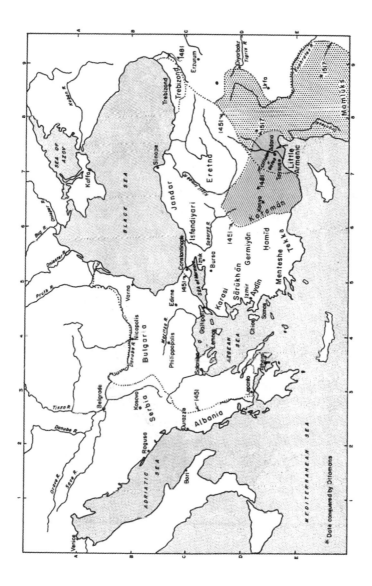

Ottoman conquests to 1451.

Courtesy of the University of Washington Press (Originally appeared in *A Near East Studies Handbook* by Jere Bacharach, 1977.)

what Muslim caliphs had sought for nearly eight hundred years—the conquest of Constantinople. He quickly moved his capital to the great city, now called Istanbul, and created a buffer by making the Danube River (northern border of modern Bulgaria) the northern boundary of direct control.

Up until the 1460s the Ottoman Empire had been a purely Anatolian-Balkan affair. Mehmed declared himself sovereign of the "Two Seas"—the Black Sea and the Mediterranean—and the "Two Lands"—Anatolia and the Balkans.[7] Mehmed's son Bayezid II (r. 1481–1512) would begin a conflict with the Egypt-based Mamluk sultanate that marked the beginning of Ottoman interest in the Arab world. The Mamluks not only claimed suzerainty over Egypt, the Hijaz, and Syria, but also over much of Anatolia as well. The tensions began in 1468 when Mehmed moved to expand eastward in Anatolia. At Mehmed's death in 1481, the Mamluks gave refuge to Bayezid's brother Cem, also a claimant to the sultanate. The very next year they facilitated his reentry into Anatolia, and this led to several inconclusive campaigns between the two Muslim powers over the next decade. Bayezid II then began to modernize his army and increase the use of firearms, which the Mamluks did not use.[8] He also oversaw an economic expansion and the improvement of the navy. The naval buildup signaled the growing ambition of the hitherto land-based Ottomans.[9]

Bayezid's son and successor Selim I (r. 1512–1520) completed the Ottoman conquest of Anatolia, and in doing so made conflict with the Mamluks inevitable. At the time the Mamluks, the primary power in the Arab world, were faring badly against a naval challenge from the Portuguese to the south in the Red Sea. Since the wealth of Egypt and much of the Arab world depended to a significant degree upon control of the east-west trade routes, the threat was deemed severe enough for the Sharif of Mecca to suggest that the Mamluks send a delegation seeking Ottoman aid, although the Mamluks rejected the idea. The delegation was not necessary. Selim was only too happy to help, and in fact sent out word to the Arabs that he would not only fight the infidel Europeans, but he would liberate them from the Mamluks as well.[10]

In 1516 Selim first moved on Aleppo in northwest Syria and defeated the Mamluk army in a battle in which Sultan al-Ghawri was killed. The Mamluks still viewed the use of firearms as degrading to their status as warriors, and it cost them.[11] In the presence of the Caliph al-Mutawakkil, previously under Mamluk custody, Selim I received the title "Servant of Mecca and Medina." He quickly overcame what remained of the Mamluk forces, taking Jerusalem and Damascus. Moving on Egypt, Selim proclaimed an amnesty for the inhabitants of the province, stating that only the Mamluks were his enemies. The new Mamluk sultan refused to submit and was defeated in 1517. The sharif sent Selim I the keys to Mecca and Medina, exactly as he had wanted. Selim then appointed a new governor in Egypt and returned to Istanbul.

In many ways, the conquest of Arab lands transformed the empire even more than that of Constantinople. The Ottoman ruler, previously sultan of Anatolia and the Balkans, was now the caliph, successor to the prophet Muhammad as head of all Muslims. As such, he now was owed loyalty by Muslims in the Arab world, and he bore the chief responsibility of being the protector of the holy cities. Yet Arab lands had more than symbolic value. Control of the trade routes brought new wealth, and revenue doubled.[12]

Selim's successor Suleyman I (r. 1520–1566), known in history as Suleyman the Magnificent, used this new wealth to expand the *jihad* into Europe. Ottoman forces made it all the way to the Hapsburg capital of Vienna in 1529 before their three-week siege was called off. Suleyman also moved aggressively in the Mediterranean, first seizing Algiers (c. 1520) as a naval base. France had taken Tunis in 1535, and was thus a threat to Ottoman control of the western Arab lands. The Ottomans moved to take Tripoli (c. 1550) and Tunis (1574), and defeated a major European fleet in 1538.[13]

Up until the 1530s one major area of the Arab world was still beyond Ottoman power—Iraq, and with it control of the Persian Gulf. In 1533 Istanbul intensified efforts to woo local amirs in Iraq into its fold and away from the Shi'a Safavids of Persia. The next year Suleyman led his army into Iraq, occupied Baghdad, and annexed both Iraq and Azerbaijan. Local rulers pledged submission to the Ottomans. This gave them complete control of the Arabian trade routes, as they now had taken both the Red Sea and the Persian Gulf.[14]

In 1548 the Persians attempted to take advantage of an Ottoman campaign in Europe by invading Iraq, but Suleyman again led his armies against Iran and secured control of Iraq over a seven-year

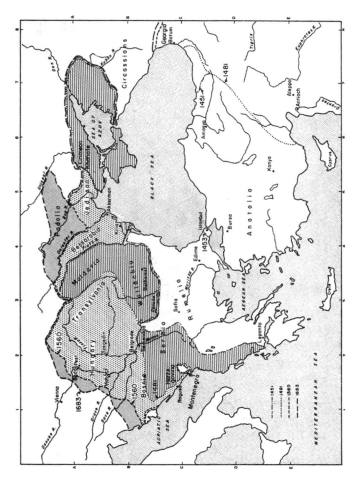

Ottoman Empire in Europe and Anatolia, 1415–1683.

Courtesy of the University of Washington Press. (Originally appeared in *A Near East Studies Handbook* by Jere Bacharach, 1977.)

conflict. The Treaty of Amasya in 1555 formalized Ottoman rule in Baghdad. At the same time the Ottomans began using the Persian Gulf as well as the Red Sea as bases for their naval war against the Europeans in the Indian Ocean. However, the Portuguese held on to the strategic island of Hormuz, which lies between the tip of the Arabian Peninsula and Persia, thus controlling the outlet into the ocean.[15]

The sixteenth century saw a massive expansion of Ottoman might on land and sea, financially as well as militarily. Although they suffered setbacks, none were catastrophic, and the Ottomans grew from a regional to a genuine world power, playing a key role in the international balance of power from central Europe to North Africa, and from central Asia to the Indian Ocean. The new Ottoman self-perception, molded in part by control of Arab lands, is here expressed by Suleyman the Magnificent himself:[16]

> I am God's slave and sultan of this world. By the grace of God I am head of Muhammad's community. God's might and Muhammad's miracles are my companions. I am Suleyman, in whose name the *hutbe* [Friday sermon] is read in Mecca and Medina. In Baghdad I am the shah, in Byzantine realms the Caesar, and in Egypt the sultan; who sends his fleets to the seas of Europe, the Maghrib and India. I am the sultan who took the crown and throne of Hungary and granted them to a humble slave. The voivoda Petru raised his head in revolt,[17] but my horse's hoofs ground him into the dust, and I conquered the land of Moldavia.

Arab Societies during the Ottoman Age

Nearly all the urban areas of the Arab world spent almost four full centuries under Ottoman suzerainty. Even where local elites managed to gain autonomy from Istanbul for long periods, the Ottoman way of life and administration still had its impact.

The general pattern for a newly conquered province was for Istanbul to appoint its own officials, including a *bey* acting as the governor and *qadi*s to act as the judiciary. Each *bey* would have his own Janissary regiment in order to keep control. The division of power between the executive and judicial branches was viewed as central to Ottoman justice, so the *bey* could have people arrested, but only a *qadi* could sentence a suspect. The basic element of the economy was the Timar system, in which revocable land grants were given to subjects who fought in wars, raised taxes, kept order, and fulfilled other functions for the empire. However, the only aspect of the Timar system implemented in the Arab provinces was, in some areas, tax farming, the practice of giving individuals the responsibility for collecting taxes for a given region.[18]

The composition of the political elite varied by province. In Egypt and the Hijaz, the previous rulers, the Mamluks and the sharifs, were left in place. Whereas most provinces sent—or were supposed to send—tax money to Istanbul, the empire actually subsidized the sharifs to maintain control so that the Ottomans would not find themselves in endless warfare with Arabia's Bedouin tribes. Most provinces received appointed rulers, and Algiers (capital of modern Algeria) was built due to the Ottoman need for a naval base in the Western Mediterranean. Algiers thus represented the opposite extreme on this spectrum, with its elite overwhelmingly Ottoman.[19]

The Ottoman class system exhibited a four-tiered hierarchy. First, the "Men of the Pen" comprised scholars and other educated professionals. These included the *ulama*, judges, administrators, teachers, and others. The highest-level *qadi* would be an Ottoman, but much of this class was Arab. However, as with European empires, colonization by Turkish families sometimes provided the mid-level administration and buttressed Ottoman rule by their presence. Second, the "Men of the Sword" were the military and security forces. These were mostly Ottoman, and where governors were able to establish themselves they sometimes developed their own military caste systems, giving them greater independence. Third, the "Men of Negotiation" included merchants, tradesmen, craftsmen, and the like. They tended to be Arab. Significant elements of this class were Christian or Jewish. Fourth, the "Men of Husbandry" included farmers and other agricultural workers. These were largely Arab, although military and administrative officials often exploited this class for their own benefit. One phenomenon that did not occur is notable: whereas in the West the first and last of these categories came to converge in the tradition of the educated farmer (e.g., George Washington), this never happened in the Arab world. Thus, elsewhere agriculture came to be viewed as a science with which farmers could experiment according to local conditions, but this was much less the case in the Middle East.[20]

As suggested above, these categories, which under Ottoman law were strictly separate, often overlapped in practice. The *ulama* sometimes controlled *waqf* funds, and at times used them for capital investment. Administrative officials often formed joint ventures with merchants. Janissaries began to enter the guilds illegally, and officers sometimes took over tax farming. The incentives toward corruption in this overlapping system are obvious, which is why the classes were supposed to be separate. Yet in distant provinces especially, there was little Istanbul could do to prevent it.[21]

Ottoman political legitimacy in the Arab world was insured by the appropriation of the caliphate. After the conquest of Egypt in 1517 the last of the Abbasid line was taken to Istanbul, from whence he later returned as a private citizen.[22] The Ottoman sultan simply added "Caliph" to the list of his titles, as demonstrated by the quote from Suleyman the Magnificent above.

Nationalist sentiment in the contemporary sense did not exist in the Arab world at this time. However, locals often protested over food prices or abuses of power, and could succeed in having local governors replaced.[23] Provincial notables came to play a prominent role in local affairs, one which they retained to modern times.[24]

Egypt and Syria were essential to the Ottoman treasury. Due to conflicts with Persia, trade with the east largely came through Egypt, and to some degree through Syria. As of 1528 these two provinces alone provided one-third of the budget income of the entire empire. There also was a good deal of bilateral trade between the central Asian provinces and the Arab provinces—most prominently, Arab provinces imported timber and iron, while they exported linen, rice, and sugar.[25]

Arabic was able to maintain itself during the Ottoman period due to its status as the language of the Quran, Sunna, and classical scholarship. While non-religious writing might be in Turkish, Arabic dominated the preeminent fields of law and religion. This was true in Istanbul as well as in the Arab provinces. The Ottomans thus confirmed its status as the *lingua franca* of Islamic thinking, a status it has maintained to this day across the Muslim world.[26] Further-more, while Istanbul could appoint the judicial authorities, societal influence in the provinces was primarily held by the local Arab *ulama*, not the *qadis*.[27] This allowed Arab religious thought to flourish in the absence of political power.[28]

Ottoman rule also increased the strength of Sufism. After con-quering Syria, Selim II built an elaborate memorial over the grave of the Sufi master Ibn al-Arabi in Damascus, and the Ottomans facilitated the spread of the originally Indian Naqshbandiya broth-erhood through much of the empire.[29]

Sufism in the Arab provinces took a different course from pre-vious times. Whereas before Sufis often were viewed with suspicion by the *ulama*, now the twin "ways" of Islam began to converge. Building upon al-Ghazali's attempted synthesis of legalism and mysticism, the Ottoman period saw an increase in hadith scholars, intent upon strict adherence to the *shari'a*, who used Sufi orders to revitalize Muslim societies, which they believed to be in spiritual decline. In addition to the Naqshbandiya *tariqa*, the Khalwatiya *tariqa* held the most sway in Arab lands. The Khalwatiya focused less on strict adherence to the *shari'a*, and over time it was split into sub-orders by various Sufi masters. Both *tariqa*s were especially strong in North Africa, but also had a strong following in the Hijaz and Cairo.[30]

Cairo played a special role in the development of Islamic thought. Al-Azhar University had a permanent group of resident teachers and welcomed students and scholars from near and far. They would come and study or teach for a while before moving on to spread their ideas elsewhere. Mecca and Medina, domi-nated by families that boasted scholarly traditions, held a similar role. That both the *ulama* and Sufi traditions, with their partial convergence, were so wide-ranging helped to give the Arab world itself a sense of religious community and also tied it to other Muslim lands.[31]

The Shi'a found life harder under the Ottomans. The cities were Sunni-dominated and intolerant of Shi'a teaching. Suleyman the Magnificent set the tone by summoning a prominent Shi'a scholar to Istanbul and having him executed. If religion cannot thrive without government, then the Shi'a needed a guardian. That guardian appeared with the adoption of Shiism by the Safavid

Al-Azhar, founded by the Fatimids, has been an international institution of Islamic study and prayer from Mamluk times until today.

Caroline Williams, photographer. CMES.

Empire in Persia. To this day the overwhelming majority of Shi'a worldwide are concentrated in Iran and Iraq.[32]

It was during this period that modern trends in Arab Christianity became established. Starting in the sixteenth century and accelerating afterward, Catholic missions proliferated among what remained of Christian populations in Syria, Palestine, and Iraq. This increased the number of congregations who gave their allegiance to the Pope, while by the eighteenth century virtually all the rest aligned themselves with the Orthodox Patriarch of Constantinople, with Antioch being their local base.[33] Along with the Egyptian Copts, these two groups have made up the overwhelming majority of Arab Christianity to the present time.

Morocco and Arabia: Arabs outside the Empire

From medieval times to the twentieth century, only one Arab society produced a relatively stable state ruled by Arabs— Morocco. Situated at the western edge of the Arab world, the people of Morocco bordered three worlds: the Ottoman Empire, which tried to expand at their expense; Europe, which wanted to use Morocco as a way-station for its mercantile empires; and West Africa, which provided an outlet for their own expansion.

The Spanish retaking of the Iberian Peninsula provoked a grave crisis for Muslim northwest Africa, and a number of factions attempted to gain control, fearing a Christian invasion. The Almohads, having been beaten in Spain, were replaced in 1269 by the Marinid dynasty. The Marinids also thwarted a takeover by the Hafsids of Tunis. Although the Marinids were not able to expand their power, they did succeed in implanting Islam and the Maliki legal tradition in what would become Morocco.[34]

After a long period without sustained centralized rule, in 1510 a dynasty of sharifs (descendants of Muhammad), the Sa'dids, were able to establish a stable state and fight off European encroachment. They then expanded their control southward into the Sahara and sub-Saharan Africa. One might even speak of a sharifian mini-empire, as the Sa'dids took control of the Saharan trade in gold and slaves, for a brief time as far as Timbuktu in east Africa.[35]

The Tinmel Mosque in Morocco (circa twelfth century).

Ron Baker, photographer. CMES.

The Sa'dids developed a dual army—a slave army constituted from African slaves, and a regular army made up from local tribes. With the support of the *ulama* and the merchant class, the Sa'did state successfully withstood the Ottomans as they swept across North Africa, but its population base simply was not large enough for it to do anything more than hold on. The main city, Fez, was only about half the size of Tunis or Damascus and not remotely comparable to Cairo or Istanbul.[36]

Due to a family rift, in 1670 a new dynasty, the Filalis, were able to take control of the entire country by presenting themselves as a bulwark against Ottoman expansion. The Maliki school was maintained, but the primary source of religious inspiration came from a Sufi brotherhood founded by one al-Shadhili (d. 1258). It penetrated virtually every level of Moroccan society, and the tombs of holy men became places of pilgrimage.[37]

The *ulama* continued to promote the *shari'a*-based vision of an Islamic society. A famous essay by al-Hasan al-Yusi (1631–1691) described the role of the state and the *ulama* in relation to society. He outlined three responsibilities that a ruler had to fulfill in order to maintain legitimacy: just collection of taxes, *jihad*, and prevention of oppression of the weak by the strong. With the early caliphs as his model, the ruler should engage in consultations with the *ulama* while carrying out his duties.[38] What is notable about this essay is its sense of continuity, building upon precedents set, or thought to have been set, in earlier times. Despite Morocco's isolation, its culture was set within the framework of a wider Islamic vision. The Filali sharifs managed to maintain their rule into modern times and constitute the oldest continuous state in the Arab world.

At the other end of the Arab world in the Arabian Peninsula, Arab tribes faced some of the same challenges, but none created a centralized state. Ottoman power extended down into the Hijaz, controlling the Red Sea and the pilgrimage routes to Mecca, but little more. The southern and eastern sides of the peninsula had a number of important ports, including Aden in Yemen, Muscat in Oman, and the island of Bahrain. Naturally, they were tempting targets for larger powers. Muscat was taken over by Portugal and then retaken by the Omanis in the mid-seventeenth century. Omani merchants themselves were wide-ranging, establishing outposts in

A view of Fez, Morocco. The historical building is the Abu Inaniyya
School founded by the Sa'dids in the sixteenth century.

Caroline Williams, photographer. CMES.

The ramparts of the Portuguese fortress El-Jadida in Morocco.
Ron Baker, photographer. CMES.

A different view of the fortress of El-Jadida.
Ron Baker, photographer. CMES.

east Africa. Bahrain was taken by Persia in 1602, but became independent again in 1783.[39]

The rest of the peninsula was controlled by a number of tribes
who achieved leadership locally but could not project power
regionally. The first serious attempt to unify the peninsula under a
single tribe was made by the clan of the Al-Sa'ud. This early movement is of special significance because after some reversals it led
to the creation of the modern state of Saudi Arabia.

In 1727 Muhammad ibn Sa'ud became the leader of al-Dir'iya, a
sub-region within the Najd, the central region of the peninsula. His
tribe, the Al-Sa'ud, belonged to the landowning merchant class of
the Najd, but its power did not extend beyond the settlement. The
most prominent tribe in the eastern half of Arabia was the Banu
Khalid. The Al-Sa'ud lacked both the wealth and the tribal lineage
to challenge them. [40]

Yet the Al-Sa'ud were able to compensate for their weakness
through an alliance with Muhammad ibn Abd al-Wahhab (1703–
1792). Abd al-Wahhab was a reformer with a passion for the strict

145

enforcement of the *shari'a*. He believed that the practices of the Shi'a were the epitome of *bida'*, or innovation from Islam, and should be eliminated by whatever means necessary. Soon he became too much for local leaders, whom he condemned as lax in Islam. In response, they banished him from the tribe. He then turned to an alliance with the Al-Sa'ud in 1744. This Saudi-Wahhabi Pact became the basis for a partnership that has endured to this day:[41]

> [Ibn Sa'ud:] This oasis is yours, do not fear your enemies. By the name of God, if all Najd was summoned to throw you out, we will never agree to expel you . . . [Abd al-Wahhab:] You are the settlement's chief and wise man. I want you to grant me an oath that you will perform jihad (holy war) against the unbelievers. In return you will be imam, leader of the Muslim community and I will be leader in religious matters.

The alliance sealed, the Al-Sa'ud would raid and the Wahhabis would preach, and settlements only would find peace by agreeing to pay tribute to the Al-Sa'ud and by accepting Wahhabi judges to ensure strict adherence to the *shari'a*. After pacifying the Najd, Ibn Sa'ud's son Abd al-Aziz I (1765–1803) moved eastward and defeated the Banu Khalid, taking the region of Hasa. Qatar and Bahrain capitulated in 1797. As much of the population in this part of eastern Arabia was Shi'a, this offered the Wahhabis an opportunity to further purify the peninsula. They then turned east and subjugated the Hijaz, taking Mecca in 1803 and Medina the following year. The sharifs, since 1517 vassals of the Ottomans, now came under the rule of the Al-Sa'ud.[42]

The alliance had its setbacks, however. The rough, unfamiliar terrain of Yemen allowed Yemeni tribes to rebuff the invaders. Turning north, the Al-Sa'ud began raiding Iraq. Besides bringing in plunder, this also allowed the Wahhabis a chance to wreak destruction on Shi'a holy sites, including Karbala, where Ali's son Hussein had been martyred. Yet this proved to be their undoing. A Shi'a retaliatory raid plundered Dir'iya in 1803 and assassinated Abd al-Aziz. Even more seriously, in 1811 the Ottomans sent an army into the Najd from Egypt to end the nascent threat for good.

Many local tribes sided with the Ottomans, having tired of Al-Sa'ud's punitive raids. Sa'ud ibn Abd al-Aziz died in 1814, and in 1818 his son Abdullah was forced to surrender. Ottoman forces massacred many of the Wahhabi *ulama* and took captive all they could find. Abdullah himself was eventually sent to Istanbul where he was beheaded. Thus ended the first Saudi-Wahhabi emirate.[43]

The Decline of the House of Osman

At the end of the sixteenth century, having swallowed the vast majority of the Arab world, a large section of southeastern Europe and huge swaths of land around the Black Sea, the Ottoman Empire was at its peak. Superior on land and feared across Europe, their armies barely failed to take Vienna in 1529, and that primarily due to the weather. Yet in the seventeenth century the decline of Ottoman power was palpable, and despite desperate attempts at reform the eighteenth only saw the deterioration accelerate. To a large degree this decline was merely relative—the Ottomans actually stagnated while Europe moved ahead. Yet much of it, especially in the Arab provinces, was real decline, measured in decreasing trade, wealth, and military power, concomitant with a loss of effective control of local authorities.

Disparities in sea power became obvious first, and these in turn contributed to other aspects of the empire's long-term decay. The Ottomans had succeeded in fending off Portuguese naval attacks on Yemen and the Hijaz, but had lost the Indian ocean. At the Battle of Lepanto in 1571 Europeans demolished their Mediterranean navy, sinking 200 out of 230 ships.[44] The Ottomans boasted that they had such wealth that they could easily rebuild all that was lost, and did so, but replacing inferior ships with inferior replicas still left the Ottomans with an inferior navy. The balance of power on land shifted in the following century. Whereas the previous failure to take Vienna had been followed by an orderly retreat, the defeat at the gates of Vienna in 1683 was followed by a headlong rout and another defeat near Belgrade in 1697 in which virtually the entire army was wiped out.[45]

The Treaty of Carlowitz that followed in 1699 had special significance in regard to the changing balance of power. Not only did

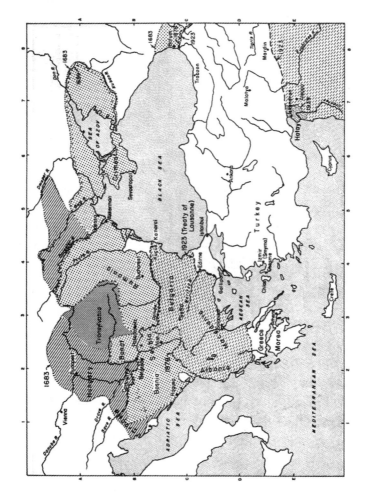

Ottoman Empire in Europe and Anatolia, 1683–1923.

Courtesy of the University of Washington Press. (Originally appeared in *A Near East Studies Handbook* by Jere Bacharach, 1977.)

Istanbul cede a significant portion of its European territory, but for the first time was lowered to the point of having to engage in diplomacy. Whereas before Istanbul could merely dictate the terms of peace to an enemy, it now had to use persuasion to mitigate the consequences of a defeat.[46]

Naval weakness played a key role in the economic decline. European nautical engineering and navigational techniques, developed to better survive the Atlantic, gave them a decisive advantage. European control of eastern trade, signified by the founding of the British East India Company in 1600, cut the Arab provinces out of much of international commerce. Ottoman records at this time show a drop in the number of trade ships arriving in the Red Sea annually from twenty previously to just three or four.[47] The expansion of European empires in the Western hemisphere also eliminated Europe's need to import products from the Middle East. Christopher Columbus' mission was expressly founded upon the need to find a way to circumvent the Muslim world.[48]

All this was exacerbated by the illogic of Ottoman trade policy, which taxed exports at the same rate as imports and prohibited the export of certain goods on the theory that this would lead to shortages.[49] Most international trade that remained was constituted by luxury items, not the kinds of products that could lead to aggregate economic expansion.[50] Internal economic growth was further hampered by the guild system and its place in Ottoman regulation. The guilds, as in Europe, were organizations of craftsmen with a common trade and interest in protecting their control of it. The Ottoman state gave guilds monopolies within their towns, thus preventing external competition. Moreover, the fact that guild membership passed from father to son prevented competition within the guild. Geographical limitations also prevented the development of economies of scale. Finally, prices were fixed by common agreement between the guilds and the government.[51] If the intent had been to prevent commercial innovation, the Ottomans could not have designed a better system.

Of the trade and industry that did survive, a disproportionate amount came to be controlled by European powers and religious minorities through what became known as the Capitulation System. The capitulations essentially were rights given to European powers to protect non-Muslim minorities in the empire while

149

gaining exemptions from Ottoman control and taxation for their activities. For example, the French became the protectors of Catholics. Originally granted as an act of magnanimity by the sultan, over time these agreements allowed Europeans and their clients to gain complete economic and legal immunity from Ottoman regulation.[52]

The loss of naval power in the Mediterranean also accelerated the tendency toward *de facto* independence for the Arab provinces. The Mamluks in Egypt began to reassert themselves, and the North African provinces were beyond control. Originally the sultan had maintained a tight hand on the provinces by keeping Janissaries there and by rotating appointees. Eventually local troops and officials became a self-perpetuating elite.

Perhaps the most important factor in the decline was the Ottomans' all-encompassing attitude of self-sufficiency regarding their own ways and disdain toward anything Western. This changed over time, but all too slowly. Although they were quick to adopt European techniques of war, both by purchasing weapons and by hiring European experts, the cultural, social, economic, and political aspects of European civilization most closely associated with the Renaissance, the scientific revolution, and modernity were rejected. The Ottomans would import the products of Western civilization, but not the cultural capital that had generated the innovations in the first place. The concept of *bida'*, or innovation, had always been considered one of the worst of sins in Islam, but the Ottomans made the prohibition on innovation holistic. Their long-standing prohibition on the printing press illustrates this. Since the process was first fully developed in Europe, the concept of printing was known but considered sinful, at least when used for Islamic languages such as Arabic and Turkish. The first Turkish printing press was established in 1729, and even then religious material was off-limits. It printed only a small number of volumes and was shut down in 1742. After a few more false starts, it was not until after 1795 that printing presses in Arabic and Turkish became permanently established.[53]

During the centuries of dominance by governments formed out of central Asian military classes, the peoples of the Arab world underwent an extended "Rip Van Winkle" experience. Around the beginning of the second millennium A.D., the Muslim civilization of

150

the Middle East was in virtually every way more advanced than, or at least the equal of, that on the northern side of the Mediterranean. This still was a defensible worldview when Ottoman rule began, although Europeans were beginning to exceed them in some areas. By the end of the eighteenth century Europeans outclassed the Muslim Middle East in every measurable way. The Ottomans were sinking, and Arabs were going down with the ship.

Notes

1. Halil Inalcik, *The Ottoman Empire: The Classical Age 1300–1600* (London: Phoenix Press, 2000) 6–8.
2. Ibid., 9.
3. Ibid., 7, 10–1.
4. Ibid., 13.
5. Ibid., 12.
6. Ibid., 20–1.
7. Ibid., 29.
8. Ibid., 33.
9. Ibid., 32–3.
10. Ibid.
11. Hitti, *History of the Arabs*, 703–4.
12. Inalcik, *Ottoman Empire*, 34.
13. Ibid., 36–7, see also Hourani, *History of the Arab Peoples*, 215.
14. Ibid., 38.
15. Ibid.
16. Ibid., 41.
17. This vague reference likely refers to the successful attempt by Russia's Ivan IV (r. 1533–1584) to use the Cossack horsemen to raid and plunder Muslim lands under Ottoman suzerainty. See Geoffrey Hosking, *Russia and the Russians: A History* (Cambridge, Massachusetts: The Belknap Press of Harvard University Press, 2001) 115–7.
18. Inalcik, *Ottoman Empire*, 104–8.
19. Hourani, *History of the Arab Peoples*, 234.
20. Lewis, *Middle East*, 164.
21. Itzkowitz, *Ottoman Empire and Islamic Tradition*, 39. See also, Hourani, *History of the Arab Peoples*, 235–8, and Inalcik, *Ottoman Empire*, 161–2.
22. Lewis, *Middle East*, 150.
23. Hourani, *History of the Arab Peoples*, 238.
24. Inalcik, *Ottoman Empire*, 161.
25. Ibid., 127–8.
26. Hourani, *History of the Arab Peoples*, 239.
27. John Obert Voll, *Islam: Continuity and Change in the Modern World*, 2nd ed. (Syracuse, New York: Syracuse University Press, 1994) 37.
28. Ibid., 31–56; 65–79.

29. Hourani, *History of the Arab Peoples*, 240.
30. Voll, *Islam*, 37–41.
31. Ibid., 41–53.
32. Hourani, *History of the Arab Peoples*, 240.
33. Ibid., 242.
34. Hodgson II, 270–1.
35. Hourani, *History of the Arab Peoples*, 244–5.
36. Ibid.
37. Ibid., 245–7.
38. Ibid., 247.
39. Ibid., 243.
40. Madawi Al-Rasheed, *A History of Saudi Arabia* (Cambridge: Cambridge University Press, 2002) 15–6.
41. Ibid., 16–7.
42. Ibid., 19–22.
43. Ibid., 23–4.
44. Inalcik, *Ottoman Empire*, 41–2.
45. Alan Palmer, *The Decline & Fall of the Ottoman Empire* (New York: Barnes & Noble Books, 1995) 25.
46. Bernard Lewis, *What Went Wrong?: Western Impact and Middle Eastern Response* (New York: Oxford University Press, 2001) 18–9.
47. Inalcik, *Ottoman Empire*, 45.
48. Felipe Fernández-Armesto, *Columbus and the Conquest of the Impossible* (London: Phoenix Press, 1974) 31.
49. Inalcik, *Ottoman Empire*, 52.
50. Ibid., 62.
51. Ibid., 150–60. See also Hourani, *History of the Arab Peoples*, 112.
52. Bernard Lewis, *The Muslim Discovery of Europe* (New York: W.W. Norton & Company, 2001, 2nd ed.) 48–9.
53. Lewis, *What Went Wrong*, 142–4.

Chapter IX

Sick Man of the Middle East: The Arab World in the Age of Ottoman Decline and European Ascendance

(1798–1920)

From the first European incursion in 1798 to the present, most areas of the Arab world went through a series of stages which may be broadly outlined as follows. First, some event or series of events would shock the inhabitants of the region into recognition of the vast differentials that existed between the West and the Muslim Middle East. By every measure—in wealth, technology, industrialization, political and legal development, education, and perhaps most obviously, military power—the West now clearly had the advantage. Second, some movement, religious or secular, would arise and attempt to revive or reform the region to face the challenge. Third, the hope of revival would be crushed and the province would come under either the direct control or indirect influence of some European power. Fourth, this would engender a nationalist reaction, leading to independence and hope for revival under the banners of nationalism, secularism, and socialism. Fifth, the joy of independence would give way to frustrations with the economic failure of most Arab states and the political authoritarianism of all. Sixth, Islamist movements would rise, filling the void left by the failures of secularist ideologies. Seventh, the current period would find autocracies able to stay in power but unable to satisfy the demands of their populations, thus resulting in a stagnant *status quo*.

In some regards these stages developed concurrently rather than sequentially, and naturally the details differ by region, but broadly speaking this periodization provides a useful paradigm for understanding the modern Arab world.

The late Ottoman Empire has become known in history as the "Sick Man of Europe," a moniker given it by Tsar Nicholas I.[1] For our purposes, it may also be said that the empire was the Sick Man of the Middle East as well. It was against this backdrop that the first stages of the previously described schematic played themselves out. Aside from having regional influence in its own right, Egypt was a microcosm of this process of impact, change, and reaction. It is thus with Egypt that we begin.

An Egyptian Saga

In 1798 the Mamluks, who had ruled Egypt in the name of God for 548 years, were confronted by a Frankish infidel who declared that God was really on the side with the most artillery. Napoleon Bonaparte demolished Mamluk forces with ease, and he not only used Pharaonic monuments for target practice, but had the audacity to tell Egyptians that the French were the true Muslims.[2] No one believed him. French troops became known for their public drunkenness and debauchery with local women. They even fired their cannons on the venerable al-Azhar Mosque in response to a riot. The French also took over the Mamluk administrative system, significantly improving the efficiency of tax collection, thus making it all the more oppressive.[3]

Ottoman forces prevented Napoleon from taking Palestine, but could do nothing to regain Egypt. The sultan requested the aid of the British, who were concerned with French control of an area so vital to their trade. In 1801 the British navy sank Napoleon's fleet, forcing the French to leave. This marked the beginning of a policy, upheld by successive British governments, of protecting the Ottoman Empire as a check on the expansion of other powers—especially Russia. Presaging the Cold War in many ways, British policy sought the containment of Tsarist expansion beyond a line beginning in Tibet in the east, running through India, Afghanistan, Persia, the Ottoman Empire, and up through central Europe. Ottoman control of the Arab world played a central role in this grand design, and British policy in the region must be seen in this context. [4]

The tomb of Sultan Hasan in Cairo; also a school.
Drawing by David Roberts. CMES.

Once the British withdrew, Egypt fell into chaos, with various factions fighting for control. In 1805 Istanbul appointed as governor an Albanian tobacco dealer named Muhammad Ali Pasha. After consolidating power, in 1811 Ali invited all remaining Mamluk officials to a ceremony, killed all who attended, and hunted down the rest.

Ali was a rapacious innovator. He is credited as being the first to fully grasp the pivotal role of industrialization in European power. He initiated a series of educational, industrial, economic, administrative, and military reforms, attempting to close the gap. He had students learn European languages and study in the West so as to imitate European methods, and hired French officers to train his military.[5]

From the beginning Ali harbored vast ambitions and had no intention of remaining a local Ottoman lackey. As he put it,[6]

I am well aware that the [Ottoman] Empire is heading by the day toward destruction, and that it will be difficult for me to save her. And why should I seek the impossible. . . ? On her ruins I will build a vast kingdom . . . up to the Euphrates and the Tigris.

The Ottomans seem to have sensed this, because they tried to transfer him the year after his appointment, and at one point sent a Georgian slave girl to poison him.[7]

A variety of circumstances gave Ali his chance. First, in order to pit one threat against another, Istanbul entrusted Ali with the job of defeating the nascent Saudi-Wahhabi Emirate in Arabia. Ali crushed the rebellion and took the Hijaz for himself. Next, believing that the source of the Nile contained vast deposits of alluvial gold, Ali sent his army south and occupied the Sudan and Ethiopia. He found no gold but the venture vastly increased the size of his empire. However, his plan to build a new Mamluk army from African slaves faltered when too many died. A third opportunity presented itself when a Greek revolt forced Istanbul to ask Ali for help again. Ali took advantage of this and occupied Crete and territory on the Greek mainland. Unfortunately, the European powers became involved and crushed his navy at the Battle of Navarino in 1827. He just barely got his troops back to Egypt.[8] This led to the independence of Greece.

Yet Ali's indomitable spirit would not be deterred. Beginning in 1829, he began conspiring with the French to take the key Ottoman cities in North Africa: Tripoli, Tunis, and Algiers. Istanbul refused to extend Ali's mandate to cover them, and negotiations with the French were aborted when the British intervened. Again undeterred, Ali initiated his endgame: his son Ibrahim Pasha marched into Syria with a force of fifty thousand troops. He took Palestine and successfully laid siege to Acre. Damascus fell shortly thereafter.[9]

Ali requested that Istanbul confirm his rule of the Levant. Sultan Mahmud II refused, and after being spurned by Western powers, he turned to his arch-nemesis to the north, signing a treaty of alliance with Russia. The sultan sent his army to take back the Levant, but again met defeat at Ibrahim's hands near Aleppo. As a result, the sultan succumbed to despair and drank himself to death, elevating the sixteen-year-old Abdulmejid to the throne. Even worse, the Ottoman navy then sailed for Alexandria, not to fight the upstart Albanian, but to defect to him.[10]

This was enough to stir the British into action, and they mobilized in the Mediterranean. Since Ibrahim depended upon the use of coastal ports for communication and supplies, the British shut them down, while also threatening Russia with war. Then in 1840 Britain, Russia, Prussia, and Austria signed the London Convention for the Pacification of the Levant, securing Ottoman control. Furthermore, while the sultan stripped Ali of his title, the Arab populations of the Levant were growing rebellious, finding Ali's liberation from Ottoman "oppression" oppressive. The French initially had supported Ali, but they now joined the pro-Ottoman consensus, and with the Royal Navy threatening Alexandria, he had no choice but to retreat. Istanbul reinstated Ali as governor of Egypt, and the *status quo ante* was restored.[11]

Muhammad Ali's grandson and successor Abbas (r. 1848–1854) lacked his ambitions, but those that followed after, Sa'id (r. 1854–1863) and Isma'il (r. 1863–1879) did not. Sa'id's grand initiative was what would become the Suez Canal, which, completed in 1869, would link the Mediterranean with the Red Sea. Almost immediately after his ascension, Sa'id reached an agreement with a French company to build it. Britain opposed the plan, in part because it threatened their overland trade route, and in part simply because it

157

involved the French. Istanbul also opposed it, but the Sick Man's opinions were given due consideration and ignored.[12]

Sa'id was succeeded in 1863 by Isma'il. Isma'il had his grandfather's ambition but neither his intelligence nor his common sense, and his particular lack of the latter quality would bring Egypt to ruin. He continued reform of virtually every aspect of Egyptian life—the legal system, the military, agriculture, administration, education—and imported foreign advisors by the boatload. Even American officers were brought over. Moreover, he gave major cities themselves a face-lift, with European-style streets lined with European-style hotels, opera houses, restaurants, and so on. Street signs were in French, and top hats were worn instead of the Arab *keffiya* (headdress) or Turkish-style hats.[13] Envisioning himself as a European colonialist (perhaps with Cairo as Paris), he expanded Egypt's control into Ethiopia and Somalia. Isma'il's self-perception—his own "White Man's Burden"—is demonstrated in a letter he wrote to the governor of the Sudan:[14]

> The prerequisite for [civilization] lies in the subjects' acquisition of the sciences . . . so that they may excel in them and be always disposed to love of the homeland, and eager to obtain the wealth of excellence and progress in knowledge and the arts.

This national makeover, naturally, cost quite a lot of money. However, the American Civil War had brought about a dramatic increase in cotton prices, vastly but temporarily increasing Egypt's export earnings. This encouraged Isma'il to spare no expense; he spent all he had and much more, taking out massive loans from Europe, apparently thinking that the conflict would last forever. Fortunately for the United States it did not, and after 1865 Egypt's export boom became a bust while Isma'il kept on borrowing. The army's poor showing in the Ethiopia War of 1875–1876 also dimmed his hopes. The national debt went from £3 million in 1863 to almost £100 million in 1875, of which two-thirds was short-term debt.[15]

Isma'il's creditors in London and Paris soon tired of this, and in 1876 they forced him to accept European controllers to supervise his treasury. This humiliation simply amplified existing popular anger over the legal and financial privileges of foreigners in

158

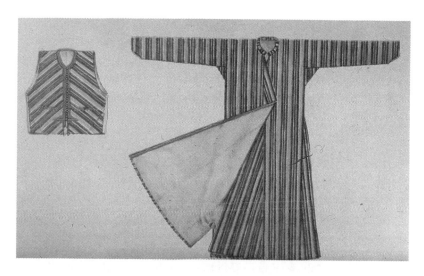

Traditional Egyptian dress, the kaftan.

Traditional Egyptian dress, a cloth overcoat called the *binish*.

Egypt. And it was not merely Europeans who were resented; the army rank-and-file was Egyptian, but the officer corps was overwhelmingly Ottoman (Isma'il himself being Albanian). Isma'il temporarily regained popular support by replacing the European controllers with Muslims. Britain and France demanded his resignation, and the sultan agreed. Isma'il's son Tawfiq Pasha took charge with the sultan's approval.[16]

Tawfiq managed the situation no better, and an outburst of Egyptian nationalism led by the Egyptian officer Urabi Pasha (1839–1911) swept the country. The Ottoman elite was trapped between the irresistible force of Egyptian nationalism and the immovable resolve (and navies) of their European creditors. This led to a complex and less than artful diplomatic dance between the anti-imperialist British Prime Minister William Gladstone, the French Prime Minister Léon-Michel Gambetta, and Sultan Abdulhamid II. Gladstone merely wanted to keep the British and (more importantly) the French out of Egypt, and the Ottomans in. Gambetta wanted to revive French imperial glory. Abdulhamid desperately wanted the Europeans to save his empire from imploding. After the nationalists largely had taken control, the European navies arrived off Egypt's coast in 1882. Tawfiq demanded that Ottoman troops be sent, but the sultan refused and instead proposed a British-Ottoman treaty in which the former would take over Egypt and the sultan would retain his current—and effectively meaningless—sovereign rights. Gladstone rejected the proposal out of hand.[17]

Yet events would force his hand. Urabi appeared to be close to control, and when Tawfiq tried to remove him, Urabi produced a fatwa from al-Azhar deposing Tawfiq himself. Afraid for Britain's lifeline to India, Gladstone reversed course. With an understanding that the sultan first would condemn Urabi and then send in troops, British forces landed to prevent him from blockading the canal. At the last moment the sultan drew back, but British forces already had routed Urabi. Britain now occupied Egypt, but declared that it planned to withdraw immediately upon being relieved by the Ottomans.[18]

Beginning as an attempt to restore Ottoman control, the occupation took on a life of its own. Although the prevailing opinion in London remained in favor of ending the occupation, provincial officials felt otherwise. The Consul-General from 1893 on, Sir Evelyn Baring (later Lord Cromer), persuaded successive governments of the necessity of the occupation, primarily by emphasizing the strategic importance of the Suez Canal as well as the economic benefits of preferential access to Egyptian exports.[19] Agricultural development became focused on cotton and other products needed by British industries, and no more progress was made toward industrialization than during the Ottoman era.[20]

The defeat of Urabi was not the end, but rather the beginning, of nationalism in Egypt. The primary vehicle for opposition to British rule prior to World War I was the National Party, founded by Mustafa Kamil (1874–1908), a French-educated lawyer. Kamil viewed modernization as the key to the nationalist struggle.[21] To the extent that Islam had any political role, Kamil and many other European-educated reformers viewed it as a means of strengthening the nationalist cause, not as an end in itself. Egypt's nationalist movement was still gathering strength at the beginning of World War I.

Curing the Sick or Raising the Dead? Islamic Revivalism and the Tanzimat Era

Although Islamic revivalism predated Western dominance of the Arab world, the nineteenth century gave new impetus to revivalists. While some focused their efforts on the regions in which they lived, others pushed a pan-Islamic agenda. Only a few representative examples are given here.

Revivalists in the Sufi orders continued, but by the end of the century leadership had largely passed to the *Salafiya* ("the way of the ancestors") movement. The salafs were at once both modernists and fundamentalists, attempting to discard traditional ways in favor of early Islam, and then apply original principles to the modern world.

The most prominent Arab salaf was Muhammad Abduh (1849–1905), an Egyptian scholar who became the head of the religious court system and who attempted to reform the curriculum of al-Azhar. His goal was "to liberate thought from the shackles of *taqlid* [tradition], and understand religion as it was understood by the elders of the community before dissension appeared; to return, in the acquisition of religious knowledge, to its first sources, and to weigh them in the scales of human reason . . . and to prove that . . . religion must be accounted a friend of science."[22] Although his emphasis was on internal reform, Abduh also framed salafism in nationalist terms during conflicts with the British. The pan-Islamic side of salafism was epitomized by Jamal al-Din al-Afghani (1839–1897). His name suggests he was of Afghan origin, but he traveled widely through Iran, the Arab world, and Ottoman Anatolia and Europe, propagating the idea of Muslim unity as a source of strength against European power.[23]

Abd al-Aziz al-Tha'alibi, a contemporary of Abduh, played a similar role in Tunisia. Being fundamentalist rather than conservative, he angered the *ulama* establishment by attacking traditional Islamic practices that he considered innovations, while rejecting Westernization as a means of reform. He viewed modernization as a means of strengthening Islam rather than as a means unto itself. This also led him to merge his Islamism with nationalism in opposition to French rule (1881–1956).[24]

Some Sufi revivalists retained the initiative, including Muhammad ibn Ali al-Sanusi (c. 1787–1859). A scholar of the Quran and hadith, al-Sanusi laid the foundation for modern Libya. Through his Sanusia *tariqa*, he developed a network of schools and social centers that created a loosely structured system among the various tribes of the region. He angered conservatives, pushing the fundamentalist aspects of the *Salafiya*, but he lacked Abduh's emphasis on modernization. Amir Abd al-Qadir (d. 1883) was perhaps the most significant Sufi revivalist in Algeria, although circumstances made his movement differ from others. Abd al-Qadir was the head of a Sufi order, and he used it to organize the main opposition to the French occupation (1833–1960), fighting almost two decades before being defeated in 1847. Because the French aimed to eradicate Islamic culture from Algeria, his focus was not reform but merely the preservation of Islam.[25]

Sufi revivalists in the Sudan faced a different dilemma. From 1820 to 1882 the foreign imperial power was Muslim Egypt, and its administration in the Sudan was explicitly Islamic. Nevertheless, local revivalists chose opposition, and could not be eliminated. Just before the British takeover, a Sufi teacher named Muhammad

162

Ahmad (d. 1885) declared himself the awaited Mahdi (an Islamic figure with apocalyptic overtones) and established an Islamic state. The Mahdist state was maintained by his successor until the British invaded and terminated the movement in 1899.[26]

The Ottomans were not blind to the need for reform, but their perspective differed. Whereas Arab revivalists emphasized the need to return to the Golden Age of Islam represented by the early caliphs, the Ottomans believed that they themselves were the Golden Age and had merely slipped in recent times. The corruption of the system was chronicled repeatedly over a long period by high-level advisors to the sultan.[27] Yet despite various initiatives over time, wholesale reform did not begin until the 1830s, by which time it was recognized that a return to the old ways was not a solution.

What is now called the "Tanzimat Era" (*tanzimat* is an Arabic loanword that can mean "reform," like the Russian *perestroika*[28]) was initiated by Sultan Abdulmejid (r. 1839–1861). The young sultan kept his father's foreign minister, Mustafa Reshid Pasha, in power to implement the changes. It was Reshid and his assistants who structured a wide-ranging system of reforms in every aspect of the empire—taxation, administration, finance, education, civil rights, and religious equality.[29]

In practice this meant tax farming was abolished in favor of more systematic taxation. This required administrative improvements that would specify the duties of local authorities more clearly and make them more accountable to Istanbul. An attempt at a paper currency was made but with little success. Restrictions on the slave trade were introduced. Education was viewed as essential, and Reshid pushed to introduce a new system of non-Islamic education more appropriate to the needs of a modern bureaucracy and economy. This faced intense hostility from the *ulama*, and by his death in 1858 there were only forty-three secondary schools with less than four thousand students in the entire realm. Even more controversial was the move toward religious equality. In 1856 Abdulmejid's Imperial Rescript proclaimed the equality of all Ottoman citizens regardless of religion, a gross violation of the *shari'a*. Violence against Christians increased dramatically, an official condemnation by the sultan notwithstanding. The violence especially destabilized the Arab provinces of the Levant.[30]

There was also a move to secure greater property rights, but this threatened the interests of the military class.

The Tanzimat Era was widely viewed by its European contemporaries as a period of enlightened reform. This is not surprising, as the British and French themselves were advising Reshid, but historians now take a dimmer view. Aside from the fact that the reforms fell far short of their stated goals, they carried some severe negatives. The other side of greater accountability was a stronger autocracy, as the empire moved toward a statist command-and-control model. Local independent elements, especially the urban notables and the *ulama*-controlled *waqf*s, in time might have provided for a dispersal of power and what is today called "civil society." Now they saw their power reduced in favor of Istanbul, although it was increased vis-à-vis the Arab countryside, as badly administered social restructuring impoverished the village economy.[31] The *tanzimat* were followed by a series of retrenchments and ever more urgent reform initiatives, culminating in the abolition of the caliphate itself by Kemal Ataturk (Mustafa Kemal) in 1924. They left the Arab provinces of the empire ill-prepared for the twentieth century.

The Struggle for Arabia to 1914

In examining tribal power struggles in Arabia, a cultural point must be kept in mind. Where the leader of a tribe was viewed as being the ruler of a region, the legitimacy of this authority resided in the lineage as a whole, not the individual ruler.[32] Such was the case for the Al-Sa'ud, who now made a revival. The first Saudi emirate was extinguished in 1818 and a second was formed six years later. It would last until 1891, but it never was able to maintain either internal unity or significant external expansion outside the Nadj.

In 1824 Turki ibn Adbullah (r. 1824–1834), the son of the beheaded former ruler, cobbled together a coalition, put his neck on the line, and took Riyadh. From this base he expanded his power through much of central and eastern Arabia. Although himself a strict Wahhabi, he took care not to run afoul of Ottoman authorities. Yet he faced dissension within the family, and when he was assassinated in 1834 his son Faisal (r. 1834–1838; 1843–1865) came to power with the help of Abdullah ibn Rashid, the ruler of Ha'il in the northern Najd. In 1837 Faisal refused to pay tribute to the Ottomans. Shortly thereafter, he was taken captive and held in Cairo while the Ottomans appointed a rival member of the family as ruler of the Najd. This governor was overthrown by another member of the Al-Sa'ud. In 1843 Faisal escaped from Cairo and returned to Riyadh where he regained power. He was succeeded by his son Abdullah (r. 1865–1871).[33] Abdullah's death led to a power struggle among his half-brothers, allowing the Rashidi tribe, based in northern Arabia, to encroach. One of the half-brothers, Abd al-Rahman, kept power only by accepting Rashidi dominance. He eventually attempted a revolt, but was defeated in 1891 and fled to the protection of the Al-Sabah of Kuwait.[34]

The end of the second Saudi emirate brought the possibility that the Rashidi leader, Muhammad al-Rashidi (r. 1869–1897), might become the new great power in Arabia. At its greatest extent, the Rashidi emirate stretched from parts of Syria in the north to Oman in the southeast, and included the Saudi stronghold in the Najd. Allied with the Ottomans, the Rashidis could have become the main Arabian power in the twentieth century. Yet due to a variety of factors, including internal strife and a renewed challenge from the Al-Sa'ud, they were unable to maintain their dominance.[35]

A major reason for the decline of the Rashidis was the rise of one of the twentieth century's most important figures, Abd al-Aziz ibn Abd al-Rahman Al-Sa'ud. Known as Ibn Sa'ud, he retook Riyadh in 1902 and began a final revival of the Saudi-Wahhabi emirate. The standard formula, calling for raids that would be ended only upon acceptance of Wahhabi Islam and Saudi rule, allowed Ibn Sa'ud to expand outside the Najd to much of Arabia. He reached a stalemate with the Rashidis and signed an accord with the Ottomans in 1913 recognizing Saudi rule. Because the British viewed the Ottoman-Rashidi alliance as a threat to their commercial interests in the Persian Gulf, especially Kuwait, they agreed to aid for Ibn Sa'ud in 1915 which included a £5,000 per month subsidy plus provision of modern firearms, giving him a key advantage.[36]

Beside the Rashidi domain in the north, two areas of Arabia remained beyond Saudi control. In the east, the emirates of the

Persian Gulf had all signed protection treaties with the British by around 1900. Their eventual independence would lead to the creation of the modern states of Kuwait, Bahrain, Qatar, Oman, and the United Arab Emirates. In the west, the Hijaz was still ruled by the sharifs, descendants of Muhammad and the clan of Hashim (they are thus known as the "Hashimites"). Unlike other Arabian leaders, Sharif Hussein of Mecca accepted Ottoman rule. He was responsible for the internal administration of the holy cities and relations with the surrounding tribes. The Ottomans provided a subsidy and were responsible for trade and foreign relations. Hussein was also implicitly protected by the British, who threatened to cut off Ibn Sa'ud's subsidy if he attacked the Hijaz.[37] The eve of the First World War thus found Arabia divided between these three tribal powers at the core—the Al-Sa'ud, the Rashidis, and the sharifs—with the Gulf emirates remaining independent at the periphery.

Two southern coastal regions also remained outside Saudi control. One was the territory around the port of Aden, which the British took in 1839. Even prior to this, the region's strongest ties were to the Indian Ocean trade network that included India and east Africa, rather than to the rest of the peninsula. This was true politically and religiously as well as commercially. Britain developed a network of alliances with local tribes, further tying Aden to the world of maritime trade. Yemen (which today includes Aden) also stayed independent of Ibn Sa'ud. Istanbul controlled it for much of the century, but the independent religious orders survived, and resistance increased until in 1911 the Ottomans granted independence to a movement favoring a strict application of the *shari'a*.[38]

Zionism and the Seeds of Arab Nationalism (1881–1914)

The contemporary Jewish-Palestinian conflict is not an ancient one, but essentially can be traced to events in and around the year 1881. As of that date Ottoman records show the population of Palestine to have included 400,000 Muslim Arabs, 20,000 Jews, and 42,000 Arab Christians (primarily Greek Orthodox).[39] Although

Jewish longing for a return to *Eretz Israel*—Arab Palestine—had existed continually over the centuries, the immediate impetus for the modern Zionist movement came from Russia.

Although the past two centuries had seen steady progress in western Europe for Jews in their struggle for acceptance, much of world Jewry lived in the east, where conditions were very bad, especially in Russia. Under Nicholas I (r. 1825–1855), over six hundred Jewish laws were passed. Many, such as a prohibition on Jewish education, essentially constituted an attempt at compulsory assimilation. Things changed under Alexander II (r. 1855–1881), who eased or eliminated many restrictions. His assassination in 1881 marked a clear turning point. Jews were accused of being the assassins (only one was), and a wave of violence swept Russia as rioters beat, raped, and killed Jews. Anti-Jewish legislation was reintroduced, although annihilation rather than assimilation now seemed to be the goal. Jews all over eastern Europe struggled to emigrate. Thousands began pouring into Palestine, although the vast majority went elsewhere, especially to the United States.[40] Later waves of pogroms in 1903–1905 (when an embattled Tsar attempted to refocus popular anger against the Jews) and 1917–1920 (concurrent with the Bolshevik revolution) accelerated this process.[41]

In the years between 1881 and the First World War the Zionist movement grew steadily. Theodor Herzl (1860–1904) played the most important role in the development of Zionism as an ideology. For Herzl (who lived on the same street in Vienna as Sigmund Freud), the turning point was not the Tsarist pogroms but the fraudulent persecution of an assimilated Jewish officer in the French military (the Dreyfus Affair). His 1896 book *The Jewish State (Der Judenstaat)* was the most influential Zionist publication up to that time. Although not committed to Palestine himself, Herzl came to realize that the preponderance of Zionist passion was focused on the ancient homeland. He concentrated his efforts on obtaining patronage for a Jewish homeland there, petitioning every influential sovereign in Europe.[42]

Jewish rabbis in Vienna sent representatives to Palestine to study the situation. Their cable from Palestine stated: "'The bride is beautiful, but she is married to another man.'"[43] Others began to notice what would become the "Arab Problem." One attendee at the Second Zionist Congress in 1898 brought notice of the "'established fact that the most fertile parts of our land are occupied by Arabs . . . 650,000 souls, but this figure is not verified.'" Few paid attention to this at the time.[44]

Meanwhile, Jewish settlement in Palestine increased. During the first wave ("Aliyah") of 1881–1903 around twenty-five thousand immigrants arrived. The pogroms of the early twentieth century accelerated the trend.[45] The primary method by which Jews obtained land was to purchase it from Arab landlords. This became an issue of violent contention among Arabs, as landowners uniformly denied they were selling land, when in fact they were doing so on a substantial scale. Ironically, given the widespread belief that Jews controlled much of the world's wealth, the primary obstacle to Jewish land purchases quickly became lack of money. They never had trouble finding Arabs willing to sell.[46]

Initially, this did not lead to the large-scale dispossession of Arab peasants, as the new Jewish owners still needed workers. Things began to change for two reasons. One, as Jewish settlement increased, settlements made a concerted effort to use Jewish labor whenever possible. This was partly because of Arab violence against the settlements, but since the violence existed partially because Arabs sometimes were deprived of their jobs or homes, replacing Arab workers with Jews accelerated the cycle. Two, after the turn of the century the "Second Aliyah" took place, and the new migrants were largely socialist visionaries intent on creating collectivist communities (the kibbutzim). Since socialists do their own work, Arab laborers lost their employment, and often their homes.[47]

Arab nationalism, previously an intellectual fashion limited to urban notables, received a huge boost from Zionism and began to become a mass movement. In 1905 Najib Azouri, a former Ottoman civil servant, published a book titled *Le Reveil de la Nation Arabe* (*The Reawakening of the Arab Nation*). He advocated independence from Istanbul and resistance to the Jews. Previously, opposition had been limited to sporadic attacks on settlements. Although published in France, the book resonated strongly in Palestine, and in the six years leading up to 1914 there was a growing awareness of a common threat. Petitions were sent to Istanbul, pleading for stricter measures to restrain Jewish immigration. The Ottomans indeed attempted to clamp down, but immigration and land sales increased despite legal prohibitions. Ruhi Bey al-Khalidi, a representative from Jerusalem in Istanbul, emphasized that the problem was not simply immigration but colonization. He warned that the Jews "'will be able to buy many tracts of land, and displace the Arab farmers from their land, and their fathers' heritage.'"[48]

Palestinian Arabs, who if nationalistic at all had identified with Greater Syria (which included modern Lebanon, Jordan, and Palestine), began to organize as Palestinians. In 1911 Palestinian notables petitioned Istanbul for help, and by the eve of the First World War they had become an organized bloc.[49] Slowly they began to realize that their lack of national consciousness vis-à-vis the Zionists was putting them at a disadvantage. The problem was not episodic conflicts caused by displaced peasants, but a fundamental clash in the interests of the two peoples. Zionists had recognized this much earlier. In 1882 one Russian Zionist wrote: "'The ultimate goal . . . is, in time, to take over the land of Israel and to restore to the Jews the political independence they have been deprived of for these two thousand years . . . '"[50] A better sense of identity and organization would work in their favor when the real conflict came.

The Great War and the Creation of the Modern Arab State System (1914–1922)

The entrance of the Ottoman Empire into the First World War and the negotiations that followed would eventually give the Arab world the shape that it has today. As this was not at all inevitable, it is important to see why it happened.

Having taken over the Ottoman Empire in 1908, a party called the Young Turks became controlled by a nationalist faction called the Committee for Union and Progress (CUP), which brought the empire neither. In 1912 Bulgaria declared itself independent, and Bosnia-Herzegovina was annexed by Austria-Hungary. In 1911–1912 the Ottomans lost Libya, the only remaining North African province over which the empire had even formal control. In 1912–1913 an alliance comprising Bulgaria, Greece, Serbia, and Montenegro attacked and handed the Ottomans a humiliating defeat. Only the

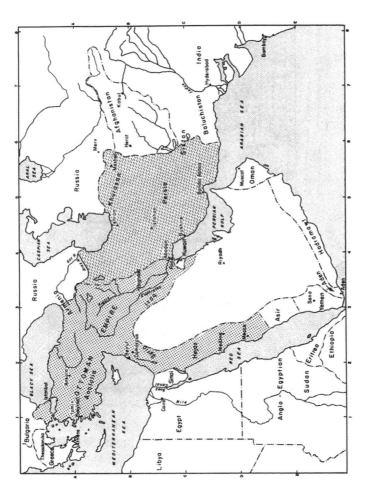

Egypt and southwest Asia, circa 1914.
Courtesy of the University of Washington Press. (Originally appeared in *A Near East Studies Handbook* by Jere Bacharach, 1977.)

great powers kept the Balkan alliance from taking Istanbul. The CUP itself was ousted in 1912 but returned to power in January 1913. Later in 1913, during the Second Balkan War, the Ottomans were able to reclaim a small amount of territory in Greece. Although few Ottoman subjects wanted a new war, the *coup d'etat* returning the CUP to power was driven entirely by three individuals bent on expansion—Talaat Bey, Djemal Pasha, and especially Enver Pasha, the new Defense Minister. The losses of the previous five years only fed Enver's imperial ambition and propelled Istanbul into the war.[51]

Internally, the CUP kept a tight grip. In Syria-Palestine there was a genuine attempt to suppress all independent elements. This meant repression of not only Zionist activities but also the extermination of the burgeoning Arab nationalists as well. Arab notables also found themselves under tight control.[52]

The triumvirate first signed a secret treaty of alliance with Germany, aiming to take advantage of the approaching war to take back territory. When First Lord of Admiralty Winston Churchill seized two battleships that Britain had built for Istanbul, fearing correctly that the Ottomans were likely to side with Germany, the CUP had its *casus belli*. The Arab world soon became a battleground for the First World War.[53]

As part of their agreement with Germany, the Ottomans would attack Russia in the Black Sea area and Britain in Egypt, cutting their "lifeline" to India.[54] For their part, the British reversed their long-standing policy of upholding the Ottoman Empire, thus ensuring that it, and its control over the Arab world, would come to an end.[55]

Lord Horatio Herbert Kitchener, the new Defense Minister, would mold British strategy in the Arab theater. Kitchener was the greatest British general since Wellington; one of Kitchener's highlights was his defeat of the Mahdist troops in the Sudan. He viewed the Middle East as a secondary front and was determined to use Arab troops to defeat the Ottomans to avoid committing British troops. Furthermore, British officials feared that the Ottomans might use the caliphate to undermine the British Empire in India and Egypt. From these twin concerns was born a plan to have Sharif Hussein of Mecca lead an Arab revolt. Hussein then would become the spiritual head of a new caliphate that would be internally independent but essentially an appendage of the British Empire.

Kitchener's plan was flawed from the beginning due to a fundamental lack of understanding of the Muslim world on the part of himself and his subordinates. Doctrinally, they thought they could make Hussein the "Pope" of the Muslims, with only nominal temporal power. They did not realize that such a separation between religion and state did not exist in Islam. Furthermore, on a tactical level they were wrong to think that a caliphal call to *jihad* still mattered. The sultan in fact already had declared a *jihad*, and it produced almost no response in the Arab world or anywhere else (the German Foreign Ministry had expected a massive anti-British revolt).[56] Finally, they failed to understand the fragmented nature of the region. Arabia itself was then in a three-way civil war between Hussein, the Al-Sa'ud, and the Rashidis.[57]

This is not to say that an Arab revolt could not have succeeded. The major Ottoman offensive in the war, an ineptly led drive against Russia in the Caucasus, resulted in an 86 percent fatality rate (out of one hundred thousand troops).[58] With a premodern transportation system, the Ottomans would not have been able to quickly mobilize their remaining forces anyway. Arabs constituted a sufficiently large percentage of the security forces in the provinces that their defection likely would have been decisive.

A series of negotiations thus took place that would redraw the map of the Arab world. In early 1915 what has become known as the "McMahon-Hussein Correspondence" (after Sir Henry McMahon, the High Commissioner in Egypt) continued a negotiation Kitchener had begun. Hussein repeatedly demanded an independent state including all of the Arab world, and British support for his assumption of the caliphate. McMahon essentially responded that, yes, Britain would support him on both points, but of course the final frontiers would have to be worked out with the French, and naturally the new state would need British protection, so a suitable relationship between the caliphate and the empire would have to be determined.

This was facilitated in part by British liaison T.E. Lawrence ("of Arabia"), whose fertile imagination provided much of the content for his famous *Seven Pillars of Wisdom*. Lawrence constantly exaggerated Hussein's importance—and thus his own—to his superiors, while telling Arabs whatever they needed to hear at any given time to keep them on board. Muhammad Sharif al-Faruqi, an

172

"Arab Lawrence of Arabia" one might say, played a similar role in the Levant. A deserter from the Ottoman army who knew little English, in late 1915 al-Faruqi became the liaison between Britain and what he described to them as a mass of secret Arab nationalist societies just waiting for Hussein to initiate the revolt. He, like Hussein, emphasized that the Arabs would accept only real independence. It is not known if al-Faruqi deliberately deceived his Arab interlocutors as to what was on offer, or whether they—or he—simply misunderstood, but in any case after the war there was no common understanding about what the agreement had been. This mess was further complicated by the fact that different departments of the empire were supporting different sides in Arabia. While the British Arab Bureau in Cairo was backing Hussein, the Foreign Office in London aided the Rashidi clan, while the Raj in India was funding Ibn Sa'ud.[59]

Eventually the Ottomans forced the issue, as Hussein discovered that Istanbul was planning to depose him. Although McMahon was unwilling to back Hussein on his terms, he offered money and weapons. Having received 50,000 gold pounds, the "Great Arab Revolt" was duly declared in June 1916, but there was no great uprising, or even a mild one, from the Arab masses. Instead, the mass of Arab society, which had supported the Ottomans since the beginning of the war, stayed loyal.[60] The revolt was led by Hussein's sons Abdullah and Faisal, and it was sustained as long as Lawrence had gold coins. It took only a few weeks for London to realize that Hussein had no popular support, and that other Arab leaders would not feel bound by his commitments. This meant that Britain was not bound by its promises, such as they were.

Ultimately, the British had to take the Arab provinces themselves. The invasion of Iraq began in 1915, backed by the Raj, but did not take Baghdad until March 1917. Later that year Sir Edmund Allenby invaded Palestine from Egypt and entered Jerusalem in December. Faisal's Arab troops played a marginal role in the fighting, but through 1917–1918 British and French forces did the bulk of the work. Faisal finally entered Damascus, the capital of his new Arab state, in October 1918, although some Australian cavalry had ruined the climax of his triumph by accidentally "taking" the city four days earlier.[61] Although successful, the use of European troops had defeated the point of recruiting the Arabs in the

173

first place. Financially, Lawrence's sideshow had cost an estimated ten million pounds, a huge sum at the time.[62]

Throughout his correspondence with the Arabs, McMahon had to be careful because Britain simultaneously was negotiating with France over the same territories. Under what became known as the Sykes-Picot Agreement (1917), the French, who wanted all of Ottoman Syria, including Palestine, would have direct control over Lebanon and a protectorate over Syria, with shared responsibility for Palestine. Britain would have protectorates in Egypt, Transjordan, and Iraq, and would maintain its defensive treaties with the various factions of Arabia. Once Allenby took Jerusalem, the British made it clear that they would have sole rule in Palestine, but in broad detail the agreement stood.

During the war the Zionists finally began to win Great Power support for their cause. The ascension of the pro-Zionist David Lloyd George as Prime Minister in 1916 was vital. Lloyd George recalled that as a child he knew the names of more cities in ancient Israel than in Europe, and is said to have still referred to the area by its Biblical name of "Canaan." Much of British support for Zionism was driven by the belief that Jews secretly controlled vast amounts of the world's capital. They also were thought to have been behind the Russian Revolution in 1917 and to have taken control of the Ottoman Empire through the CUP (many Russian Jews were involved in socialist movements, but few joined the Bolsheviks; there were no Jews running the CUP). President Woodrow Wilson's support certainly helped. In fact, British and American Jews overwhelmingly opposed or were indifferent to Zionism. Edwin Montagu, secretary of state for India and the highest ranking Jew in the British government, led the opposition to Zionism, fearing that it would threaten the progress of assimilated Jews.[63]

Nevertheless, in November 1917, Foreign Secretary Lord Balfour sent an open letter to Lord Rothschild in which he declared British support for "the establishment in Palestine of a national home for the Jewish people . . . it being clearly understood that nothing shall be done which may prejudice the civil and religious rights of existing non-Jewish communities in Palestine. . . . "[64] This became known as the Balfour Declaration.

After the war, at the Paris Peace Accords, Britain and France set about redrawing the map of the Arab world. Perhaps the greatest irony of all, given later events, was that the British considered themselves to be patrons of both Jewish and Arab aspirations. As one diplomat put it, "'Arab nationalism and Zionism became two of the most successful of our war causes.'"[65] Churchill, who became Colonial Secretary in 1921, emphasized that Britain supported both sides, and that there was "'room for all'" in Palestine.[66]

While diplomats talked, anti-European revolts broke out in Egypt, Iraq, Palestine, and Syria.[67] Hussein's sons Faisal and Abdullah were placed in charge in Syria and Transjordan respectively, although Faisal eventually would be pushed out and sent to Iraq. Both Faisal and Abdullah were foreigners in the lands they were to rule, but the British thought nothing of it; after all, foreigners had ruled these lands for centuries. Meanwhile, Jewish immigration to Palestine increased, as did Arab hostility. Faisal originally had excluded Palestine from Arab demands at Paris, but he renounced the agreement upon realizing the intensity of local Arab opinion. A new world was being born, and it was not shaping up well. In the words of one British officer: "After 'the war to end war' they seem to have been pretty successful in Paris at making a 'Peace to end Peace.'"[68]

Notes

1. Alan Palmer, *Decline and Fall of the Ottoman Empire*, 115. He originally made the remark regarding the Austrian Empire, and then later more famously applied it to the Ottomans. See also Alan Palmer, *Metternich: Councillor of Europe* (London: Phoenix Press, 1972) 290–1.
2. *Nous sommes les vrais musulmanes* is the famous phrase.
3. Goldschmidt, *Concise History of the Middle East*, 151–2.
4. Goldschmidt, *Concise History of the Middle East*, 151–2; Efraim Karsh and Inari Karsh, *Empires of the Sand: The Struggle for Mastery in the Middle East 1789–1923* (Cambridge, Massachusetts: Harvard University Press, 1999) 10–1. For a detailed and fascinating description of a different front in the Anglo-Russian rivalry, see Karl E. Meyer and Shareen Blair Brysac, *Tournament of Shadows: The Great Game and the Race for Empire in Central Asia* (Washington, D.C.: Counterpoint, 1999).
5. Karsh and Karsh, *Empires of the Sand*, 28.
6. Ibid., 29.
7. Ibid.
8. Ibid., 29–31.
9. Ibid., 32.

10. Ibid., 35–40.
11. Ibid.
12. Ibid., 42–4.
13. Ibid., 44–5; Goldschmidt, *Concise History of the Middle East*, 165.
14. Karsh and Karsh, *Empires of the Sand*, 44–5.
15. Ibid., 48.
16. Ibid., 50–1.
17. Ibid., 54–63.
18. Ibid.
19. Afaf Lutfi Al-Sayyid-Marsot, "The British Occupation of Egypt from 1882," in *The Oxford History of the British Empire: The Nineteenth Century*, Andrew Porter, ed. (New York: Oxford University Press, 1999) 654.
20. Ibid., 658–61.
21. Voll, *Islam*, 96.
22. Ibid., 95.
23. Ibid., 94–106.
24. Ibid., 97–9.
25. Ibid., 119–20.
26. Ibid., 140.
27. Lewis, *Islam in History*, 209–22.
28. Palmer, *Decline and Fall*, 110.
29. Goldschmidt, *Concise History of the Middle East*, 158–9.
30. Benny Morris, *Righteous Victims: A History of the Zionist-Arab Conflict, 1881–2001* (New York: Vintage Books, 2001) 12–3. See also Palmer, *Decline and Fall*, 157.
31. Lewis, *What Went Wrong*, 53–4; Lewis, *Islam in History*, 67–86.
32. Al-Rasheed, *History of Saudi Arabia*, 34.
33. Ibid., 23–4.
34. Ibid., 24–6.
35. Ibid., 26–8.
36. Ibid., 29–44.
37. Ibid.
38. Voll, *Islam*, 134–5.
39. Morris, *Righteous Victims*, 4.
40. Morris, *Righteous Victims*, 17, 18; Avi Shlaim, *The Iron Wall: Israel and the Arab World* (New York: W.W. Norton & Company, 2000) 4.
41. Morris, *Righteous Victims*, 25.
42. David J. Goldberg, *To the Promised Land: A History of Zionist Thought* (London: Penguin Books, 1996) 30–72.
43. Shlaim, *Iron Wall*, 3.
44. Goldberg, *To the Promised Land*, 60.
45. Morris, *Righteous Victims*, 19–25.
46. David Fromkin, *A Peace to End All Peace: The Fall of the Ottoman Empire and the Creation of the Modern Middle East* (New York: Henry Holt and Company, 1989) 522.
47. Ibid.
48. Ibid., 63.
49. Ibid., 64.
50. Ibid., 49.
51. Karsh and Karsh, *Empires of the Sand*, 94–108.
52. Ibid., 101.

53. Fromkin, *A Peace to End All Peace*, 54–6. It also took a few gold shipments from Germany and an Ottoman provocation against Russia before war was formally declared, but this event created the momentum that Enver needed.
54. Karsh and Karsh, *Empires of the Sand*, 116.
55. Fromkin, *A Peace to End All Peace*, 75.
56. Ibid., 109.
57. Ibid., 104.
58. Ibid., 121.
59. Ibid., 107–8.
60. Ibid., 219–20.
61. Ibid., 337–40. The Australians were merely using it as a shortcut to chase down some Ottoman soldiers, but Faisal felt that it ruined his triumphal entry all the same.
62. Ibid., 311.
63. Ibid., 284–301.
64. Ibid., 297.
65. Morris, *Righteous Victims*, 81.
66. Ibid., 100.
67. Fromkin, *A Peace to End All Peace*, 415–64.
68. Ibid. Taken from the introductory quote by Archibald Wavell (later Field Marshal Earl Wavell).

A skyline picture of Cairo.

Caroline Williams, photographer. CMES.

CHAPTER X

The Hope of Revival: Arab Nationalism, Secularism, and Socialism

(c. 1920–1950)

The Mandate System

U.S. President Woodrow Wilson's grand scheme, the League of Nations (which the U.S. Senate voted not to join), established what became known as the Mandates, a system under which a European Mandatory Power would be obligated to guide the Mandate province toward independent self-rule. In order to prevent exploitation, the European power would have the duty to report to the League. An outgrowth of Wilson's notion of self-determination, the system was seen as a compromise between continued imperial rule and immediate independence. This concept, along with the exposure to Western political concepts that came with colonialism, ensured that the European concept of nationalism would become firmly implanted in the Arab world. (Except where clearly centered on a particular state, the terms nationalism, Arabism and pan-Arabism are interchangeable).[1]

Nationalists attempted to form an organized opposition to the Mandates but hardly got off the ground. In June 1919 a Syrian Arab Congress was formed under Faisal's auspices. It demanded full independence for the Arab lands, including Palestine. Their demands were rejected, and the French forced Faisal out of power the next month.[2]

France obtained the Mandate for Syria-Lebanon in 1922. Alongside the region's history as the homeland of Arab nationalism was an extreme degree of social fragmentation. The main subgroups were the Sunnis, the Shi'a, Maronite Christians, and two heretical Muslim sects, the Druze and the Alawis. Sunnis formed the largest group, while the Maronites predominated along the coast. The Maronite Church, although institutionally separate, gave allegiance to Roman Catholicism. This fact, along with their loathing of Muslim domination, made the Maronites favor French control.

The French took advantage of this, making Lebanon into a separate country, but in doing so they stretched its boundaries to include the southern port cities and some of the other surrounding areas, making the population balance fairly even. The French census showed a 51/49 ratio of Christians to Muslims, and the constitution was crafted to maintain Maronite control. However, the census likely over-counted urban areas, which are known to be more Christian. In any case, because Muslim population growth rates were higher, Muslims were a majority before long.

French authorities placed minorities, especially the Alawis, in key military and administrative positions, giving them an incentive to support French rule. The French further attempted to gain support by funding social services, hospitals, and schools, including, *naturellement*, the teaching of French. Constitutions and elections were instituted in Lebanon in 1926 and Syria in 1930, in both cases rigged to ensure victory for friendly candidates. These measures did little to stem opposition, as protests swept Syria in 1925–1927. Various resistance groups coalesced into the National Bloc, forming a political opposition. Learning French meant reading not only about subjects useful for administration, but about democracy as well. Throughout the 1930s numerous trade unions and social clubs sprang up, and demands for more public services were made.[3] Empire was becoming more expensive.

Having been kicked out of Damascus by the French, Faisal was able to persuade the British to give him Iraq after the Cairo Conference of 1921. He brought with him some Iraqi supporters from the anti-Ottoman revolt, his most important ally being Satia' al-Husri, a Syrian considered to be one of the fathers of pan-Arabism. Al-Husri took over the educational system, helping to ensure Iraq's move toward nationalism.

Faisal was placed in an extremely difficult position from the start. He depended on the British, and an Anglo-Iraqi Treaty in 1922 (updated in 1930) preserved Britain's role in the country while preparing it for independence. Independence was duly achieved in 1932, but the stability of the country deteriorated. The next year the army, under General Bakr Sidqi, began massacring Iraq's Assyrian Christians despite Faisal's opposition. Faisal soon died, and was succeeded by his son Ghazi, who favored the pogroms.

The 1930s and 1940s also saw the rise of more radical nationalist movements than had previously been present in Iraq. In 1936 Sidqi overthrew the government and advocated social reform under an Arab national socialist platform. Six more coups took place in the next five years, when a pan-Arabist government took over and aligned itself with the Axis. Britain retook the country within a month and restored Hashimite rule. Although relatively pro-British until another coup in 1958, Iraq had achieved independence. It was in the backdrop of serial instability that the Ba'athist form of Arab nationalism took root, and it came to dominate Iraq until 2003, and Syria to the present.

The Struggle for Palestine (1920–1947)

While the First World War provided a breakthrough for the Zionists, it was a catastrophe for Palestinian Arabs. The local economy was destroyed, with severe malnutrition being widespread. British officials were shocked to find a crisis of mass starvation on their hands after taking the area in 1916.[4] Moreover, the Ottoman governor of Syria-Palestine, Jamal Pasha, spared no means in rooting out Arab nationalists. Arbitrary arrest, torture, and exile became common. Ottoman conscription may have been more damaging, as many able-bodied males were sent off to war. Any Arab club favoring a greater Arab role in governance was persecuted. Aside from a small number of families within the urban elite, Arab society was decimated.[5] The Jews also suffered, as Jamal considered Zionists subversives as well. However, they did better, as many were foreign nationals or otherwise exempt from military service, and their communities were more self-sufficient and more able to bribe their way out of persecution.[6]

The British, led by Allenby, formed the Occupied Enemy Territory Administration (OETA) in April 1818. It lasted for two years, during which time it severely restricted Jewish immigration. It was working against the Zionist Commission, which was charged by London with the job of fulfilling the Balfour Declaration. The Zionist Commission was replaced in 1921 by the Palestine Zionist Executive (PZE), which was to be the official Zionist organization pursuant to the League of Nations Mandate. Throughout the Mandate, local British officials, fully aware of the depth of Arab hostility, would remain hostile to Zionism, regardless of policy preferences in London.[7]

Arab protests became louder after the war. The U.S.–sponsored King-Crane Commission came to the region in 1919 to survey local opinion and make recommendations. As one Arab told the commission, "[i]t is impossible for us to make an understanding with them [the Jews] or even live with them . . . If the League of Nations will not listen to the appeal of the Arabs this country will become a river of blood."[8] Zionist leaders came to think so as well, although they would not state so openly. Throughout the 1920s their official line was that Jews and Arabs could live together, and that Arabs actually would benefit economically from Jewish investment. Prior to the war, some sincerely believed this, but realism set in afterward. David Ben-Gurion saw this early, privately declaring in 1919: "No solution! There is a gulf, and nothing can bridge it . . . We, as a nation, want this country to be ours; the Arabs, as a nation, want this country to be theirs."[9] The Commission recommended that Palestine be incorporated into Syria as a united Mandate, effectively rejecting the Balfour Declaration. It was ignored.

In 1919 the crushing of the Syrian Arab Congress in Damascus was followed by the defeat of a low-level rebellion against the French in the area around Galilee in northern Palestine and southern Lebanon. The attacks spread southward and took on a more anti-Jewish character, culminating in a siege that forced the withdrawal of two settlements.[10] This was the most organized attack against the Jews yet seen. The following March saw a far greater escalation of the conflict: during Passover a Muslim mob ran through Jerusalem, attacking Jews, while Palestinian police on hand either did nothing or joined in. Order eventually was restored by British security and Jewish militia. This incident and its fallout saw the birth of the Haganah—an organized Jewish defense force.

A 1922 Churchill White Paper reinterpreted the Balfour Declaration, limiting it in three ways: it endorsed the creation of a legislature based on proportional representation, meaning that Arabs would have a majority; it prohibited Jewish settlement in territory east of the Jordan river (modern Jordan); and it limited further Jewish immigration to the land's absorptive capacity.[11] While the majority of Jewish leaders reluctantly voted to accept the White Paper (some rejected any compromise), Arab leaders at the time were unwilling to consider any negotiation with Zionism at all. Most importantly, they demanded a complete halt to Jewish immigration, not merely a limiting of it.

A relative peace for most of the 1920s was broken by a series of riots in 1929 in which mobs attacked Jewish communities. The Shaw Commission, charged with investigating the violence, placed the blame squarely on the Arabs, saying the riots arose from "their political and national aspirations and fear for their economic future."[12] Jewish immigration had continued above the limits placed by British officials, and it was clear that the Yishuv, as the Jewish sub-state entity was known, was growing stronger.

Britain's political response, however, was pro-Arab. As one official put it, "All British officials tend to be pro-Arab . . . The helplessness of the *fellah* [peasant] appeals to the British official."[13] The government issued the Passfield White Paper, blocking any further Jewish immigration and promising a legislative council based upon proportional representation. This effectively repudiated the Balfour Declaration. However, the Yishuv threatened to sue Britain at the Hague for violating the terms of the Mandate by restricting immigration, causing Prime Minister Ramsay MacDonald to back down and reiterate support for the Declaration.

The upshot was that both sides concluded that Britain was against them, and both escalated the conflict. The British had provided only partial and inadequate protection from the rioters, and although some Arab policemen had protected Jews, virtually all Jewish leaders now viewed peaceful coexistence as a fantasy. They began in earnest to develop the Haganah into a national army. Some Jewish officers split with the Haganah and formed the Irgun, a militia favoring a more offensive military strategy.[14]

Arabs likewise saw a more urgent situation arising. Land sales and tenant evictions continued apace, reflected in a land price increase of almost 450 percent from 1929 to 1935. There were also other trends unrelated to Zionism, including famine and the worldwide economic depression, which increased Arab distress, but all ire was focused on the Jews. The influence of German National Socialism on Palestinian politics did not help. The dominant Palestinian faction formed the Palestinian Arab Party in 1935, led by the long-dominant Husseini family. Its leader, Amin al-Husseini, wrote the German consul that "'the Muslims inside and outside Palestine welcome the new regime in Germany, and hope for the extension of the fascist, anti-democratic governmental system to other countries.'"[15] The opposition, led by the Nashashibi family, formed the National Defense Party (NDP) in 1934 and was publicly conciliatory. It was even more accommodating in private, making clear its willingness to accept a Jewish state. The upsurge in nationalism also was fed, logically despite the apparent irony, by the success of the colonial administration. British efforts at expanding education were flourishing, and the huge increase in literacy meant an increased national consciousness. Even more explosively, those who learned English could read about the concept of popular sovereignty from British writers. This phenomenon existed across the Arab world, and in Palestine it resulted in the Istiqlal (Independence) Party, based on the concepts of pan-Arabism, independence, opposition to Zionism, and unity with Syria.[16]

Militias engaging in clandestine violence, or *jihadiya* societies, also formed. The most important was led by the Syrian-born Shaikh Izz al-Din al-Qassem (1882–1935). Al-Qassem was sentenced to death *in absentia* by the French, fled to Palestine, and formed a peasant fighting society. Most notable during this time is the fact that the Palestinians, whether moderate or otherwise, took virtually no practical steps toward building the institutions necessary for founding and maintaining a state. By contrast, the Jews were busy building the Yishuv into a state-in-waiting.

Tensions exploded in 1936, beginning a three-year conflict Arabs referred to from the first as the "Great Arab Rebellion." It began with isolated attacks by Palestinian youth, but was joined by the elite in April with a united front called the Arab Higher Committee (AHC). The AHC, headed by al-Husseini, declared that first it would call a general strike to force Britain to turn against Zionism, and if it failed to do so, Arabs would begin armed resistance. The

British responded by offering to restrict immigration further, but the AHC wanted a complete ban, opting for continuance of the strike and armed attacks both in the cities and the countryside. In September the British declared martial law and switched from appeasement to repression, driving the rebels from the cities. Arab disunity was a source of weakness for the rebels. Because the British had both lowered taxes and improved public services, they were not universally hated. By contrast, Jewish leaders decided it was best to simply sit back and defend themselves, allowing Britain to crush the insurgency while cooperating with the British against Jewish militants. The first stage of the rebellion was a clear defeat for the rebels.

The second stage of the rebellion was set off after the Peel Commission report was released in July 1937. The Commission immediately cut immigration from 4,500 to 1,800 per annum, and proposed a partition that would give Jews a state of less than a fifth of Palestine. Arabs would receive most of the rest, with a small portion, including Jerusalem, remaining in British hands. Zionists reluctantly voted to accept the Peel plan.

Apparently operating on the premise that the only acceptable compromise was one that achieved 100 percent of their goals, Arab leaders rejected the Peel plan forcefully, and the rebellion continued. Now the fighting was mostly rural, and the toll on Palestinian society was severe, as the strike was strangling the economy. An upswing in Jewish terrorism led by the Irgun increased Arab casualties, which previously had been caused primarily by British forces. Because the opposition Nashashibis began negotiating with the British, the Husseini faction began attacking them. For their part, the Arab rebels, always short of funds, began using "gun barrel taxation" in order to raise money. Arab villages thus faced not only starvation, but assaults from Jewish terrorists, British reprisals, and the rebels themselves.

Yet the rebellion continued and by October 1938 the British realized their partial restraint was making them look weak internationally. They simply could not afford another "Munich" (coming shortly after their total humiliation at the real one in Germany). They significantly increased the severity of their counterinsurgency measures, while Arab villagers began cooperating with British intelligence and forming militias to protect themselves—

185

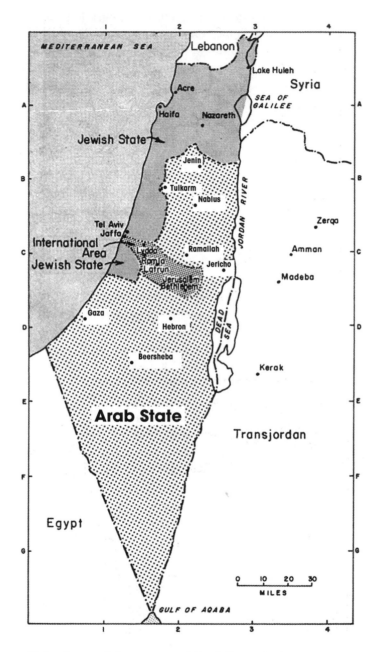

Palestine and the proposed Peel Commission partition
plan, 1937.

Courtesy of the University of Washington Press. (Originally appeared
in *A Near East Studies Handbook* by Jere Bacharach, 1977.)

from the rebels. Rebel bands that escaped over the Jordan River were cut down by the Jordanian Arab Legion. Meanwhile, the Yishuv escaped unscathed and used the Arab strike to increase its own economic self-sufficiency.

For all the harm that the "Great Arab Rebellion" did to Palestinians, it was entirely unnecessary. The Jews were correct in believing that the British were now pro-Arab. They had been moving in that direction since 1922, when the Churchill White Paper had restricted immigration. Their incessant fear was that Muslims across the empire would revolt against them. The Peel Report was fairly evenhanded, yet London's pro-Arab tilt caused it to distance itself immediately. Another White Paper was issued in 1939, after the rebellion had been crushed, completely gutting the Balfour Declaration.

The Yishuv also made better use of the World War II period, despite the catastrophe that befell world Jewry. Despite the 1939 White Paper, Jewish leaders overwhelmingly supported the Allies[17] and were able to persuade Britain to form and arm Jewish regiments. Despite the fact that Arab North Africa was the setting for some of the greatest tank battles of all time, Arabs themselves played a minimal role. Most sympathized with the Axis because they believed Britain to be still pro-Zionist. This was ironic, since not only did the Nazis consider the Arabs themselves to be racially inferior, but they had encouraged Jewish immigration to Palestine when Britain was restricting it. Very few were active on the Axis side, but Palestinian leader Amin al-Husseini became a Nazi functionary and played a bit part in the Holocaust by lobbying east European governments to deport Jews to camps in Poland.[18]

Once the war ended and the world awakened to the horror of the Holocaust, international sympathy for Zionism increased dramatically. The Yishuv had prepared itself well for war, and Jews now believed that they had to fight for their very existence. The Palestinians, meanwhile, had done little to prepare for statehood, and they soon would pay the price for the sins of the West.

The Triumph of Ibn Sa'ud

The aftermath of World War I left Ibn Sa'ud in an excellent position. His main rivals, the Rashidis, lost their patron with the collapse of the Ottomans, and with it, the British lost their rationale for cultivating them. Ibn Sa'ud maintained his British subsidy until 1924, and although Hussein had been promised a state, his uncompromising demands for complete independence irritated British officials, and they did nothing to stop Ibn Sa'ud from encroaching on him. Ibn Sa'ud declared himself "sultan" of all the Najd and its dependencies in 1921, and was able to take Mecca in 1924.[19]

At this time, the Al-Sa'ud were in the process of reshaping Arabian ideals of governance, paving the way for the modern Saudi state. There were three concepts of governance then in play: the traditional view based on tribal autonomy; that of the *mutawwa'a* (ideological shock troops), who viewed the Al-Sa'ud as mere instruments for the expansion of the Muslim *umma*, and Ibn Sa'ud's view, based on the dominance of his own lineage over Arabia.[20] Ultimately the Wahhabi-influenced *ulama*, a crucial element, supported Ibn Sa'ud.[21]

Ibn Sa'ud's rule, once established, met with criticism. The complaints included his relations with infidel Britain, his concept of kingship, the Islamic legitimacy of some of his taxes, his personal conduct, his reluctance to extend the *jihad* outside the peninsula, and his laxity in purifying Islam domestically.[22] On the latter point, his refusal to force the conversion of the Shi'a, or to end Wahhabi-prohibited practices (like music and singing) by pilgrims to Mecca from outside the peninsula, were criticized. The sore point with his conduct was his insatiable desire for women, or at least new wives. Ibn Sa'ud followed the rule limiting him to four wives at a time, but this required rapid repudiation to allow for turnover. He eventually had an estimated two hundred and fifty or so wives, plus an indefinite number of concubines. This was not to secure alliances, given the turnover rate, and the few hundred women combined produced "only" around one hundred or so children, and so was not an efficient method if progeny was the goal. Tribal leaders, many polygamous themselves, considered Ibn Sa'ud's behavior unseemly.[23] More vexatious was his alliance with the British combined with the limit on *jihad* against neighboring territories, such as Iraq or Kuwait. Since each was protected by a defensive treaty with Britain, the two problems were different sides of the same coin.

At least as early as 1907–1908 Ibn Sa'ud had realized that the traditional tribal system was an impediment to his goals, given that it was based upon the politically autonomous tribe as the basic unit of society. Fighting tribal rebellions convinced him to create a permanent military force called the *Ikhwan* (Brotherhood). Ibn Sa'ud used the *Ikhwan*, indoctrinated by the *mutawwa'a*, to expand his power. However, the *Ikhwan* became impatient with Ibn Sa'ud's willingness to subordinate the struggle for the expansion of a purified *umma* to political realities. The conflict intensified in the 1920s and the British intervened when it appeared that the *Ikhwan* were infecting territories such as Kuwait with their militant ideology. In 1932 Ibn Sa'ud capped his defeat of the old system when he declared the founding of the Kingdom of Saudi Arabia.[24]

A key event in Saudi history was the 1933 signing of a concession with Standard Oil of California to explore for oil and the subsequent discovery of that resource in great quantities. Production increased quickly and in 1943 President Franklin Roosevelt designated Saudi Arabia as a country "vital to the defense" of the United States. This was the beginning of the end to Britain's role as the primary Western power in the Arab world.[25]

Thus began the transformation of Arabia by a sudden and overwhelming inflow of wealth. Members of the elite began to live ostentatiously, offending Arabian society. The new wealth also brought new technologies, and the radio ushered in the age of information globalization. For the first time, Bedouin became interested in the everyday politics of other areas, in particular Palestine and Egypt. Ibn Sa'ud, himself indifferent to the situation, soon was forced to begin pressuring the United States on the state of affairs in Palestine. Thus, all of the elements of the modern Saudi conundrum—the contradictions of austere religiosity with elite corruption, resentment of a foreign alliance, autocratic governance, and Westernizing influences—were present by the 1950s.

Islamic Revivalism and the Golden Age of Arab Nationalism

Two broad movements, each with a variety of undercurrents, dominated the Arab world in the twentieth century: Islamic revivalism and secular nationalism. In theory, the two exist in complete mutual exclusivity—in Islam the basic unit is the Islamic nation, or *umma*, which unites believers without regard to language or ethnic background, while nationalism binds together people of a particular background, regardless of their religious identity. This theoretical contradiction often has been borne out in practice as well, as Islamists and nationalists have fought over control of Arab states. Yet the two movements must be understood together, for their paths of development were like two half-brothers from the same household; having been made from only some of the same genetic material, they grew up together and then fought over the family patrimony. Furthermore, whatever contradictions intellectuals might see between the two, the masses often have seen none, and Arab Muslims in particular often view them as one and the same.

Islamic revivalists prior to the twentieth century largely thrived on domestic concerns—the revival of Islamic belief and practice. As Western penetration of the Arab world continued, however, Islamists were compelled to respond to the challenge of European influence. Many followers of Muhammad Abduh who emphasized the need for internal reform eventually chose nationality rather than Islam as the primary binding force for renewal. One was Muhammad Kurd Ali (1876–1952), who founded the Arab Academy in Damascus. He used Arabic literature to remind Arabs of their glorious past, and thus their potential for the future. Amir Shakib Arslan (1869–1946), an Islamist, reconciled Arabism with Islam by arguing that although nationalism was otherwise incompatible with religion, Arabs were so central to the *umma* that their revitalization was essential to the revival of Islam.[26]

Nationalism was very much a Western import to the Arab world, but this is not to say that the Arabs previously had lacked a sense of community. It is not difficult to find examples of Arab identification with Arab culture dating from before the nineteenth century. One bilingual Arab writer expressed a common sentiment in stating that he would rather be abused in Arabic than praised in Persian. However, in the early twentieth century, group identity had greater political consequences. Even after four hundred years of Ottoman rule, opposition to Ottoman rule itself—as opposed to policies viewed as oppressive or unjust—was very limited. This changed very quickly after the introduction of European rule. Nationalists explicitly used the contradiction between democracy and colonialism against their colonial rulers. For example, the proclamation of Syrian leaders in the 1925 revolt against French rule demanded "the complete application of the principles of the French Revolution and the Rights of Man."[27]

Whereas some, such as Arslan, began with Islam as the basic paradigm and Arabism as a facilitating ideology, after the middle of the century it became more common for thinkers to reverse Arslan's paradigm—they viewed Arabism as the ultimate ideology, and argued that Islam, as part of the Arab heritage, was therefore an important pillar of nationalism. Abd al-Rahman al-Bazzaz, a more secular thinker than Arslan, pictured Muhammad as a central historical figure for Arabs, and Islam "as a religion which enabled the Arab nation to assert its place in the world."[28]

The events stirring nationalist opposition to British rule in Egypt before World War I afterward gave rise to the Egyptian Wafd Party founded by Sa'd Zaghlul (1857–1927). Zaghlul was educated at al-Azhar and like many nationalists had a strong Islamic background. After the war, however, Zaghlul framed his arguments primarily in nationalist terms. In a flare of initiative, he attempted to organize a delegation (*wafd*) to the Paris Peace Accords in 1919 in order to negotiate on behalf of Egypt.[29] His arrest and exile by the British led to the greatest popular upheaval Egypt had ever seen.

Perhaps the most important nationalist thinker in the first half of the century was Satia' al-Husri, whose influence was magnified by his official position in Faisal's government in Iraq. His stature was such that after World War II he became responsible for the Arab League's cultural section. Al-Husri was a thoroughgoing secular nationalist. He believed language and a common historical heritage were the essential elements of Arab identity. In his mind religion was not an essential element, and in fact it could be counterproductive, disrupting Arab unity. A native of Syria, he emphasized the importance of including Egypt within the Arabist fold (prior to the 1950s Arab nationalism was concentrated in the Levant). Another influential secularist was the Egyptian Taha Hussein (1889–1973). One of Hussein's central ideas, expressed in his book *The Future of Culture in Egypt*, was that Egypt was not an oriental culture at all, but primarily an occidental one in which Islam was simply one element of the Egyptian identity (he was obviously not a pan-Arabist). Even more radical was another Egyptian, Ali Abd al-Raziq (1888–1966). Abd al-Raziq was educated

191

A camel market in Cairo.

Caroline Williams, photographer. CMES.

at al-Azhar and held the position of *qadi*. In his controversial book, *Islam and the Principles of Government*, Abd al-Raziq argued that Islam as originally conceived by Muhammad was essentially apolitical and that the caliphate and the *shari'a* were later distortions of the faith. They were, he contended, maintained as mechanisms by which rulers could oppress the popular will.[30]

Along with mainstream nationalists, a number of more radical secular movements arose, especially in Iraq and Syria. The radical secularists largely drew upon Marxist thinking, and some were specifically Communist. A crucial difference between the two strands of nationalism was that the more Marxist-oriented groups not only downplayed Islam, but were forthrightly anti-Islamic. One important role that the radicals played was to focus attention squarely on the need for practical reform of Arab societies at a time when most nationalist movements were based on fashionable intellectual trends and anti-colonial sloganeering.[31]

From these currents developed two movements that may be described as constituting the Golden Age of Arab nationalism— that of Gamal Abd al-Nasser in Egypt and the Ba'ath (Renaissance) Party in Syria and Iraq. Both movements were based upon the three pillars of nationalism, secularism, and socialism.

By the early 1950s Egypt had been independent for three decades, but was not fully free from its colonial past. Its monarchy, headed by King Farouk, still was constituted by the Ottoman-era dynasty of Muhammad Ali. Moreover, the Suez Canal Zone still was controlled by Britain. In 1952 a group of "Free Officers" (which included Nasser, who took control in 1954) ousted Farouk and declared the dawn of a new age. It was not merely independence that they wanted, but a transformation of Egypt from a traditional, peasant society to a Westernized, industrial society through the force of socialist revolution. The economy would be developed, the landed elite humbled, and the poor empowered. The Free Officers themselves were of relatively humble origins. Their primary policies revolved around the expansion of education, the redistribution of wealth, the nationalization of industry, and the integration of women into the workforce.[32]

The Syrian Ba'ath Party was formed out of the Arab societies of the late Ottoman period. It was founded by the Greek Orthodox Michel Aflaq and a Syrian Muslim named Salah al-Din al-Bitar in

1943. Both men had studied in France, and although attracted by socialism, they rejected Communism and de-emphasized class struggle as being divisive and counterproductive to the nationalist cause. Branches of the party also formed in Jordan (1948), Lebanon (1949), and Iraq (1950).

Syria's course after independence following World War II was extremely turbulent. Nationalists had taken control by 1946, but they were overthrown by the military three years later. This was followed by a period of unstable parliamentary rule from 1954–1958 in which the Ba'ath and the Communists took the forefront. Fearing a Communist takeover, the Ba'ath engineered a union with Nasser's Egypt in 1958, forming the United Arab Republic. Given the population imbalance between the two countries, and the domineering force of Nasser's personality, the project was bound to have problems, and it ended three years later. The Ba'ath took complete control in 1963 through a military coup. Internal division led to another coup in 1966, a "self-coup" of sorts, in which more stridently Marxist Ba'athists took control of the party and the state.

Iraq went through a similar process. In 1958 the Hashimite monarch was assassinated and nationalist forces took over. Through a series of military coups, the Iraqi Ba'ath was able to consolidate its rule. A party member named Saddam Hussein used his position within the security services to take control, first behind-the-scenes, and then formally in 1969.

In the countries of the Maghrib, reaction to European rule had an ideological context similar to that of the Arab east. Morocco, Tunisia, and Algeria all had come under French control, and whereas the British were content to leave domestic affairs largely undisturbed, French rule followed a very different pattern. As part of *la mission civilatrice*, the French undertook an intense effort of "Francophonization," almost eradicating Arabic as an official language and limiting it to use as a peasant dialect. Nowhere in the Arab world was French penetration deeper than in Algeria. Its conquest completed by the end of the 1840s, France formally annexed the province as a department of France, heavily colonizing it with French settlers. This made the separation process all the more difficult. The Algerian *Front de Liberation Nationale*, or FLN, arose in the 1950s and from 1952–1960 waged what the Algerians came to

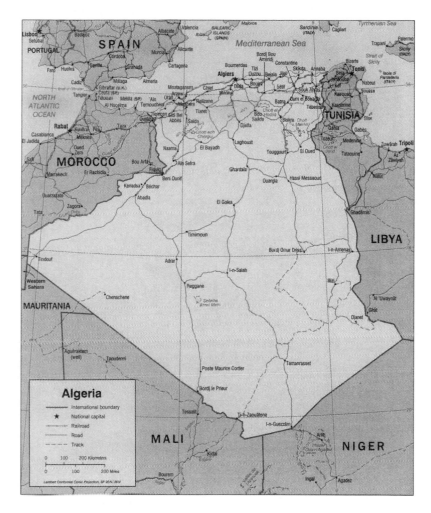

Algeria, 2001.

Courtesy of The General Libraries, The University of Texas at Austin.

call the "War of a Million Martyrs." The bloody struggle toppled the French Fourth Republic in 1958 and gave Algeria its independence. The ideology of the FLN also emphasized secularism and statism.

In part because of the conflict in Algeria, both Tunisia and Morocco gained independence more peacefully. Following independence in 1960, the Tunisian nationalist Habib Abu Raqiba (Bourguiba) was "elected" president. Bourguiba, who was educated in France, essentially wanted to continue *la mission civilatrice* but under native auspices. Intensely anti-Islamic, he banned polygamy and tried to abolish the Ramadan fast. He once appeared on television drinking orange juice during the day, arguing that Tunisia was on an economic *jihad* and that fasting could be done away with. He had a point, since productive work does come to a virtual standstill in the Arab world during the month of Ramadan, but Tunisians would not give up their beliefs. He was also a socialist, and Tunisia began the socialist revolution in earnest in the 1960s.

Morocco likewise won its freedom without violence, but its sharifian monarchy had little taste for secularism or socialism. Morocco's monarch King Muhammad V (d. 1961) and his long-ruling son, King Hassan (r. 1961–1999), formally based their legitimacy on their descent from Muhammad and defense of Islamic values, and had no radical visions comparable to the rulers of other Arab states. Hassan, although in his twenties upon his ascension, received "on-the-job" training by leading the suppression of a revolt under his father. While maintaining control over the territory of the western Sahara (a conflict that simmers to the present), Hassan was openly allied with the West and secretly so with Israel, and developed a record of stable stagnation for decades.

Although the tripartite nationalist-secularist-socialist ideology of both Nasserism and Ba'athism were usually described as being the outgrowth of indigenous Arab heritage, its origins were clearly European. Its basic ideas had come from Western writers, especially those writing in English and French. The rise of German National Socialism in the 1930s also became attractive to Arab nationalists for a variety of reasons. Hitler was viewed as an enemy of the colonial powers, Britain and France. After Germany's withdrawal from the League of Nations in 1936, it was seen as an enemy of the organization that had created the hated Mandate

The skyline of the famous Casablanca in Morocco.
Ron Baker, photographer. CMES.

system. Nazi anti-Semitism was also a major draw as the Zionist-Arab conflict escalated in the 1930s. The Fascist powers engaged in an extensive propaganda campaign in the Arab world. Future Egyptian president Nasser and his successor Anwar Sadat were on record as supporters (Sadat actually worked for Nazi intelligence).[33] Yet, in addition to the final defeat in 1945, overt Nazi influence was limited by the third element of Adolf Hitler's elixir, his occultic, racist Aryan ideology (socialism and nationalism being the other two).[34]

It was into this ideological void that the Soviet Union stepped in the 1950s, inspiring Arab leaders with its Marxist ideology, while sending military advisors and weapons to train and equip their armies. Syria and Egypt were the primary beneficiaries. Although now it may be difficult to comprehend how Marxist economics could have inspired such enthusiasm, at the time the illogic of Marxism was not so clear. The rapid industrialization of the USSR and other Soviet bloc countries had been impressive indeed, and the Soviets were passionate champions of the anti-colonial struggle in the Third World, notwithstanding their own repression of central Asian Muslims. The revolutions in technology and information services that eventually would make command economies obsolete were just beginning. The United States under Truman and Eisenhower was also strongly anti-colonialist, and unlike the USSR, it was able to bring practical pressure to bear on England and France to end their empires, but this was hardly noticed.

Notes

1. Throughout the last two chapters I have chosen to only use footnotes for factual references that would not necessarily be obvious to someone with a general familiarity with the period.
2. Morris, *Righteous Victims*, 88.
3. Elizabeth Thompson, "The Climax and Crisis of the Colonial Welfare State in Syria and Lebanon during World War II," in *War, Institutions, and Social Change in the Middle East*, Steven Heydemann, ed. (Berkeley: University of California Press, 2000) 59–99.
4. Tom Segev, *One Palestine, Complete: Jews and Arabs under the British Mandate*, translated by Haim Watzman (New York: Metropolitan Books, 2000) 13–32.
5. Morris, *Righteous Victims*, 83–4.

198

6. Ibid.
7. Ibid., 88–91.
8. Ibid., 90–1.
9. Ibid.
10. Ibid., 92–3.
11. Shlaim, *Iron Wall*, 10.
12. Morris, *Righteous Victims*, 116.
13. Ibid., 117.
14. Ibid., 120.
15. Ibid., 124–5.
16. Ibid.
17. Ben-Gurion expressed the view: "We shall fight the White Paper as if there is no war, and we shall fight the war as if there is no White Paper." Ibid., 164.
18. Ibid., 161–6.
19. Al-Rasheed, *History of Saudi Arabia*, 63–5.
20. Ibid., 65.
21. Ibid., 67.
22. Ibid., 66.
23. Ibid., 75–80.
24. Ibid.
25. Ibid., 91–95.
26. Voll, *Islam*, 162–5.
27. Ibid., 165.
28. Ibid.
29. Ibid., 166.
30. Ibid., 166–70.
31. Ibid., 170–2.
32. Ibid., 173–7.
33. Lewis, *Middle East*, 349; Lewis, *What Went Wrong*, 154, 158.
34. Hitler once referred to Arabs as "Half-Apes." Morris, *Righteous Victims*, 165.

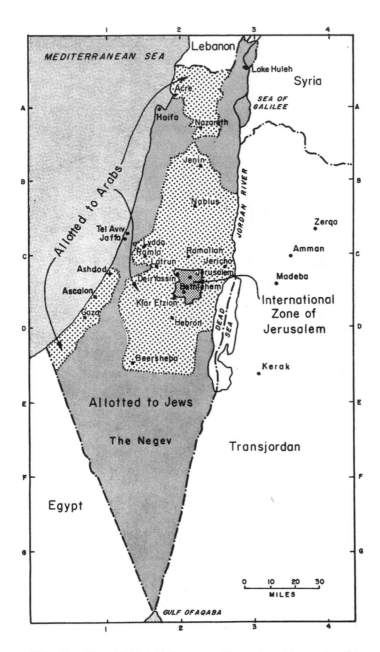

Palestine: The United Nations partition plan, November 29, 1947.

Courtesy of the University of Washington Press. (Originally appeared in *A Near East Studies Handbook* by Jere Bacharach, 1977.)

CHAPTER XI

Hopes Betrayed:
The Contemporary World

The Israeli-Palestinian Conflict (1947–1990)

After World War II, Britain made it clear that it could not shoulder the burden of Palestine any longer, and that it would withdraw. The first Arab-Jewish war began after the United Nations General Assembly passed a resolution partitioning Palestine in November 1947. The partition gave the Jews 55 percent of the land for a state, albeit one with almost a 40 percent Arab population; it gave the Arabs almost all the rest, and internationalized Jerusalem. The state of Jordan had been created in 1946 out of Britain's Palestine Mandate east of the Jordan River, with Sharif Hussein's son Abdullah as king.

Who actually started the war is immaterial; the conflict was essentially an escalation of the low-level fighting that had been going on intermittently since 1929. The first stage of the war was between the Yishuv and local Palestinian militias, and it was not even close. The Yishuv had huge advantages in training, organization, and motivation, while the Palestinians engaged in random attacks against settlements. Neither side spared civilians, and perhaps two hundred and fifty thousand Palestinians fled their homes.

The second stage of the war began as Britain was pulling out the last of its forces. On May 14, 1948, Yishuv leader David Ben-Gurion declared the founding of the State of Israel against threats of invasion from Egypt, Jordan, Syria, and Lebanon. The Egyptian and Syrian armies were sizeable enough to scare Ben-Gurion, but were ill-trained, unorganized, and badly led. They were also decisively defeated. By contrast, Jordan's Arab Legion, led by a British officer corps, was a real army. Yet King Abdullah merely wanted what is now the "West Bank" and Arab East Jerusalem, the latter of which contains holy sites of both Islam (the Dome of the Rock) and Judaism (the original site for Solomon's Temple).[1] The Legion fought the Israeli Defense Force (IDF) to a standstill and achieved its objective just as it was running out of ammunition. The Lebanese never wanted to fight and agreed with the Israelis that they would fire a few shots over their heads and then sign an armistice. Eventually all four Arab states did so, and the armistice lines became Israel's permanent borders. Crucial to Israel's victory was a large arms shipment from the Soviet bloc, and financial support from American Jews (and some non-Jews, but the U.S. government gave no support).

What Israelis call the War of Independence, Arabs call *al-nakba*, or the catastrophe. Aside from the territory lost and the collective humiliation of the defeat itself, the Arab states now were burdened with refugees who would be a source of instability for decades. Only Jordan has made a real effort to help resettle them.

Israel quickly faced a massive infiltration problem.[2] Arabs, mainly Palestinian refugees, began crossing Israel's border in small groups. Some came from Egypt, but most came from the West Bank or Jordan itself. Most did so for economic reasons: to retrieve cattle or other property, gather crops, or stay and reclaim land that had been lost. In addition, armed groups set out to attack Jewish settlers or ravage their crops.

Infiltration quickly became a serious problem for the young state, as settlements increasingly came under attack and Israel faced a growing Arab minority (Israel's population of about 900,000 included 150,000 Arabs[3]). Israel adopted two responses: first, security forces implemented a tough deterrence policy, often firing on unarmed infiltrators. Second, as this was ineffective, Israel began launching punitive raids, mainly in Jordan. The severity increased with time and included attacks on both civilian and military targets. The most notorious of these was carried out by Major Ariel Sharon on the Jordanian village of Qibya in 1954. About sixty villagers were killed, and evidence seemed to indicate that they were

202

Omar Moschee   Mosque of Omar

The Dome of the Rock.
CMES.

An old city gate in Jerusalem.
CMES.

trapped inside their homes, which then were blown up.[4] Increasing domestic and international criticism of Israeli retribution exploded after Qibya. Thereafter Israel focused on military targets, but with increased force.

Diplomatically, all four Arab states showed a willingness to make peace with Israel if it was willing make territorial concessions. Prospects for peace were best with regard to Jordan, because King Abdullah feared the Palestinians much more than he did Israel. As the combined Palestinian population of Jordan and the West Bank was significantly higher than that of the Jordanians themselves, Jordanian officials feared that an independent Palestinian state might turn on them and annex Jordan. Then in 1951, as discussions were ongoing, Abdullah was assassinated for negotiating with Israel.

Abdullah's eighteen-year-old grandson Hussein came to power in 1953, and he also wanted peace. In addition to Israel's unwillingness to part with any substantial plot of territory, relations were strained by Israel's reprisals to infiltration. Jordanian officials put more troops at the border to curb infiltration; King Hussein himself wondered why Israel kept attacking Jordan, when the infiltrators were a threat to Jordan as well.[5]

Syria was also open to a deal, but it too wanted territorial concessions. The dispute revolved around the demilitarized zones that just happened to run adjacent to the Jordan River, which was essential to Israel's water supply. At one point Syria offered 70 percent of the disputed territory, but Israeli officials believed that the territory Syria wanted to keep was crucial to their water supply. Resisting U.S. pressure to accept, Israel rejected Syrian overtures, and after a 1949 coup Syria became less compromising. Political upheaval also played a role in Egypt's dealings with Israel, although it had the opposite effect. King Farouk took a hard line against Israel, but his overthrow by the Free Officers in 1952 led to serious peace talks. Yet as before, Egypt offered peace only with territorial concessions, while Israel offered only peace for peace.

The public diplomacy overshadowed two undercurrents that significantly restricted each side's freedom to compromise. The first was that, while Israel's willingness to make peace, albeit without giving up territory, reflected public opinion, the pragmatism of the Arab governments was totally at odds with Arab opinion. Arab leaders were in a double bind; they needed to secure peace so that they could consolidate power domestically, yet negotiating with Israel could itself be destabilizing. In fact, the rulers of all three states were either killed or overthrown during the 1948–1955 period.

The second factor limiting diplomatic flexibility was an expectations gap. Arabs considered themselves flexible if they were demanding only a small portion of the land that they had just lost. By contrast, Zionists traditionally had dreamed of a Jewish state including the lands of Biblical Judea and Samaria—that is, the West Bank—along with much of Jordan. Most Israelis, including Ben-Gurion himself, still wanted to find a way to take the West Bank. Only reluctantly, if at all, would they give up this goal. Jerusalem, with its centrality to Jewish history, they would never give up.

By the mid-1950s peace talks had failed, and Nasser became more bellicose with time. Given the shift in his foreign policy, Nasser probably had intended at first to focus on domestic policy. Yet he discovered that leading the charge against Israel gave him fame and adoration far beyond Egypt's borders. The Suez Canal Zone offered him a chance to strike a blow to European colonialism and Zionism at once. In 1956 he nationalized the Suez Canal and closed the straits to Israeli shipping. Along with continued raids across the armistice line, Israel, along with Britain and France, began to look for a way to attack Egypt.[6]

The situation was made more urgent by Nasser's announcement of a large arms deal with the Soviet Union (through Czechoslovakia). This announcement was greeted with acclaim across the Arab world, as the United States was incorrectly thought to be pro-Israel. In fact, the United States refused Israel's request for a similar deal. From the beginning of the Cold War, the greatest fear of U.S. officials, especially Eisenhower, was that association with the colonial powers would taint America in the eyes of the Third World, and that the world's population would tilt toward the Soviet Union.[7] Thus it was U.S. policy to pressure Israel to compromise and to refrain from giving Israel military aid.[8]

Having been spurned by Washington, Israel found ready allies in Britain and France. Both still clung to their empires, and both hated Nasser. Under their plan, Israel would first invade the Sinai

A Cairo street that leads to the Pharonic City of the Dead.
Diane Watts, photographer. CMES.

Peninsula. Britain and France would then invade the canal zone, ostensibly to force a cease-fire, but in fact to reverse Nasser's nationalization.

Beginning October 29, 1956, the first stage went well as the Israeli army cut through Egyptian lines like butter, but the ineptness of the scheme soon became apparent. Too much time went by before the Anglo-French attack, and the United States and the USSR demanded a cease-fire first, making the invasion unnecessary. When it came anyway, Eisenhower condemned the attack with enough force to shock Britain and France into capitulation. It was Nasser's good fortune that the attack came at a time when Soviet forces were savagely repressing a popular uprising in Hungary, making it impossible for the West to mount a unified response to the double crisis. Israel quickly withdrew.

The Suez crisis and its aftermath had two primary consequences. One was to make Nasser the hero of the Arab world, allowing him to intimidate other Arab leaders. The other was to show that the age of European preeminence was over.

After nearly a decade of uneasy peace, by 1965 the Arab states were moving back to war. The founding of the Palestinian Liberation Organization (PLO) in 1964 had given the Palestinians a means of taking control of their future. They began attacking Israel with increasing frequency in 1965. Most of the attacks were launched from Jordan or Lebanon, but they were supported by Syria. The rise to power of a more radical element within the Syrian Ba'ath in 1966 further strained relations, and tensions mounted. A highly visible Israeli reprisal against a West Bank town in November 1966 sparked massive anti-Hashimite protests among Palestinians, and Hussein felt forced to act.

The journey to war accelerated in May 1967, when Syria erroneously suggested—and Soviet intelligence confirmed—to Egypt that Israel was preparing an attack on Syria, and that Egypt needed to mobilize in the south (this was likely an honest mistake on the part of the Syrians, but may not have been for the Soviets[9]). Nasser promptly ordered mobilization. Thereafter King Hussein signed a mutual defense pact with Egypt, as did Iraq, and Iraqi troops began to move toward Israel. Israel itself then mobilized its forces.

Having mobilized militarily, Israel now faced a "use-it-or-lose-it" situation. Israel's military structure comprised a small permanent force backed up by a much larger reserve force. Once called up, the reserves were an unsustainable drain on the economy, so Israel could not stay mobilized. Egypt faced no similar dilemma; if it remained mobilized, Israel would have to attack. This corresponded with threats of another Holocaust. State-controlled media in Egypt, Syria, and Iraq began talking about liquidating Israel, while PLO Chairman Ahmad Shukeiry declared that "there will be practically no Jewish survivors."[10]

On the morning of June 5, the Israeli Air Force (IAF) executed one of the most flawless performances in the history of air warfare. Fully 95 percent of the entire fleet was launched, leaving at different times and striking at eleven different air bases across northern Egypt—all precisely at 7:45 A.M. The Egyptian Air Force was destroyed virtually to a plane. IDF tank regiments then attacked with full force, sending opposing troops, being strafed from above by the now unopposed IAF, fleeing headlong across the Sinai. The Egyptian army was in complete disarray, military command had no real idea where its units were, and large numbers were cut off.

Having decisively defeated Egypt, Israel then turned on Jordan and Syria in turn. Both were vastly outmatched, and with Egypt having capitulated, they lacked the will to fight. In six days of fighting, Israel vastly increased the territory under its control, taking the Sinai, the West Bank, including East Jerusalem, and Syria's strategic Golan Heights.

Despite the mythology that has grown up around Israel's victory, Israel won the 1967 war for the same reason most victors do—the balance of military power favored itself. Fully mobilized, Israeli manpower was about 75 percent of the combined forces of the three Arab states. However, in terms of training, equipment, leadership, intelligence, motivation, and air power, Israel vastly overpowered its neighbors.

Nasser's humiliation was so severe that his health began to fail. Knowing that his power depended upon his status as Arab champion, he initiated what became known as the War of Attrition. In 1968 Egypt began launching small-scale raids on Israeli positions in the Sinai, and with Soviet aid it was able to neutralize IAF reprisals. Although Egyptian losses were significantly greater, Egypt could afford them, while Israel could not. Tensions heightened nearly to

209

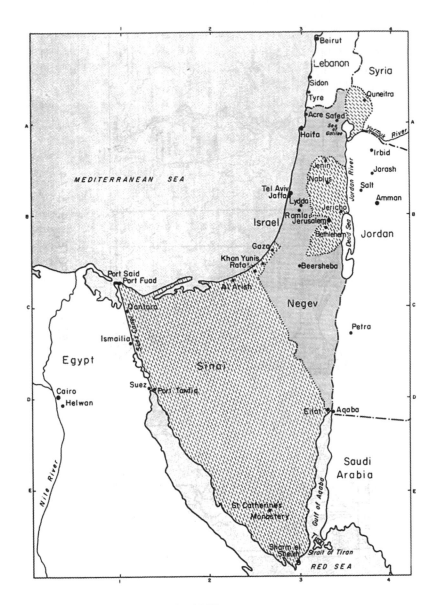

Israel and Occupied Lands, 1967.

Courtesy of the University of Washington Press. (Originally appeared in *A Near East Studies Handbook* by Jere Bacharach, 1977.)

all-out war before the United States brokered a cease-fire in 1970. U.S. foreign policy had taken a decisive turn by this point. The shift toward Israel began under Kennedy, but the Johnson administration fully committed the United States to resupplying Israel in order to balance Soviet influence in the region.

The second front in the War of Attrition was opened up by the Palestinians from Jordan and Lebanon in January 1965, backed by Syria, and in a sense has never ended. The main Palestinian organization was still the PLO, now dominated by al-Fatah, a group led by an engineer named Yassir Arafat. Although some wanted to limit targets to the Middle East, more militant groups emerged, including the Popular Front for the Liberation of Palestine (PFLP), which specialized in airline hijackings. Syria and Iraq also sponsored militant groups called Al-Sa'iqa ("lightning") and Abu Nidal ("father of conflict"), respectively. Funding from Persian Gulf states also supported militant activity.

The country facing the greatest crisis, however, was not Israel but Jordan. Palestinian attacks not only brought Israeli reprisals on Jordanian soil, but they also began challenging the Jordanian state directly. Most of the Arab world sympathized with the Palestinians. After tolerating low-level conflict, King Hussein decided to clamp down after two assassination attempts. In September 1970 Hussein replaced his civilian cabinet with a military government, and by July 1971 he had eradicated Palestinian resistance.

Jordan's war against the PLO did not sit well with its main backer, and Syria invaded Jordan in September 1971. The United States threatened to have the IAF wipe out Syria's vulnerable tank columns. Since the United States was at that time bombing Vietnam around the clock, it was no idle threat, and Syria retreated.

Their defeat in Jordan forced the PLO to relocate to Lebanon, a move that would have portentous consequences for the region. The political balance in Lebanon had been precarious anyway, and Muslims used the influx of Palestinian militants to destabilize the Maronite-dominated government. The PLO created a virtual state-within-a-state, and in 1974 helped unleash a bloody civil war between the country's main factions—Maronite Christians, Druze, Sunnis, and Shi'a Muslims—that has made Beirut an internationally recognized byword for "war zone." The situation also afforded the PLO a new base from which to build a regular army.

211

A typical apartment building in Amman, Jordan.

Ann Grabhorn-Friday, photographer. CMES.

The War of Attrition had allowed Egyptian forces to regain respectability. Then in October 1973, on Yom Kippur, the holiest day of the Jewish year, Egypt and Syria launched a well-planned, well-disguised attack in the Sinai and the Golan. Anwar Sadat had taken over power in Egypt after Nasser's death in 1970, and Hafez Assad, Syria's defense minister during the disastrous 1967 war, had come to power in Syria. They now were bent on regaining Arab prestige by catching Israel off guard, and they succeeded. Israel's only partially mobilized forces barely were able to hold back a Syrian advance.

In the Sinai the IDF had no choice but to fall back, and a counterattack was repulsed. Had Egyptian forces simply held their ground, the toll of full mobilization would have worn Israel down. Egypt then launched a clumsy, staggered tank assault against IDF lines, and it was decimated. Israel took advantage of the opening and launched a devastating counteroffensive that cut Egypt's army into pieces and forced Sadat to call on Moscow to demand a ceasefire. Israel also launched a counteroffensive against Syria, but backed up against their capital city, the Syrians held firm.

Militarily, the October War (Yom Kippur War) was a moderate victory for Israel. The IDF had suffered losses as never before, but overall losses were much heavier on the Arab side. Psychologically, however, it was a powerful boost to Arab morale. It was Egypt's "victory" in 1973 that allowed Sadat to travel to Jerusalem in 1977 and reach a peace agreement with Israel in 1979.

In July 1972 Anwar Sadat had ejected Soviet advisors from Egypt. He did this in part to lull Israel into a false sense of security, but also because he knew that an alliance with the United States would be more useful. The 1979 Camp David Peace Accords brought to Egypt a return of the Sinai, an alliance with the United States, and a formal peace with Israel. U.S. aid to Israel and Egypt has essentially been frozen at $3 million and $2 million respectively. U.S. military aid has improved Egypt's strategic position in Africa, enabling its Air Force to deter its southern neighbors, Sudan and Ethiopia, from diverting water from the Nile.[11]

The next Arab-Israeli war took place in Lebanon. Syria had entered the Lebanese civil war in 1977 and carved out a buffer zone in the Bekáa Valley. In 1982 Israel launched an attack framed as a limited incursion to push the PLO away from its northern border,

213

The Egyptian Tomb of the Unknown Soldier, Sadat Memorial Pyramid.
Caroline Williams, photographer. CMES.

but actually intended to drive the PLO and Syria out of Lebanon and to put in power an Israel-friendly government. The first stage went well, as all Arab factions stepped aside and watched the IDF smash PLO forces. Israel managed to provoke a fight with Syria and won it decisively. Then the IDF encircled Muslim West Beirut until the PLO accepted a U.S.–brokered deal allowing them to evacuate. The IDF also arranged for the election of its Maronite ally, Bashir Gemayel, as president of Lebanon.

Having achieved its objectives, Israel's house of cards began to collapse. The intervention led to a new Shi'a Lebanese militia, Hizbullah (Party of God), focused on fighting Israel rather than other Lebanese. Financed by Syria and Iran, Hizbullah stepped up attacks on the IDF, while also carrying out a number of attacks against U.S. peacekeepers—perhaps misnamed since there was no peace to keep. This included a 1983 bombing that killed 241 American marines. The breaking point to Israeli morale came when militias allied with Israel entered refugee camps protected by the IDF and massacred about eight hundred Palestinians. It appeared that Israeli Defense Minister Ariel Sharon had arranged for the operation. Israeli public support for the war always had been weak, and the country was shaken by a wave of revulsion. The IDF soon pulled back to a thin buffer zone in south Lebanon.

The conflict ended the 1980s with a spontaneous Palestinian uprising in the West Bank and Gaza called the intifada. Although by some indications their material conditions had improved since 1967, this also had led to a demographic explosion. Furthermore, Palestinians lived under the firm hand of Israeli security forces, with their economy held captive and exploited. Most threatening of all was the settlement expansion. Israel had begun building settlements in the West Bank and Gaza after 1967, but this accelerated after the election of Menachem Begin's Likud in 1977. The reason for Palestinian rage is clear when one considers that between 1967 and 1987 irrigated land decreased by 30 percent in the West Bank, and in the Gaza Strip by 1987 Jewish settlers, who made up 0.4 percent of the population, controlled 28 percent of the land.[12]

Although it featured some armed attacks, the intifada mainly consisted of Palestinian youths throwing stones at tanks and armed soldiers. More threatening in the long term was the rise of an Islamist opposition, mainly represented by the organization

215

Hamas.[13] Yet while Palestinians lacked the means to be a serious threat, the international publicity seriously demoralized Israel and led to increasing pressure for change.

Development and Stagnation: Contemporary Socio-Economic Issues[14]

The failure of the economic pillar of the Arab nationalist-socialist project was not as sudden and perhaps not as visible as the failure of its military pillar in 1967, but over time it was just as complete and much more widely felt. The final result itself is indisputable: today the non-fossil fuel exports of the entire Arab world are less than those of Finland, which has a population equivalent to that of Jordan.[15] Per capita GDP of non-oil exporting Arab states is only about a tenth that of the United States ($35,000), and about a sixth that of Israel ($18,000). How did the economic picture turn out so badly?

Bad agricultural policy is part of the answer. In Tunisia the failure was clear by 1969. During the 1960s the government instituted an intense program of farm collectivization that brought all of the "benefits" to Tunisia that Stalin's similar program had brought to the Ukraine in the 1920s. Tunisia's agricultural sector was decimated, and after a decade of socialist sloganeering, literally overnight the government changed course. The state proclaimed that henceforth it would now follow the free market. The fact that the elite could reverse its ideology so abruptly probably lowered the Tunisian public's confidence as much as the failure itself.

While Egypt and Tunisia were the first to take the socialist plunge, other countries that followed included Algeria, Iraq, Libya, Syria, the Sudan, and Yemen. All Arab states became statist and "top-heavy," but this was sometimes for pragmatic rather than ideological reasons. Where private actors failed to take the initiative, officials felt they had to fill the void. Moreover, they needed to keep people employed, for nothing is more dangerous than having a lot of jobless young men wandering around. As a "solution," Nasser made an explicit pledge to provide every Egyptian with a job. This resulted in a bureaucratic state glacial in its immobility (one study concluded that the average Egyptian bureaucrat works

A modern café in Amman with the old city in the background.
John A. Williams, photographer. CMES.

Loading up the wheat at harvest time in southern Iraq.
Robert Fernea, photographer. CMES.

A merchant of brass in Cairo.

Caroline Williams, photographer. CMES.

only eighteen minutes per day). Even where other states have not made such an explicit promise, the tendency existed everywhere.

Another problem was the practice of import substitution. Dependency theory, which was very popular in the developing world in the decades after World War II, posited that poor countries were being kept poor by exporting raw materials and importing finished products. The solution was to institute tariffs on imports and focus on producing finished goods for the domestic market. The basic concept itself is sound—no country creates a developed economy just by exporting commodities. Yet this policy insulated inefficient industries from competition, whereas countries that did develop quickly (i.e. Japan and South Korea) did so by exporting value-added goods. Furthermore, very often the companies that dominated the market were state-owned.

State-owned companies, aside from being costly and inefficient, brought other negatives. Banks were forced to give low-interest loans to them, keeping in business companies that were not producing anything. This in turn undermined the banking system itself, and lack of confidence in the banking system—along with war risks and a lack of financial transparency—has led Arab investors to keep most of their money in the West.

The lack of a genuine export strategy left Arab consumers with little hard currency with which to purchase goods that were not available at home. This led to dependence on barter with Eastern European states, which were producing goods that no one wanted to buy. The fall of Communism ended this option.

Imposing price controls on various items also helped keep a lid on a short-term problem by mortgaging future development. Low prices on basic foods were viewed as essential to social peace. Nothing could lead to riots more quickly than an increase in the price of staple foods. Yet this also stunted agricultural development, making it harder for farmers to buy the land they rented. If they owned the land, controls made it difficult for them to increase their holdings to create economies of scale and to make capital investments that would lead to greater productivity. Likewise, rent controls were popular with renters, but they stunted investment in real estate that might have increased the supply of apartments, thus easing the price problem.

219

Currency controls have been used, producing a variety of distortions. The controls did not effectively prevent individuals from stashing money outside the country, which was their goal, but they did discourage foreign investors worried about getting money out of the country. Combined with the lack of well-functioning financial markets, controls meant individuals had no alternative to state banks, allowing governments to take out loans subsidized by depositors in the form of low returns for deposits.

Even the successful aspects of many policies have had drawbacks. In purely statistical terms, education reform has been an astounding triumph. Literacy rates rose significantly, and higher education has achieved a spectacular increase in graduates. Yet due to lagging economic growth, these graduates had few jobs available to them. Another bright spot has been health care, most clearly shown in declining rates of child mortality. Yet along with the economic difficulties, this has led to problems associated with population growth. It is commonly believed that the Arab world is overpopulated, but this is not technically correct. Arab countries are far less densely populated than those of Western Europe. Egypt has a population of 61 million, about that of France, while the second most populous, Algeria, has only 31 million inhabitants. Most Arab states have fewer than 10 million. The problem is an imbalance between population and economic growth rates. Population control programs are widely in place, and fertility rates have fallen, but the lack of expansion in the private sector has led to very high levels of unemployment. Arab fertility rates are not much higher on average than those experienced by the United States as recently as the 1950s, but the United States has had productive agricultural and industrial sectors for most of the past two centuries.

As in so many other areas, Egypt is a paradigm for the Arab world's economic-demographic problems. Roughly 95 percent of its 61 million people live on 5 percent of the land, cramped around the Nile River. To deal with both the land and the water scarcity issues, Egypt built the Aswan Dam, completed in 1970. This increased irrigation and led to a significant increase in useable land and agricultural production. However, even this has backfired, since disturbing the natural rise and fall of the Nile has led to excess mineral deposits, and the increased salinity has damaged

A busy Egyptian market.
Caroline Williams, photographer. CMES.

A narrow passage through an Egyptian market.

Caroline Williams, photographer. CMES.

the fecundity of the soil. It also is undermining the limestone foundations of many historic buildings in Cairo.[16]

Water scarcity certainly is not limited to Egypt. It exists over most of the Arab world and is an especially acute issue in the Levant, where Israel and its neighbors share water sources and inevitably attempt to monopolize them.[17]

Internal problems have not been helped by international crises. As of the mid-1970s, fully 14 percent of public expenditures went to military purposes (the figure for the United States in 2002 was less than 4 percent). In addition to the Arab-Israeli wars, there have been significant military conflicts between Morocco and Algeria, Egypt and Sudan, Syria and Lebanon, Libya and Chad, Iraq and Iran, Egypt and Saudi Arabia (in Yemen), Jordan and the PLO, Iraq and Kuwait, as well as ruinous civil wars in Algeria, Yemen, Iraq, Sudan and, worst of all, Lebanon. Aside from the direct human and material costs of the conflicts themselves, the very risk of war acts as a strong disincentive to investment.

Ironically, given all the regional conflicts, one of the most persistent rallying calls in Arab politics has been that of Arab unity. The Arab League Pact of 1945 created the Arab League, and, aside from (at least rhetorically) opposing Israel, its major theme has been a succession of attempts at increasing economic and, occasionally, political unity. It has had little success, and inter-Arab trade continues to be beset by tariffs and other regulatory obstacles.[18] Today Arab countries conduct most of their foreign trade with Europe and the United States.

The oil-producing states of the Persian Gulf went through a very different economic experience. The rise of the Organization of Petroleum Exporting Countries (OPEC) as an independent organization in the early 1970s and a dramatic worldwide increase in prices (1973 was a watershed year in that regard) led to hundreds of billions of dollars flowing into Gulf state treasuries. Oil revenues stayed high for the duration of the 1970s, allowing for lavish expansion of state-sponsored welfare and creating a system in which citizens were not only guaranteed a job, but a comfortable living as well.

Yet the oil bust in the early 1980s made the Persian Gulf look like Isma'il's Egypt in the wake of the post-Civil War cotton boom. Saudi Arabia's oil revenues, for example, went from $120 billion to

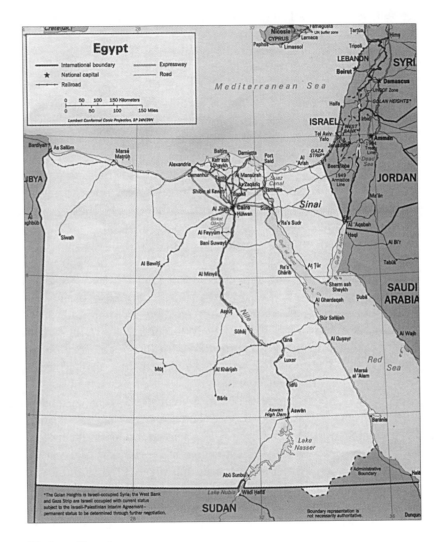

Modern Egypt.

Courtesy of The General Libraries, The University of Texas at Austin.

$17 billion between 1981 and 1984.[19] The Gulf states' economies were barely more efficient than Egypt's during that time. The Saudi state is still so pervasive that the kingdom cannot qualify for membership in the World Trade Organization (WTO), and maintains debt levels so high that a drop in oil prices would engender an economic crisis. Kuwait, Qatar, Bahrain, the United Arab Emirates (UAE), and Oman, by contrast, have made progress at economic reform in recent years and are the best placed of all the Arab states to compete in the global economy at the present.

The Islamic Resurgence and the Islamist-Secularist Struggle for Power

To continue a metaphor introduced earlier, Arab national socialism and Islamism were like half-brothers—the building blocks were only partially the same, and after growing up together, they began fighting over the inheritance. At first this was not so clear. Even where the two were mutually exclusive, both were resisting colonial powers, and thus had a common enemy. In addition, neither movement held power, and thus they had little ability to repress one another. The inevitable conflict occurred first in Egypt.

In 1928, an Egyptian school teacher named Hasan al-Banna founded al-Ikhwan al-Muslimun, or the Muslim Brotherhood. The Brotherhood was different from any previous revivalist movement and became the prototype for modern Islamism. Its central focus was on creating an Islamic society, not through pious declarations, but by building Islamic institutions and calling Muslims to lead a more Islamic life.

The Brotherhood was extremely successful. Al-Banna's stronghold was in Ismailia, a city along the Suez that at the time still stationed British troops and was named after the Westernizing Isma'il Pasha. The Brotherhood thought that by creating an Islamic society, an Islamic state based around the shari'a could be formed, and this would also empower the Egyptian people to shake off the vestiges of European rule.

Perhaps because of its success, the Brotherhood's conflicts with the government increased, and al-Banna himself was assassinated in 1949. After the Free Officers' coup in 1952, the outlook

225

initially improved, and relations between the Brotherhood and Nasser's government were good. But pressure to make Islam more central to the state brought conflict, and in 1954 Brotherhood members attempted to assassinate Nasser during a public speech. Unhurt, Nasser showed his bravado by returning to the podium to finish his speech. He then ordered a crackdown; the Brotherhood was outlawed and members by the thousands were jailed, tortured, and sometimes executed.[20]

With such a large percentage of its most active members in jail, the Brotherhood produced a prison culture of hatred and resentment of the state. Its military wing had existed previously, but members increasingly saw violent struggle as the only solution. This increased their emphasis on violent overthrow of the government.

The central figure in this movement was Sayid Qutb (1906–1966). Qutb had visited America in the early 1950s and was disgusted with its materialism and secularism. He feared modernizers in Egypt were moving his country in the same direction. Qutb was arrested in 1954 as part of Nasser's crackdown, tortured, and released a decade later, only to be rearrested and hanged in 1966. Yet it was his writings from prison that made him dangerous. Qutb argued that the government itself had caused all society to revert to *jahiliya*. *Jahiliya*, which literally means "ignorance" but has a connotation of barbarism, is the term Muslims use for pre-Islamic Arabia. This meant that Muslims who did not follow the right path, including Nasser, were apostates from Islam, and thus could be killed. The doctrine, widely accepted by militants, justified the killing of those who did not agree with them—officials, tourists, secular opposition leaders, and so on.[21]

Following in the footsteps of the Brotherhood, and sometimes of Qutb as well, Islamic opposition movements mushroomed in all the other secularist states. In Tunisia the movement began as groups formed to study and promote the Quran. The repression of religion and economic failure of Bourguiba's government encouraged Tunisians to look for an alternative. In 1981 the *Mouvement pour la Tendance Islamique* (MTI) became an organized opposition under Rashid al-Ghanushi. Al-Ghanushi is representative of many Islamists in that he began as a secularist, studying in Damascus in the 1960s. He turned to Islamism after the 1967 war destroyed his faith in the vision of Ba'athism and Nasserism.

226

The skyline of Tunis, Tunisia.
Caroline Williams, photographer. CMES.

In the 1980s the Tunisian government became increasingly repressive and in 1986 al-Ghanushi and other MTI leaders were imprisoned. However, the aging Bourguiba was filled with such hatred for them that he ordered the trials annulled so that they could be retried and executed. Acting under a constitutional provision that allowed the president to be removed for mental incapacity, Prime Minister Zein al-Abidine ben Ali had him removed. In the years following, Ali began a rapprochement with the Islamists, but sensing a threat, he returned to repression and has maintained power up to the present.

In Algeria the country remained a one-party state under the secular FLN. The overthrow of independence leader Ahmad ben Bella in 1965 led to a greater emphasis on Islam by the government, although policy remained socialist. Algeria's Islamist movement got going in 1980 after Islamist-led student demonstrations rocked the country. Pressure for change grew until the regime instituted democratic reforms and legalized the *Front Islamique de Salut* (FIS—Islamic Salvation Front). The FIS was led by Abassi Madani, a philosopher who had a doctorate from Britain and who had fought in the nationalist cause against the French in the 1950s. The FIS beat the FLN decisively in regional elections in 1990, and then won the first round of national elections in 1991, at which point the military cancelled the second. This was followed by a brutal war over much of the 1990s in which tens of thousands of Algerians were killed. Many were civilians murdered brutally by either the government or Islamists for supporting the other side. Algeria's huge natural gas and oil reserves have kept the country from collapsing entirely, and the violence had practically ended by the end of the 1990s. Yet recent political reforms have failed to heal the nation's wounds.[22]

Although fighting a losing if inconclusive battle elsewhere, Syrian Islamists bit off more than they could chew in challenging the country's Ba'athist leader, Hafez Assad. From militant secularism in the 1960s, under Assad the Syrian Ba'ath began making accommodations to Islam, incorporating some Islamic trappings into the regime. Yet Islamists considered it all a show and began armed resistance. After a campaign of repression that left untold thousands of Syrians in prison, the remainder of the opposition, perhaps twenty thousand men, were concentrated in the town of Hama. Rather than fight them in a costly house-to-house campaign, Assad had the entire area incinerated, killing militant and civilian alike. This led Thomas Friedman to coin the term "Hama Rules": In Arab society, where those who lose power are tortured and left to languish in a jail cell rather than retired to a villa, you eliminate the opposition before they eliminate you.[23]

Hama Rules were applied no less vigorously in Ba'athist Iraq, although under different circumstances. After the Islamic revolution in Shi'a Iran in 1979, the new government began fermenting religious unrest among the Shi'a populations prominent in the Persian Gulf region. With financial backing from other Gulf states, Iraq under Saddam Hussein waged an exhausting war from 1980–1988 against Iran. Because Iraq's population is close to two-thirds Shi'a, Iran thought it to be ripe for revolution. But since most Iraqi Shi'a refused to cross over, Iraq held firm. Members of the Islamist opposition, mostly Shi'a, were savagely repressed, as was anyone else showing the slightest sense of independence. Although the government had managed a significant level of socioeconomic development by the 1980s, the country was often described as one big prison with Saddam Hussein as the warden. American diplomats at the time reported that it would be an improvement if they could just get Saddam to be as repressive as Assad.[24]

In addition to secular Pan-Arabists and Islamists, the third faction of the post-colonial Arab world comprised the Islamic monarchies. They represented less an ideology than an attempt to use Islam as a basis for the preservation of kingdoms and emirates led by specific families. The monarchies of Jordan, Morocco, and the Persian Gulf faced similar challenges but under different circumstances. Their "Islamic" nature helped shield them from some abuse, and the monarchies of Jordan and Morocco claimed descent from Muhammad. In several countries dynasties managed the situation by alternating repression with offering to give Islamists a greater role in society conditioned upon proper behavior. In Saudi Arabia, the Saudi-Wahhabi alliance remained intact, with the Wahhabis having a junior but nevertheless important role in running internal and religious affairs.

There was a great deal of variation in the policies of the Islamic monarchies. Whereas Saudi Arabia was intensely Islamic domestically, most of the others, especially Jordan, struggled to make incremental moves toward Westernization. All were pragmatic in foreign affairs, feeling the need to stay close to the United States.

Yemen became a junction where all three faces of the Arab world met. The long-ruling Zaydi imamate was overthrown in 1962. Yemen became a proxy battleground between secularist Egypt, which sent troops, and monarchist Yemeni tribes supported by Saudi Arabia. This conflict coincided with Soviet-backed attacks by a Marxist Yemeni group against British troops stationed there until 1967.[25] A Saudi-Egyptian agreement in that year led to the partition of the country and the creation of the Marxist People's Democratic Republic of Yemen (PDRY) in the south and the Yemeni Arab Republic (YAR) in the north. Whereas Syria and Egypt were merely Soviet clients, the PDRY became the only Arab satellite. In the north, tribal leaders pushed for greater Islamization, but President Ali Abdullah Salih kept control and mediated conflicts externally until the eventual reunion of the two states in 1990. A democracy was proclaimed with Islam and Yemeni tradition

229

A five-story house in Sana, Yemen.

John A. Williams, photographer. CMES.

as the core components of the national identity. The ruling party has managed to maintain the state through well-managed elections since that time.

Libya has been a special case. The military overthrew the Sanusia monarchy in 1969, bringing Colonel Mu'ammar Ghaddafi to power. Ghaddafi's ideology, called "The Third Universal Alternative," was expressed in three volumes of *The Green Book* (the color is associated with Muhammad), published 1976–1978. The first volume condemned parliamentary democracy as a sham, advocating the formation of local associations in which people would rule themselves directly. This system actually seems to have worked as designed at times, but of course these associations did not have the right to get rid of Ghaddafi. The second volume advocated socialism, and the third, Islam.[26]

Libya's oil wealth and alliance with the Soviet Union allowed Ghaddafi to play a much greater role on the world stage than otherwise would have been possible. Libya became a major patron of terrorism, with the blowing up of Pan Am Flight 103 over Lockerbie, Scotland, in 1988 being its greatest success (this led to international sanctions that were being lifted as Libya reached a settlement with the victims' families in 2003). Arabism became more important in Ghaddafi's mind, and he failed at repeated attempts to merge with other countries. Libya intervened militarily in Chad often during the 1970s and 1980s, and actually created a brief union with that country in 1981.[27] Ghaddafi even tried to get poor Egypt to swallow his under-populated, oil-rich state (the Egyptians might have agreed had Ghaddafi himself been left out of the bargain). The 1990s brought a genuine move away from terrorism, although it is suspected that Ghaddafi has accelerated his efforts at going nuclear.[28] Arabism also went out of style, and African unity came into vogue. In 2002 Ghaddafi renamed his Foreign Ministry the "Ministry of African Affairs," and suggested Libya might even pull out of the Arab League.

Hamas in Palestine and Hizbullah in Lebanon have also followed their own path, centered on the conflict with Israel. In addition to armed resistance, both have developed extensive social services to garner public support.[29] Hizbullah (and to a more limited extent, Hamas) has moved toward pragmatism in its dealings with other Arab factions.

231

By the mid-1990s it was clear to almost all that Islamism had hit a dead end and needed a new course. The movements had increased the role of Islam in many Arab societies, but their armed wings had been crushed ruthlessly, while their political wings remained banned in most countries. Their success at the societal level was notable. Islamization, shown by such symbolism as wearing of the veil (for women) and growing beards (for men), had increased, and Islamists had been very successful at winning elections of student unions and professional associations. Most Islamist activists are not illiterate and poor, but college-educated and middle-class. Yet for all their influence, they could not get their governments to implement the *shari'a* in its entirety, break off relations with the United States, or declare war on Israel. A new strategy had to be found.

War and Peace from 1990 to the Present

In August 1990 Saddam Hussein decided to settle an old score. With its independence in the 1930s, Iraq had recognized the borders of the nearby emirate called Kuwait, ruled by the Al-Sabah family. The precise borders had been drawn by Britain and were inconsequential at the time. It later was discovered that the border had been drawn over one of the largest oil reservoirs in the world, most of which was on Iraq's side. Iraq had attempted to realign the border by force in 1962 but was forced out by Britain. As technology improved the Kuwaitis got better at "slant drilling"—that is, drilling Iraq's oil. For Iraq there was a risk of American intervention, but Hussein must have been reassured when U.S. Ambassador April Glaspie told him that her country was not concerned with the matter.[30] They were both wrong. Iraqi forces rolled across the border, annexing the territory as one more unit in Hussein's "prison," but a reaction was brewing.

Nowhere was the reaction more severe than in the Arab world. Secular regimes and Islamists alike condemned the action and demanded that Iraq withdraw. Yet Iraq had the largest military in the Arab world, and no Arab country or countries could seriously even attempt a rollback, so the rape of Kuwait continued. A leader

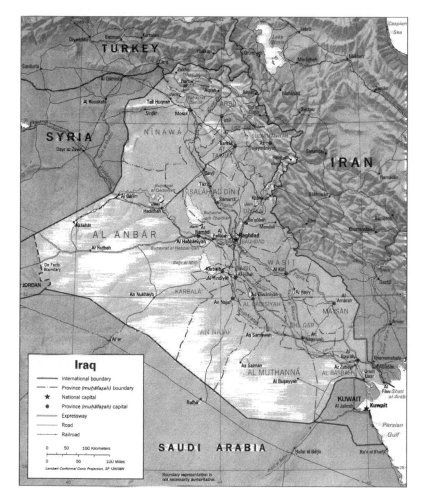

Iraq and the surrounding nations.

Courtesy of the U.S. Government, Central Intelligence Agency.

An urban scene in Baghdad.
Christy Gish, photographer. CMES.

of the Afghan *jihad* against the Soviets named Usama ibn Ladin
(Osama bin Ladin) approached the Saudi King Fahd and proposed
an all-Muslim war against secular Iraq, but he was rebuffed. Outside help was needed, and the United States quickly built up a line
of defense to protect the kingdom until enough forces arrived for
an assault. In the spring of the next year, after an intense bombing
campaign, an international coalition led by U.S. forces drove Iraq
from Kuwait but stopped short of removing Hussein from power. A
series of uprisings against Hussein took place, mainly led by Shi'a
Iraqis in the east and south and Kurds in the north. The Bush
Administration had encouraged the revolts, but then learned that
many Shi'a rebels were directly supported by Iran. Believing, probably incorrectly, that an overthrow of Hussein's regime would lead
to a Shi'a Islamic state in Iraq, the administration pulled back and
Hussein crushed the rebels.[31]

Most telling of the changing times was Hussein's war cry—his
language was expressly Islamic, with no hint of the militant Ba'athist

secularism of the past. The nationalist dream was dead and he knew it. The masses all over the region rallied in his support, protesting the participation of Arab soldiers in a U.S.-led military effort.

The first Persian Gulf war gave new impetus to the drive for an Arab-Israeli peace agreement for several reasons. Arafat and the Palestinians had supported Hussein, and were abandoned by the Gulf states, weakening their position. The ejection of Palestinian workers from the Persian Gulf was a severe economic blow, given the importance of their remittances. The recent arrival of a million Russian Jews from the former USSR strengthened Israel's hand demographically, and the defeat of Iraq had strengthened its hand militarily. Yet the pressure was on Israel as well, and the Bush Administration had been insistent on compromise even before the war with Iraq. In May 1989 Secretary of State James Baker had drawn the line:

> For Israel, now is the time to lay aside, once and for all, the unrealistic vision of a greater Israel. Israeli interests in the West Bank and Gaza—security and otherwise—can be accommodated in a settlement based on [UN] Resolution 242.[32] Forswear annexation. Stop settlement activity . . . Reach out to the Palestinians as neighbors who deserve political rights.[33]

Israel did not have the resources to assimilate the new immigrants; it needed loan guarantees from the United States, and Bush made them dependent upon Israel's not using any of the money to expand settlements. He further pressured Israeli Prime Minister Yitzhak Rabin into attending a 1991 conference in Madrid focused around the principle of "Land for Peace" as the basis of an agreement with the Palestinians. Bush was not the first U.S. President to pressure Israel into compromise since the beginning of the United States–Israeli alliance in the 1960s. Carter had pressured Begin into giving the Sinai back to Egypt, and Reagan had pushed Israel to back down over Lebanon. Bush sought to end the problem once and for all.

The Madrid Conference and the follow-up Oslo Accords in 1993 led to a torturous "peace process" by which Israel and Yassir Arafat's PLO recognized each other, with Israel making staggered

Israel and Occupied Territories, 2001.

Courtesy of The General Libraries, The University of Texas at Austin.

pull-backs from the occupied territories of the West Bank and Gaza while Arafat used his new Palestinian Authority (PA) to crack down on Palestinian terrorists. The PA might have eventually become the government of an independent Palestinian state.

Neither side fulfilled its part of the bargain. Arafat initially cracked down hard on Palestinian militants and suppressed every hint of dissent, legitimate or otherwise. When Benyamin Netanyahu led the Likud back into power in 1996 after Rabin's assassination at the hand of a Zionist extremist, Arafat let up and attacks on Israeli citizens increased. Most Arabs opposed and continue to oppose the Oslo Accords. In the Palestinian territories the public was split but the Islamic-oriented were united in opposition to any compromise. So Islamist terrorism would not subside and could not be suppressed.

Israel never halted its creeping annexation of the West Bank and continued to expropriate land, one hilltop at a time. This increased the area of the West Bank over which Israel had security control, even though the PA obtained administrative control over population centers. Perhaps the most egregious example was the 1997 settlement in Hebron. The settlement put about eight hundred Israeli settlers in the middle of a town with 100,000 Palestinians. This effectively brought Israeli security control over all of the inhabitants, who concluded that at best they were headed toward autonomy status under permanent Israeli sovereignty.

Nor was Netanyahu willing to part with any significant part of the West Bank. At one point in 1997 he offered to withdraw from 4 percent of the West Bank initially with a total withdrawal of 13 percent. The Clinton Administration pushed for an initial withdrawal of 13 percent plus a final withdrawal from most of the occupied territories. This was too much and the negotiations collapsed.

The election of Ehud Barak, Israel's most decorated soldier, in 1997 raised many hopes. Barak offered to withdraw from 95 percent of the West Bank, but Israel would still maintain partial control over certain areas, including east Jerusalem. Arafat rejected the offer, and after a visit by Likud leader Ariel Sharon to a site holy to both Jews and Muslims in November 2000, the Palestinian territories exploded into a second intifada that included both violent mass demonstrations and suicide attacks against Israeli citizens. The continued violence and the sheer intensity of the Arab world's rejection of Barak's generous offer (as Israelis saw it) made him look like a fool, and Sharon himself became prime minister three months later. The violence has continued, and Sharon, a life-long supporter of settlement expansion, showed little inclination for compromise.

The 1990s saw the rise of the most successful anti-American terrorist organization to date, Osama bin Ladin's al-Qaeda ("the base"). Al-Qaeda was developed as an umbrella organization from the remnants of Bin Ladin's allies in Afghanistan. It became a highly disciplined, organized, and motivated organization present in at least seventy-six countries. Al-Qaeda has terrorism down to a science. Its manual is seven thousand pages long and includes details on such matters as how to handle grenades, mines, and other weapons; topography and land surveys; security, intelligence, and small-group tactics. Most funding comes from contributions, with Saudi nationals being the primary source. Al-Qaeda also makes money from crime and legitimate business investments.[34]

Ideologically, the rise of al-Qaeda can be explained by two series of events. One was the palpable failure of Islamists to take power in the Arab world. The idea was that since the United States props up repressive Arab regimes, and since killing other Muslims was always unpopular anyway, it would be better to attack the source. Two, the presence of Western companies in the Arabian Peninsula had always been a point of contention for Muslims, but after 1991 having non-Muslim troops stationed there as well was unacceptable. Bin Ladin also has made use of the Palestinian issue to draw support.

After taking refuge in Afghanistan, Bin Ladin relocated to the Sudan and then back to Afghanistan in 1996. Under the protection of the Wahhabi-tutored Taliban movement, which had taken over 90 percent of Afghanistan, al-Qaeda began to launch a large number of attacks on Western targets, many of which failed, and others that simply failed to get attention. Two that received coverage were the attacks on the U.S. embassies in Kenya and Tanzania in 1997. One ambitious scheme to blow up eleven airliners at once over the Pacific was foiled when a bomb went off in a member's apartment. Then several years of careful planning paid off when al-Qaeda was able to hijack and fly airliners into the World Trade Center and the Pentagon on September 11, 2001.

The success of the September 11 attacks shocked Americans, but it should not have done so. One plot had previously attempted to fly an airliner into the Eiffel Tower, and in 1995 Filipino intelligence officials warned the United States that al-Qaeda might be planning to fly planes into the Pentagon and the headquarters of the CIA.[35] A special report commissioned by the Bush Administration publicized in mid-2001 stressed that it was only a matter of when, not if, a major terrorist attack would hit the United States.

The (second) Bush Administration responded to this challenge in three ways. First, the administration launched a wide-ranging "war on terror" intended to deprive al-Qaeda and other militant Islamists of their sanctuaries, sources of support, and funding, a central element of which was the campaign in Afghanistan to remove the Taliban. That campaign has been mostly portrayed in the Arab media as a war against the Afghan people, and the larger effort as a war against Islam. Second, the administration prepared for and in early 2003 executed an invasion of Iraq that removed Saddam Hussein from power. Third, the administration has attempted to relaunch the Israeli-Palestinian peace process through a plan called the "Road Map" which outlines a series of reciprocal concessions the two sides are to make in order to create a lasting peace.

All three of these efforts are ongoing. Al-Qaeda's network has suffered some disruption and setbacks but continues to function. The United States is still in the early stages of an attempt to help Iraqis form a government that is stable, decent, and not threatening to its neighbors. And despite some early progress, the Israelis and Palestinians are far from a final settlement. The success or failure of these endeavors will weigh heavily on the future of the Arabs, and the world, for decades to come.

An Iraqi family.
Robert Fernea, photographer. CMES.

Notes

1. For a discussion of contemporary apocalyptic politics and their role in the Israeli-Palestinian conflict, see Gershom Gorenberg, *The End of Days: Fundamentalism and the Struggle for the Temple Mount* (New York: Oxford University Press, 2000).
2. Morris, *Righteous Victims*, 269–79.
3. Ibid., 259.
4. Ibid., 278.
5. Shlaim, *Iron Wall*, 82–3.
6. Morris, *Righteous Victims*, 289.
7. Kissenger, *Diplomacy*, 402, 538. The former page citation shows that FDR had the same concern.
8. Morris, *Righteous Victims*, 284.
9. Ibid., 304–5.
10. Ibid., 310.
11. Michael T. Klare, *Resource Wars: The New Landscape of Global Conflict* (New York: Metropolitan Books, 2001) 158–9.
12. Morris, *Righteous Victims*, 565.
13. For a general description of Hamas' history and ideology, see Shaul Mishal and Avraham Sela, *The Palestinian Hamas: Vision, Violence and Coexistence* (New York: Columbia University Press, 2000). Hamas is an acronym for *harakat muqawamat islamiyya*, or Islamic Resistance Movement. It should not be confused with the more moderate Algerian Hamas, which has the same initials in Arabic but stands for Movement for a Peaceful Society. *Hamas* is also a word that means "enthusiasm."
14. Space in this work is far too limited to provide anything more than a general survey of social and economic trends in the Arab world and a few examples from specific countries. Basic statistics may be obtained from the UN Human Development Index, www.undp.org. For a detailed evaluation see the *Arab Human Development Report 2002*, sponsored by the United Nations; http://www.undp.org/rbas/ahdr/english.html. For background on some issues mentioned herein, see Michael Field, *Inside the Arab World* (Cambridge, Massachusetts: Harvard University Press, 1995) 112–26.
15. Lewis, *What Went Wrong*, 47.
16. Robert D. Kaplan, *The Ends of the Earth: From Togo to Turkmenistan, From Iran to Cambodia—A Journey to the Frontiers of Anarchy* (New York: Vintage Books, 1997) 97.
17. For a detailed discussion of state conflict and water scarcity in the Arab world and elsewhere, see Klare, *Resource Wars*, 138–89.
18. See Michael C. Hudson, ed., *Middle East Dilemma: The Politics and Economics of Arab Integration* (New York: Columbia University Press, 1999).
19. Kiren Aziz Chaudhry, *The Price of Wealth: Economies and Institutions in the Middle East* (Ithaca: Cornell University Press, 1997) 7.
20. Anthony Shadid, *Legacy of the Prophet: Despots, Democrats and the New Politics of Islam* (Boulder, Colorado: Westview Press, 2001) 50–1.
21. Ibid., 56–61.
22. FIS leaders Madani and Ali Belhadj were released from prison in July 2003. Madani is probably too old to be a threat, but as described by *The Economist* (July 12–18), the younger Belhadj seems to have lost none of his fire: "[Belhadj]

stayed defiant throughout his prison years. His first act on release was to go to the television building in Algiers, where he was arrested in 1991 as he was about to reply to some allegations against him. He is said to have demanded from astounded employees the right of reply that was denied him by his arrest."

23. Thomas L. Friedman, *From Beirut to Jerusalem* (New York: Anchor Books, 1990) 76–107.

24. Robert D. Kaplan, *The Arabists: The Romance of an American Elite* (New York: The Free Press, 1995) 275.

25. Brian Crozier, *The Rise and Fall of the Soviet Empire* (Rocklin, California: Prima Publishing, 1999) 323–5.

26. Guy Arnold, *The Maverick State: Gaddafi and the New World Order* (London: Cassell, Wellington House, 1996) 12–22.

27. Ibid., 72, 74–78.

28. Ray Takeyh, "The Rogue Who Came in from the Cold" (*Foreign Affairs*, May/June 2001) 62–72.

29. See Shadid, *Legacy of the Prophet*, 111–50.

30. Kaplan, *Arabists*, 295.

31. It is only fair to note, however, that after the fall of Saddam Hussein in 2003, the faction still has influence, probably greater now than then. As reported by the *Financial Times* (July 19, 2003), Muqtada al-Sadr, a popular Shi'a clergyman, "asked the Shi'a population to set up their own governing council, supervised by clerics, to 'confront' the new body [approved by the U.S.-U.K. Coalition Provision Authority]."

32. United Nations Resolution 242, passed November 22, 1967, called upon Israel to "withdraw from territories conquered" in exchange for Arab recognition of Israel's right to exist.

33. Morris, *Righteous Victims*, 611.

34. Rohan Gunaratna, *Inside Al Qaeda: Global Network of Terror* (New York: Columbia University Press, 2002).

35. Gunaratna, *Inside Al Qaeda*, 181.

Reflections, Present and Future

Prospects for Democracy and Prosperity in the Arab World

At the beginning of the 1990s, as the Soviet bloc was collapsing, many predicted that the world was entering a new phase in human history, one in which there would be no alternative to liberal, free market democracy. This thesis was advanced most famously by Francis Fukuyama in his 1992 book *The End of History and the Last Man.*[1] In some regards, the theory appears to have been validated. The number of countries which have meaningful elections has increased significantly, and those few that stand firmly against the principle of governing with the consent of the governed seem increasingly isolated (e.g., North Korea and Cuba). In economic policy, the dominant free market approach has come under increasing attack. Yet the only models countries seriously consider seem to be variations on the same theme; the social market, the "Third Way," and so on.

Yet as the decade progressed it became clear that history would last a bit longer. Many countries held elections for the first time, and most turned to chaos, dysfunction, and, occasionally, genocide. Others appeared to make the transition, only to exemplify what Fareed Zakaria has called "illiberal democracy;"[2] countries hold elections, and those elected begin to restrict the press, dissolve legislatures, or persecute ethnic minorities.

A rooftop view in the city of Minya, Egypt.

J.J. Hobbs, photographer. CMES.

Economically, most countries grew wealthier during the 1990s, but about a third actually grew poorer, in some cases significantly more so. Robert D. Kaplan encapsulated a new theory of the future in his 1994 essay "The Coming Anarchy."[3] In explaining the failure of democracy in the developing world, Kaplan emphasized the long historical process by which the West developed the social capital (e.g., respect for the rule of law), legal norms (e.g., protection of property rights), and institutions (e.g., elected assemblies, independent judiciaries) which have made democracy easier to maintain. Countries with a political culture based upon authoritarian rule, violence, or tribal loyalties were not likely to successfully adopt in a few years, or even a few decades, a system that had taken Western countries centuries to develop.

Thus we return to the Arab world. Few if any Arab countries are sufficiently democratic to even be called an illiberal democracy. Some have held elections that are not a complete sham, but in none do freely elected officials hold real power. In most economic reforms seem too little, too late to overcome the accumulated obstacles of the past. As we saw in chapter eleven, non-petroleum related growth has not been substantial in most Arab countries. The question is why, and what can be done about it.

For many in the Arab world, and some in the West, the answer to the first question is clear—Arab societies are economically underdeveloped because of the latent legacy of colonialism. An alternative theory, very popular now, is that Western countries, especially the United States, have intentionally held Arab economies down. Yet the roots of underdevelopment go much deeper. Arab societies fell far behind the West long before they came under European rule. All the factors so important to modern economies— a predictable legal system that enforces contracts and property rights, an entrepreneurial culture, widespread literacy, a free market in both goods and labor—are just beginning to take shape. Moreover, the political elite in Arab societies has largely consisted of military juntas for over a thousand years before the United States entered the region. Since the 1950s, those countries that have had a close relationship with the United States are, on average, no more authoritarian than those hostile to the United States. Some argue that without American support some Arab states would have been forced to democratize earlier, but this seems unlikely. Egypt, which receives more U.S. aid than any other Arab country, was not on the verge of democratization in the late 1970s when it became a U.S. ally. Kuwait, which arguably has the most open elections, only began holding them after 1991 due to American pressure.

Perhaps, as Zakaria argues, we are looking for the wrong things. Focusing on elections, we confuse democracy with liberty and forget that historically economic progress has driven political development, not the other way around.[4] The more successful developing countries—such as South Korea, Taiwan, Singapore, and Malaysia—have provided their citizens with a great deal of liberty, including property rights, freedom to travel, and significant economic freedoms, without having democratic political systems (South Korea and Taiwan democratized in the 1980s and the 1990s, respectively). Japan has the rule of law, economic freedom, independent courts, and a free press, but Japan is not a democracy if that term includes having competitive elections. Thus constitutional and economic liberalism, a tandem Britain had during the eighteenth century when few in its middle class could vote, may allow countries to escape the trap of illiberal democracy.

It is not that European influences have not been significant. As we have seen, Arab leaders who came to power in the mid-twentieth century largely adopted their ways of thinking from the West. Nazism and fascism were rising in influence in the 1930s and 1940s,[5] and thereafter Soviet influences increased, and socialism became widely popular among elites. Another European ideology that took root was anti-Semitism. Historically, what we think of as anti-Semitism did not exist in the Arab world. Conflicts between Muslims and Jews existed, but they were less frequent than between Christians and Jews for certain. Today, in the Arab world one finds a visceral hatred of Jews that cannot be explained by real differences in national interests. Together, fascist-statism, socialism, and anti-Semitism have made for a dangerous mix. Tragically, having decided to adopt European ideologies, Arab elites adopted the wrong ones.

Furthermore, in addition to the challenges that all developing countries face, in the Arab world there is also the issue of Islam and democracy. As noted in chapter four, the *shari'a* political model was based upon Muhammad's rule in Medina and that of his

246

early successors. The caliph would rule the Islamic nation, or *umma*, as Muhammad's political successor, advised by the *ulama*, who inherited his authority to declare what the will of God was. The caliph's chief duties were the implementation of the *shari'a* domestically and the execution of *jihad* externally. The concept of democracy was known to the medieval *ulama*, as many Muslim scholars were well read in the Greek classics. But unlike the philosophical musings of Plato, Aristotle, and Socrates, they had no need for democracy, as it was viewed as inconsistent with the divine model (and it could not have helped that the great philosophers themselves were critics of democracy[6]). Indeed, in Islamic law, there could be no democracy, for there was, politically speaking, no *demos*. The concept of popular sovereignty did not exist, nor did the principle of having individual rights that could be enforced against the ruler, enshrined in the Anglo-American tradition by the Magna Carta in 1215.

In modern times many Muslim intellectuals have rethought the issue and sought to reconcile Islam and democracy.[7] One theory is that Muhammad only took on a military role due to the persecution early Muslims faced. It may be that had he been allowed to propagate his religion peacefully, Muhammad would never have taken up the sword, and Muslim history would have been radically different. However, history being what it is, Islam and the military-religious state grew up together, and untangling them is going to be very difficult. Whereas Christianity did not get entangled in martial matters until three centuries after its founding, Islam had warfare as its background from its second decade.

Another argument for congruency is the unstructured nature of Islam. There is no formal religious structure in Islam, no mechanism by which orthodoxy can be enforced; therefore, Muslims ought to be able to make their own way. Yet this fails to consider the opposite implication. In the absence of a non-state religious unit, the conceptualization of the *umma* as the basis of political identity leads to the state itself merging state functions with religious ones by default, for there is no other institution to fulfill them.

For those thinking that democracy can be easily transplanted globally (such as in Iraq), an analogy to a previous experience in Vietnam might be useful. As Henry Kissinger wrote in explaining why America failed to build democracy in that country,[8]

The underpinning of a pluralistic society is consensus on underlying values, which implicitly sets a limit to the claims of competing individuals and groups. . . . In the West, political pluralism had thrived among cohesive societies where a strong social consensus had been in place long enough to permit tolerance for the opposition without threatening the survival of the state.

Thus, to the extent that Islamists base their agenda on the *shari'a* (and all important Arab ones do), I do not believe that they are compatible with democracy, because the *shari'a* rejects the possibility of a social consensus broader than itself. Indonesia and Turkey have often been given as examples of the compatibility between Islam and democracy. Yet in both countries Islamic legal norms were ruthlessly repressed before democratic norms took hold (Turkey's current prime minister, Tayyip Erdogan, a former Islamist, explicitly rejected implementing the *shari'a* before taking office). Herein lies the paradox of applying Western norms of religious freedom in the Muslim world; where Islamists seek to implement the *shari'a*, it does no good to tell them not to restrict the religious freedoms of others, for building an Islamic state is itself part of their religion. Therefore, whereas elsewhere the problem is the imperfection of democracy in practice, in the Muslim world there is a model that claims to be a superior alternative to liberal democracy. It is only fair to note that there are well-informed observers who hold a different opinion in regard to Islam and democracy.[9] It should also be noted that there is no similar debate about Islam and capitalism; the two are clearly compatible.

The best approach is to encourage economic liberalization, the development of independent and transparent financial institutions, the securing of property rights, the protection of basic civil freedoms, and the slow and incremental but steady opening of public space for non-governmental, non-Islamist political, commercial, and civic organizations. Where all dissent has been suppressed, Islamists have gained influence because their insuppressible religious networks make them the focal point of discontent. By encouraging the development of a bourgeois middle class with an interest in stability and progress, Arab states may be able to escape the dilemma of over-rapid democratization or stagnation through

A single-family home in Jordan.
Ann Grabhorn-Friday, photographer. CMES.

repression. This approach does not guarantee development, as economic growth also requires intangible social capital that cannot be created by governments, but it is probably the safest route.

Since the study of the past would be of little practical use if it were no help in dealing with the future, some prognostications are in order. The Persian Gulf countries other than Saudi Arabia—Kuwait, Oman, Bahrain, Qatar, and the United Arab Emirates—are the best placed to compete in the global arena. Absent a resurgent Iran or Iraq destabilizing the region, they may do well. Outside the gulf, Tunisia, with its growing economy, proximity to Europe, and distance from Palestine, is well placed to enter the ranks of moderately developed nations. Lebanon has recovered well in the last decade, and with the withdrawal of Israel in 2000, it may again earn the moniker "The Switzerland of the Middle East" if Hizbullah can be contained. Jordan's enlightened despotism may lead it to

Looking east across the Nile in Cairo.
Caroline Williams, photographer. CMES.

greater growth if the situations in Iraq and Palestine ever settle down, but until then the kingdom will continue to struggle. Egypt's fiscal position improved significantly in the 1990s and its reforms accelerated, so there is some hope there. Elsewhere, dramatic changes would have to take place for optimism to be justified.

War and Peace in the Middle East

In diplomacy, it is first necessary to identify the fundamental interests of the opposing party, not as one wishes them to be or thinks they ought to be, but as they are objectively. Thus, for Israel, it makes no difference that Palestinian nationalism was invented as a reaction to Zionism, or that Arab countries easily possess sufficient land and resources to resettle the three million Palestinians now in the occupied territories. What matters is that even moderate Palestinians will accept nothing less than a sovereign, territorially viable state in Palestine. Likewise, for the Palestinians, it makes no difference that their families lived for centuries in what is now the state of Israel, or that in some cases their parents and grandparents were forced out at gunpoint by Jewish soldiers. What matters is that the return of Palestinian refugees to Israel proper would destroy Israel as a Jewish state. Thus, it is not reasonable to expect anything more than monetary compensation for the refugees. To demand that the other side abolish itself is not negotiation.

As much as many Americans find involvement in the conflict undesirable, the reality is that there is nothing either side can do unilaterally that will bring peace; a firm hand from the outside is necessary. If Israel were to pull back from the occupied territories unilaterally, this would encourage Hamas and the Al-Aqsa Martyrs' Brigade to step up attacks on Israeli citizens. It must be remembered that although there are Palestinians who are willing to compromise, the purpose of the terrorist attacks is to destroy Israel, not pressure a more reasonable settlement. Indeed, some attacks have been timed to coincide with Israeli elections in order to ensure the election of hard-line Israeli parties, such as the Likud, which are less willing to make compromises necessary for peace.

On the other hand, throughout the 1990s Israel continued to expropriate Palestinian land, expand West Bank settlements, and, in some cases, bulldoze Palestinians' homes to make way for them. There are now 250,000 Israelis living in the West Bank. Hence, Palestinians would argue that even when they were suppressing terrorists, Israel maintained its expansionism. In order for there to be any chance for peace at all, a firm outside hand is necessary in order to ensure reciprocal compliance.

That American involvement is in the national interest cannot be doubted. Although the United States, unlike Britain, bears no culpability for creating the problem, America will be blamed in the Arab world if things go wrong. It is widely believed in the region that the United States controls both the Israeli and Arab governments. In the 1940s Ibn Sa'ud's subjects wanted him to pressure the United States over the situation, even though American governmental influence on the Zionist movement was negligible. This has changed, and since 1967 the United States has obtained significant, if often exaggerated, influence over Israel. There should be no doubt who will be blamed if no just compromise is found.

251

In order to achieve this goal, in 2002 the Bush administration, along with the United Nations, the European Union (EU), and Russia, proposed a plan called the "Road Map" that required reciprocal compromises and confidence-building measures, including a pullback of settlements and a clampdown by Palestinians on Hamas. Although sound in theory, prospects for its success are limited by the same factors that have driven enmity between the two sides in the past. Israel's prime minister, Ariel Sharon, as well as most of his coalition partners, are ardent supporters of settlement expansion. Despite some recent affectations of moderation necessary to please the United States, there is little reason to think that they will ever make the complete settlement pullbacks necessary for a deal.

Prospects for realism are worse on the Palestinian side. At least in Israel public opinion is clearly in favor of compromise. The elevation of the moderate Mahmud Abbas as prime minister of the Palestinian Authority (PA) was a positive step, and the administration's decision to sideline Arafat was both wise and long overdue. Yet the major Palestinian demand recently is that Israel release six thousand prisoners, many of whom are admittedly members of terrorist organizations. The very fact that Abbas is negotiating a cease-fire with Hamas, rather than imposing one and liquidating the organization, shows that the Road Map will go no further. Hamas accepts that tactical compromises are necessary for the achievement of its goals of destroying Israel and erecting an Islamic state over all of Palestine. Although Israeli extremists have influence, they are a clear minority of the public. But those that westerners call "extremists" among the Palestinians are perilously close to the center. Across the Arab world, in the mainstream press it is customary to describe suicide bombers as *shuhada*—martyrs.

This problem is further aggravated by the EU's refusal to criminalize Hamas' political wing. Focusing on Hamas' pragmatism in internal social and political affairs ignores a key fact—a terrorist organization with a school and a medical clinic is more dangerous, not less so, than one with just a military wing. Such institutions both garner it greater public support and give it a cover for military operations.[10]

The only plan with a chance must begin with reciprocal steps from each side that provide the other with an irrevocable indication of its good faith. Israel must withdraw all settlements from the West Bank and the Gaza Strip, and the PA must wage a relentless campaign to eliminate, not conciliate, groups like Hamas that are opposed in principle to compromise. Because Arafat's security forces far outnumber Hamas' militants, they can do the job if they have the will. Having shown its own good faith, Israel can maintain a militarized buffer zone until the Palestinians have done this. Palestinian refugees should be compensated by a fund supported by the United States, the EU, Israel, and the Arab League. Americans opposed to making payments to the Palestinians should understand that we are doing this because it is in our own interest, not out of guilt or altruism. This would resolve all major legitimate issues other than that of Jerusalem, an issue on which the two sides are so far apart that compromise in the near future is inconceivable.

Such a partial settlement could give way to an uneasy peace like that which exists between Pakistan and India in Kashmir, or between China and Taiwan, in which the two sides have irreconcilable disagreements, but implicitly agree not to resolve them by force. This scenario is not ideal (especially considering that Pakistan and India have been on the verge of war), but it is the best scenario that is realistic under current circumstances.

The United States in the Arab World

The central role of the United States globally is the maintenance of financial and economic networks, plus the protection of sea lanes and natural resources essential to the global economy. The economic element of this role is a venture widely shared with others. The security element, however, is largely borne by the United States, and is beneficial to every industrial and industrializing economy that is not resource self-sufficient. This role also requires a military presence in the Persian Gulf, creating a genuinely massive security conundrum.

Whereas in many countries American military presence is either appreciated or, if resented, is primarily so because of practical negative effects on the local population, in Muslim countries American military presence is problematic by its mere existence.

An old storyteller in Iraq.

Robert Fernea, photographer. CMES.

This should have surprised no one in the post-World War II foreign policy establishment. When Britain occupied parts of the Arab world, the negative reaction was intense, despite the fact that the British were no more brutal than the Ottomans, and in some regards improved material conditions. America would replace Britain in more ways than one.

Prior to 1991, the American commercial presence was resented by some, but its financial benefits made resentment easy to ignore. The only military presence was a naval base in Bahrain, and security concerns were handled by the "Over the Horizon" approach which provided that the United States could provide security without a significant presence merely by the threat of intervention (called the "Carter doctrine").[11] Since Iraq's invasion of Kuwait in 1991 showed this to be an inadequate deterrent, a greater military presence was maintained, mainly in Saudi Arabia, home to Mecca and Medina. This violated a 1,350-year rule, established by the caliph Umar I, against a non-Muslim presence in the Arabian Peninsula, especially a military presence. It also offended the traditional Islamic self-perception regarding the necessity of the rule of Islam. The creation of al-Qaeda was a direct consequence of this tension.

This is not to say that Islamist movements are merely a reaction to American primacy. The precursors to modern Islamist movements predated Western impact. The rise of Western power has galvanized these movements by being a permanent reminder of the Muslim world's relative weakness, and by permeating the Arab world with Western culture, much of it reasonably viewed as corrosive to traditional Arab society. Many Arabs, especially the young, find elements of American culture attractive. Globalization has vastly amplified this phenomenon, making Western power, wealth, and values unavoidable. This makes the offense to Islamists all the greater.

The other side of this tension is the unavoidability, in the short term, of Western dependence on Persian Gulf petroleum. In 1999 five Persian Gulf countries—Saudi Arabia, Iraq, Iran, Kuwait, and the UAE—held 62 percent of global petroleum reserves. Saudi Arabia alone possessed 25 percent (the United States has 2.9 percent, about the same as Libya).[12] Their aggregate share is expected to increase, not decrease, over the next fifty years. Diversification

A movie theater in downtown Amman, Jordan featuring a film by
Clint Eastwood.

J. A. Miller, photographer. CMES.

of supply by greater importation from other regions alone will not help enough to remove the security risk.

Nor can the dilemma be solved soon by increasing fuel efficiency. Technologies now exist, and can be further developed, that will reduce petroleum consumption, especially in the transportation sector. Yet transportation only accounts for about 45 percent of world consumption, with most of the rest used in industry.[13] Thus even if the United States could reduce its transportation-related consumption by a third, an ambitious target itself, that would not reduce dependence on the Persian Gulf enough. Arguably the best substitute for industrial use is atomic energy, but this option has serious drawbacks. These include its ease of transition to military purposes by developing countries, thus aiding nuclear proliferation, and the vulnerability of plants to devastating terrorist attacks.

Security analysis should therefore assume the need to intervene in the Persian Gulf until at least 2050. The pacification of Iraq is an important step in this process. The invasion was necessitated by the fact that American forces could not stay in Saudi Arabia much longer without risking a major upheaval. The United States thus has three goals in Iraq: the prevention of a Ba'athist return to power, the prevention of the rise of an Islamic state, and averting the splintering of the country. This means that American forces must stay in Iraq as long as necessary to institute a government strong enough to hold the country together, but decent enough to no longer pose a threat to its neighbors or its own people. This also means that, whatever the costs, parties based on Shi'a Islamic rule cannot be allowed.

Since the successful invasion in early 2003 there has been some criticism over the issue of Iraq's possession of weapons of mass destruction. Yet if it turns out, as Iraqi scientists have said, that Iraq destroyed all the illegal weapons in the year before the attack, this maneuver will show that only under a real threat of invasion did Saddam Hussein disarm. The United States certainly could not have pulled its forces back, allowing Iraq to reinitiate its nuclear program at a later time. In any case, the fact itself cannot be definitely confirmed given the passage of unmonitored cargo trains between Iraq and Syria in the weeks before the war. There have also been concerns raised by the increase in American

An Iraqi man harvesting wheat.
Robert Fernea, photographer. CMES.

Iraqi women carrying brush.
Robert Fernea, photographer. CMES.

casualties after Baghdad fell, with about one American dying every day, but this must be kept in perspective. In 2000, 42,000 Americans died in automobile accidents, an average of 114 per day.[14] Oil drives the modern economy, and petroleum security has its costs.

Saudi Arabia may be more difficult than Iraq. The influx of massive oil wealth has turned the Saudi-Wahhabi alliance, before essentially a zealous group of desert bandits, into the Frankenstein monster of modern Islam. The Saudi political elite has bought peace by allowing the Wahhabis to fund schools and religious foundations across the Muslim world that advocate their militant version of Islam. The Saudi elite is divided between those who favor accommodation with the contemporary world and those sympathetic to the Wahhabi cause. Recent crackdowns on militants have been taken as a positive note, but the problem has not been the direct funding of terrorism or tolerance of terrorism in Saudi Arabia, but the propagation of a dangerous ideology everywhere else. Whether the world can get the Saudis to cut off the flow remains to be seen.

The containment of the Islamic Republic of Iran is a third Persian Gulf problem that must be managed. Unlike in Iraq before the fall of Saddam Hussein, there is a chance for peaceful resolution of tensions from the inside. The Iranian people are growing increasingly resentful of clerical rule, and they may succeed in transforming Iran into a peaceful, democratic state on their own. If they fail, the United States will likely face a hostile and nuclear-armed Iran within five years. By July 2003 it was clear that Iran had produced uranium metal, a heavy-water research reactor necessary for weapons-grade plutonium but not needed for civilian purposes, and was building a uranium enrichment plant, all key elements of a nuclear program.[15] If that situation does not resolve itself, the United States will consider a preemptive attack. A nuclear armed Iran would be able to easily intimidate Persian Gulf countries, forcing the United States to maintain forces in the region, which would be both expensive and destabilizing to station there, as well as vulnerable to direct nuclear attack. Iran could also incinerate Tel Aviv, bringing about a second Holocaust.

The relationship of violence to Islam is a further issue that is relevant both to political development and regional conflicts. In terms of terrorism, the doctrinal answer is easy. There is a widely accepted hadith in which Muhammad prohibits his warriors from attacking noncombatants. This was quoted on Qatar's *Al-Jazeera* by a Muslim scholar shortly after the 9/11 attacks. Yet this does not resolve the issue, as the *shari'a* doctrine of *jihad*, while banning the killing of innocents, commands offensive war in order to expand Muslim rule. Some of al-Qaeda's attacks that have been called "terrorist" have been against military installations, and would therefore be valid if executed by a state at war. Indeed, Bin Ladin had declared war against the United States. It is worth noting that even after the bombings in Kenya and Tanzania, which Bin Ladin openly praised, he remained quite popular in the Arab world. Declaring such attacks to be the work of a few marginalized extremists is not entirely accurate.

I am not arguing that conflict is inevitable. Despite the many wars, the fourteen-century history of Western-Muslim relations has also been marked by long periods of peace and commercial cooperation. Yet this was not due to any common values held by the two sides, but was due to self-interest. Now it is mainly just Arab elites who have an interest in cooperation. As the middle classes grow, so may the basis for cooperation.

The role of the human rights movement is potentially important but indeterminate. Many contemporary Muslim thinkers have rethought *jihad*, and have recast the doctrine purely in terms of self-defense. The doctrine was certainly about self-defense when Muhammad first declared it, although this interpretation is not what *jihad* has meant under Islamic law. Of greater importance is abolishing the association between Muslim belief and political rule. As it is the function of any state to wage war, a religion that is institutionally identified with state power will inevitably feel the need to resort to violence, as any state must.

Yet westerners enthusiastic about the potential for human rights movements to resolve these issues should be cautious. It is widely believed in the Arab world that there is a worldwide cultural war against Islam that aims to replace Islamic values with Western culture.[16] Absent success by Muslim reformers at reconciling Islam with international norms, an overt attempt by Western activists to push their own liberal version of Islam is certain to cause a backlash.

An Iraqi man with his coffee pot.
Robert Fernea, photographer. CMES.

There are further problems. The Bush administration has adopted a "Domino Theory" of democracy, arguing that establishing democracy in Iraq could act as a catalyst for democratization and the peaceful resolution of conflicts throughout the region. This approach, although rhetorically appealing, is naive and will likely have negligible or negative repercussions.[17] Continued cooperation with authoritarian regimes, which will continue to be necessary, will only fuel charges of American hypocrisy. Democracy is unlikely to arise soon, and were it to do so, it would probably set the region on fire. Almost all Arab governments are more liberal than their populations. In recent elections in Kuwait, a country with close ties to the West, Islamists and tribal parties won by a landslide. Egypt and Jordan's peace treaties with Israel are opposed by a strong majority of both countries' populations. We would do well to remember how the voting publics of Britain, France, and Germany cheered the rush to war in 1914.

As this book was going to press Mahmud Abbas was resigning as Palestinian prime minister after Arafat refused to support his attempts to clamp down on Palestinian terrorists. If this turn of events continues, the "Road Map" will be at a dead end. The U.S. should respond by continuing to pressure Israel to pull back West Bank settlements in order to leave a chance for future moderation among the Palestinian leadership. However, the U.S. should not deal with Arafat, who as recently as 2002 was authorizing funding for the Al-Aqsa Martyrs' Brigade. Israeli Defense Minister Shaul Mofaz has stated that he wants to deport or otherwise eliminate Arafat. Perhaps the U.S., which has protected Arafat to this point, should allow his forced removal on condition of significant Israeli pullbacks from the occupied territories.

Ultimately, the United States will need a long-term exit strategy from the Persian Gulf. The problems with which westerners and Arabs struggle will not be solved soon, but they can be managed and their human and material costs to all minimized. Managing the Palestinian issue would relieve but not eliminate the tensions, and the recent removal of U.S. troops from Saudi Arabia should help. Yet it is reasonable to expect that the tensions which created America's security dilemmas in the region will not be resolved until, decades hence, the large-scale Western presence in that region can be withdrawn.

262

Notes

1. Francis Fukuyama, *The End of History and the Last Man* (New York: The Free Press, 1992).
2. Fareed Zakaria, *The Future of Freedom: Illiberal Democracy at Home and Abroad* (New York: W.W. Norton & Company, 2003). Zakaria first expounded the theory in his article, "The Rise of Illiberal Democracy," in the November/December 1997 issue of *Foreign Affairs*.
3. Robert D. Kaplan, *The Coming Anarchy: Shattering the Dreams of the Post-Cold War* (New York: Vintage Books, 2001). The book was an expansion of his February 1994 essay in *The Atlantic Monthly*. Kaplan gives country-specific application of this theory in three very readable socio-political commentaries disguised as travel books; *Balkan Ghosts: A Journey Through History* (New York: Vintage Books, 1994), *The Ends of the Earth: From Togo to Turkmenistan, from Iran to Cambodia, a Journey to the Frontiers of Anarchy* (New York: Vintage Books, 1997), and *Eastward to Tartary: Travels in the Balkans, the Middle East, and the Caucasus* (New York: Vintage Books, 2000). He expanded upon the argument in more strategic terms in *Warrior Politics: Why Leadership Requires a Pagan Ethos* (New York: Random House, 2001).
4. Zakaria, *Future of Freedom*, 29–58.
5. Robert S. Wistrich, "The Old-New Anti-Semitism," in *The National Interest* (Number 72, Summer 2003) 59–70.
6. This is exemplified most clearly in Plato's work, inaptly translated in English as *The Republic*, in which the state was to be ruled by a small elite of philosopher-kings called "guardians."
7. See, for example, Khaled Abou El Fadl, *And God Knows the Soldiers: The Authoritative and Authoritarian in Islamic Discourses* (Lanham, Maryland: The University Press of America, 2001), and Bassam Tibi, *The Challenge of Fundamentalism: Political Islam and the New World Disorder* (Berkeley: University of California Press, 1998).
8. Kissinger, *Diplomacy*, 655, 639.
9. John L. Esposito, *The Islamic Threat: Myth or Reality?* (New York: Oxford University Press, 1992). More recently, see Anthony Shadid, *Legacy of the Prophet: Despots, Democrats, and the New Politics of Islam* (Boulder, Colorado: Westview Press, 2001), and Noah Feldman, *After Jihad: America and the Struggle for Islamic Democracy* (New York: Farrar, Straus & Giroux, 2003).
10. This may be coming to an end, as Germany has now agreed to a complete ban. However, France and Belgium continue to argue, illogically, that Hamas' political wing is only for "charity work." *The Wall Street Journal* (September 5, 2003) A7.
11. Klare, *Resource Wars*, 33.
12. Ibid., 44–5.
13. Ibid., 36–7. The percentage for the U.S. is higher than this, but not enough to affect the analysis here.
14. This is according to the U.S. Department of Transportation. www.fhwa.dot.gov/pressroom/fhwa0133
15. *The Economist*, 42 (July 12–18, 2003).
16. For example, a cover-page article in the April 11, 1997, issue of *al-Mujtama'* (The Society), a London-based Islamist magazine, was titled "The American

Plan to Limit Muslim Fertility." It dealt with the background to the 1997 Cairo conference on population control which, although supported by the United States, was most strongly supported by European countries.

17. Ironically, on the same day that President Bush gave a speech about his plan to establish democracy in Iraq on March 14, 2003, a State Department official leaked to the *Los Angeles Times* a classified report titled "Iraq, The Middle East and Change: No Dominoes," saying it would not work.

Glossary of Arabic Terms

adab: The literary culture of Arab society. *Adib* refers to a cultured person, specifically in regard to literature.

ahl al-hadith: Scholars specializing in the collection and authentification of hadith.

ahl al-kitab: Literally, "people of the book"—Jews, Christians and other monotheists; called *dhimmi* when granted autonomous religious status on condition of acceptance of Muslim rule.

Allah: "The God"; the one God of Islam.

amir: Literally "prince," but depending on context the term may refer to the ruler of a political subunit, subordinate to the caliph, or a military leader, or a political leader, as in *amir al-mu'minun*, commander of the faithful.

Ansar: "Helpers," refers to those Muslims who prepared the way for Muhammad in Medina. See *Muhajirun*.

Arab/Arabic: *Arab* is an adjective used to describe persons and most inanimate objects or concepts (culture, food, etc.). Arabic is an adjective used primarily with words dealing with language—the Arabic script, an Arabic dictionary, etc.

Dar al-Salaam/Dar al-Harb: House of Peace, and House of War, referring to the realms of Islam and non-Muslim territories, usually Europe, respectively.

dhimmi: See *ahl al-kitab*.

fatwa: A legal opinion given by a religious scholar (*mufti*), often in order to guide a judicial decision but sometimes as a general political or religious statement.

fiqh: Islamic jurisprudence; *usul al-fiqh* are the tools to understanding Islamic law, and a *faqih* is an interpreter of *fiqh*.

ghazi: Meaning "holy warrior," like *mujahid*, a term used when speaking of Turkic warriors.

hadith: A report regarding something which the prophet Muhammad either said, did, or implicitly approved by allowing it to take place in his presence.

hajj: An annual pilgrimage to Mecca, which every Muslim is obligated to perform at least once in his lifetime if circumstances permit. This is one of the five pillars of Islam.

Hanafi/Hanbali/Shafi'i/Maliki: The four primary schools of law in Sunni Islam.

hijra year: In calendrical terms, *Hijra* refers to Muhammad's immigration to Medina in A.D. 622. The Muslim calender, which is based on the lunar cycle, counts this year as the beginning of year 1. Because the lunar calender is shorter than the solar year used by the West, the two do not correspond in a linear fashion. Thus September 2003 coincided with A.H. 1423, not 1381. Most Arab newspapers today provide both dates.

hiyal: A legal device or trick by which impractical legal rules can be bypassed.

ijma': Meaning "consensus," it is a method by which Muslims can come to a rule of law where no other rule applies.

imam: A term dating from pre-Islamic Arabia which means "leader" or "model." In current usage it refers to either a Muslim leading others in prayer, or a Muslim religious leader more generally.

Islam/Muslim: The term *Islam* means "submission," and a *muslim* is one who submits, implicitly to God. Thus, *Islam* is the religion, and a *Muslim* is someone who believes in it.

isnad: Chain of human transmitters which is intended to verify the authenticity of a *hadith*.

jihad: A term meaning "struggle," which can refer to religious purification. In Islamic public law it refers to the principle that Muslims have a duty to spread Muslim rule by conquest and defend Muslim lands from conquest by non-Muslims.

jizya: A poll tax paid by non-Muslims living under Muslim rule. See *ahl al-kitab*.

Kharijite: A member of a violent and radically egalitarian Muslim sect which was very important in Islam's early centuries.

khutba: The Friday sermon which has taken on political significance because the name of the recognized ruler is often mentioned during the prayers.

mosque: Literally "a place of prostration," the term refers to a Muslim place of worship. A mosque can be a magnificent structure equivalent to a cathedral, or nothing more than a piece of ground set aside for prayer.

Mu'atezila: A rationalist philosophical school emphasizing free will which was prominent for a limited time during the Abbasid period.

mufti: A legal scholar who delivers a legal opinion, or *fatwa*, on some aspect of Islamic law.

Muhajirun: Refers to those who converted to Islam in Mecca before Muhammad's *hijra* to Medina. See *Ansar*.

mujahid: A generic term meaning "holy warrior," it is applied in any context where a Muslim fights in a religiously sanctioned war. The plural *mujahiddin* has recently come to be used to specifically refer to Afghans and other Muslims who fought against the Soviet Union, but the term is generic. See *jihad* and *ghazi*.

mujtahid: A jurisprudential expert who "struggles" to develop a rule of law. The term is sometimes used interchangeably with *mufti*.

muwali (singular *mawla*): Client; used historically to refer to non-Arab converts to Islam prior to the Abbasid period who were forced to attach themselves to an Arab tribe.

qiyas: Analogy; a methodological tool used in Islamic law. See *usul al-fiqh*.

sabiqa: A term meaning "precedence" which in early Islam referred to the principle that those who converted early and suffered with Muhammad should rule the Muslim polity.

salat: Prayer; ritually it refers to the obligation to recite five set prayers during certain times of the day, and is one of the five pillars of Islam.

sawm: Fasting; another of the five pillars of Islam. It means that Muslims are to fast during the daylight hours during the lunar month of Ramadan.

shahada: Testimony; in Islamic terms, it is the first pillar of Islam: "I testify that there is no god but God, and Muhammad is the messenger of God." It must be repeated twice in front of Muslim witnesses in order for one to become a Muslim.

shari'a: Refers to substantive law regulating many aspects of Muslim life, including family law, inheritance, criminal law, and commercial relations.

sharif: a descendent of Muhammad.

Shi'a (also Shia, Shiite, or Shi'ite): Refers to Muslims who believe that leadership of the Muslim nation rightfully belonged to Ali and his descendants. Today most live in Iraq or Iran.

shura: A term meaning "consultation" which refers to a rule of governance derived from a verse in the Quran describing how believers manage their affairs. In historical practice it has meant only consultation, but in the modern period has been advocated by some as a principle of Islamic democracy.

Sufi/Sufism: Refers to a mystical form of Islam that emphasizes asceticism and spiritual connection with God. Usually viewed as a supplement to observance of Islamic law, Sufism has sometimes been practiced as an alternative.

Sunna: A term that means "tradition" and refers collectively to all traditions about Muhammad. This is the origin of the term *Sunni Muslim*.

tariqa: Literally "a way," in religious terms it refers to a Sufi brotherhood.

ulama (singular *alim*): Religious scholars collectively viewed as having the authority to declare and delineate Islamic law.

umma: A term literally meaning "nation," it is often rendered as "Islamic community." This book renders it "Islamic nation" due to its political connotations.

usul al-fiqh: Refers to the four primary sources of Islamic law; the Quran, the Sunna, *qiyas* (analogy), and *ijma'* (consensus).

zakat: Literally "alms," this term is used to refer to the Muslim obligation to give 2 percent of one's income to the poor, usually in the form of a tax to the state. *Zakat* is another of the five pillars of Islam.

Bibliography

Afkhami, Mahnaz, ed. *Faith & Freedom: Women's Human Rights in the Muslim World*. Syracuse: Syracuse University Press, 1995.

Ahmad, Akbar S. and Hastings Donnan, eds. *Islam, Globalization and Postmodernity*. London: Routledge, 1994.

Ajami, Fouad. *The Arab Predicament: Arab Political Thought and Practice Since 1967*. 3rd ed. Cambridge: Cambridge University Press, 1992.

———. *The Dream Palace of the Arabs: A Generation's Odyssey*. New York: Vintage Books, 1999.

Al-Khalil, Samir. *Republic of Fear: The Inside Story of Saddam's Iraq*. New York: Pantheon Books, 1989.

Al-Marayati, Abid A., ed. *International Relations of the Middle East and North Africa*. Cambridge, MA: Schenkman Publishing Company, Inc., 1984.

Al-Rasheed, Madawi. *A History of Saudi Arabia*. Cambridge: Cambridge University Press, 2002.

Al-Sayyid-Marsot, Afaf Lutfi. "The British Occupation of Egypt from 1882." In *The Oxford History of the British Empire: The Nineteenth Century*. Andrew Porter, editor. New York: Oxford University Press, 1999.

Ali, Maulana Muhammad. *The Holy Quran: Arabic Text, English Translation and Commentary*. Lahore: Ahmadiyyah Anjuman Isha'at Islam, 1995.

271

Angold, Michael. *Byzantium: The Bridge from Antiquity to the Middle Ages*. New York: St. Martin's Press, 2001.

Arian, Asher. *Security Threatened: Surveying Israeli Opinion on Peace and War*. Cambridge Studies in Political Psychology and Public Opinion. Cambridge: Cambridge University Press and the Jaffee Center for Strategic Studies, Tel Aviv University, 1995.

Armstrong, Karen. *Muhammad: A Biography of the Prophet*. New York: HarperCollins, 1992.

Arnold, Guy. *The Maverick State: Gaddafi and the New World Order*. London: Cassell, 1996.

Ayubi, Nazih N. *Over-stating the Arab State: Politics and Society in the Middle East*. London: I.E. Tauris Publishers, 1995.

Barakat, Halim. *The Arab World: Society, Culture and State*. Berkeley: University of California Press, 1993.

Bierman, Irene A. *Writing Signs: The Fatimid Public Text*. Berkeley: University of California Press, 1998.

Burgat, Francois and William Dowell. *The Islamic Movement In North Africa*. Austin: Center for Middle Eastern Studies, The University of Texas at Austin, 1993.

Butt, Gerald. *The Lion in the Sand: The British in the Middle East*. London: Bloomsbury Publishing, 1995.

Cameron, Averil. *The Mediterranean World in Late Antiquity A.D. 395–600*. Routledge History of the Ancient World. London: Routledge, 1993.

Chaudhry, Kiren Aziz. *The Price of Wealth: Economies and Institutions in the Middle East*. Ithaca: Cornell University Press, 1997.

Choueiri, Youssef M. *Islamic Fundamentalism*. Twayne's Themes in Right-Wing Politics and Ideology Series. Boston: Twayne Publishers, 1990.

Cook, Michael. *Muhammad*. New York: Oxford University Press, 1983.

Crozier, Brian. *The Rise and Fall of the Soviet Empire*. Rocklin, CA: Prima Press, 1999.

Dallal, Ahmed. "Science, Medicine, and Technology: The Making of a Scientific Culture." In *The Oxford History of Islam*. John Esposito, editor. New York: Oxford University Press, 1999.

Denny, Frederick Mathewson. *An Introduction to Islam*. 2nd ed. New York: Macmillan, 1994.

Entelis, John P., ed. *Islam, Democracy, and the State in North Africa.* Indianapolis: Indiana State University, 1997.

Esposito, John L. *Islam: The Straight Path.* 2nd ed. New York: Oxford University Press, 1991.

———. *Islam and Politics.* Contemporary Issues in the Middle East. 3rd ed. Syracuse: Syracuse University Press, 1984.

———. *The Islamic Threat: Myth or Reality?* New York: Oxford University Press, 1992.

———, ed. *The Oxford History of Islam.* New York: Oxford University Press, 1999.

Fernández-Armesto, Felipe. *Columbus and the Conquest of the Impossible.* London: Phoenix Press, 1974.

Fernea, Elizabeth Warnock, ed. *Children in the Muslim Middle East.* Austin: University of Texas Press, 1995.

———. *Guests of the Sheik: An Ethnography of an Iraqi Village.* New York: Anchor Books, 1969.

Field, Michael. *Inside the Arab World.* Cambridge, MA: Harvard University Press, 1995.

Fromkin, David. *A Peace to End All Peace: The Fall of the Ottoman Empire and the Creation of the Modern Middle East.* New York: Henry Holt and Company, 1989.

Glubb, Sir John. *A Short History of the Arab Peoples.* New York: Dorset Press, 1969.

Gold, Dore. *Hatred's Kingdom: How Saudi Arabia Supports the New Global Terrorism.* Washington, D.C.: Regnery Publishing, 2003.

Goldberg, David J. *To the Promised Land: A History of Zionist Thought.* London: Penguin Books, 1996.

Goldschmidt, Jr., Arthur. *A Concise History of the Middle East.* 4th ed. Boulder, CO: Westview Press, 1991.

Goodwin, Jason. *Lords of the Horizons: A History of the Ottoman Empire.* New York: Henry Holt and Company, 1998.

Gorenberg, Gershom. *The End of Days: Fundamentalism and the Struggle for the Temple Mount.* New York: Oxford University Press, 2000.

Gunaratna, Rohan. *Inside Al Qaeda: Global Network of Terror.* New York: Columbia University Press, 2002.

Heer, Friedrich. *The Medieval World: Europe 1100–1350.* New York: Welcome Rain, 1998.

Herb, Michael. *All in the Family: Absolutism, Revolution, and Democracy in the Middle Eastern Monarchies*. Albany: State University of New York Press, 1999.

Heydemann, Steven, ed. *War, Institutions and Social Change in the Middle East*. Berkeley: University of California Press, 2000.

Hippler, Jochen and Andrea Lueg, eds. *The Next Threat: Western Perceptions of Islam*. Translated by Laila Friese. London: Pluto Press, 1995.

Hitti, Philip K. *The Arabs: A Short History*. Princeton: Princeton University Press, 1943.

———. *History of the Arabs: From Earliest Times to the Present*. 10th ed. New York: Palgrave, 2002.

Hodgson, Marshall G.S. *The Venture of Islam: Conscience and History of a World Civilization; The Classical Age of Islam*. Chicago: University of Chicago Press, 1974.

———. *The Venture of Islam: Conscience and History of a World Civilization; The Expansion of Islam in the Middle Periods*. Chicago: University of Chicago Press, 1974.

———. *The Venture of Islam: Conscience and History of a World Civilization; The Gunpowder Empires and Modern Times*. Chicago: University of Chicago Press, 1974.

Hosking, Geoffrey. *Russia and the Russians: A History*. Cambridge, MA: Belknap Press of Harvard University Press, 2001.

Hourani, Albert. *A History of the Arab Peoples*. New York: Warner Books, 1992.

———, ed., et al. *The Modern Middle East: A Reader*. Berkeley: University of California Press, 1993.

Hoyland, Robert G. *Arabia and the Arabs: From the Bronze Age to the Coming of Islam*. New York: Routledge, 2001.

———. "The Rise of Islam." In *The Oxford History of Byzantium*. Cyril Mango, editor. New York: Oxford University Press, 2002.

Hudson, Michael C., ed. *Middle East Dilemma: The Politics and Economics of Arab Integration*. New York: Columbia University Press, 1999.

Humphries, R. Stephen. *Between Memory and Desire: The Middle East in a Troubled Age*. Berkeley: University of California Press, 1999.

Huntington, Samuel P. *The Clash of Civilizations and the Remaking of World Order*. New York: Simon & Schuster, 1996.

Inalcik, Halil. *The Ottoman Empire: The Classical Age 1300–1600*. London: Phoenix Press, 2000.

Itzkowitz, Norman. *Ottoman Empire and Islamic Tradition*. Chicago: University of Chicago Press, 1972.

James, E. O. *The Ancient Gods*. London: Phoenix Giant, 1999.

Kamrava, Mehran. *Democracy in the Balance: Culture and Society in the Middle East*. New York: Chatham House Publishers, Seven Bridges Press, 1998.

Kaplan, Robert D. *The Arabists: The Romance of an American Elite*. New York: The Free Press, 1995.

———. *Balkan Ghosts: A Journey Through History*. New York: Vintage Books, 1994.

———. *The Coming Anarchy: Shattering the Dreams of the Post-Cold War*. New York: Vintage Books, 2001.

———. *Eastward to Tartary: Travels in the Balkans, the Middle East, and the Caucasus*. New York: Vintage Books, 2000.

———. *The Ends of the Earth: From Togo to Turkmenistan, From Iran to Cambodia; A Journey to the Frontiers of Anarchy*. New York: Vintage Books, 1997.

———. *Warrior Politics: Why Leadership Demands a Pagan Ethos*. New York: Random House, 2001.

Karsh, Efraim and Inari Karsh. *Empires of the Sand: The Struggle for Mastery in the Middle East 1789–1923*. Cambridge, MA: Harvard University Press, 1999.

Kepel, Gilles. *The Revenge of God: The Resurgence of Islam, Christianity and Judaism in the Modern World*. Translated by Alan Braley. University Park, PA: Pennsylvania State University Press, 1994.

Kimmerling, Baruch and Joel S. Migdal. *Palestinians: The Making of a People*. 2nd ed. Cambridge, MA: Harvard University Press, 1994.

Kissenger, Henry A. *Diplomacy*. New York: Simon & Schuster, 1994.

Klare, Michael T. *Resource Wars: The New Landscape of Global Conflict*. New York: Metropolitan Books, 2001.

Kramer, Martin. *Ivory Towers on Sand: The Failure of Middle Eastern Studies in America*. Washington, D.C.: The Washington Institute for Near East Policy, 2001.

Lamb, David. *The Arabs: Journeys Beyond the Mirage.* New York: Random House, 1987.

Lewis, Bernard. *The Arabs in History.* 6th ed. New York: Oxford University Press, 1993. First published in 1947.

———. *The Crisis of Islam: Holy War and Unholy Terror.* New York: The Modern Library, 2003.

———. *Islam in History: Ideas, People and Events in the Middle East.* 2nd ed. Chicago: Open Court, 2001.

———. *A Middle East Mosaic: Fragments of Life, Letters and History.* New York: The Modern Library, 2000.

———. *The Middle East: A Brief History of the Last 2,000 Years.* New York: Touchstone Books, 1995.

———. *The Muslim Discovery of Europe.* 2nd ed. New York: W.W. Norton & Company, 2001.

———. *What Went Wrong? Western Impact and Middle Eastern Response.* New York: Oxford University Press, 2001.

Lings, Martin. *Muhammad: His Life Based on the Earliest Sources.* Rochester, VT: Inner Traditions International, 1983.

Madelung, Wilfred. *The Succession to Muhammad: A Study of the Early Caliphate.* Cambridge: Cambridge University Press, 1997.

Mango, Cyril, ed. *The Oxford History of Byzantium.* New York: Oxford University Press, 2002.

Masud, Muhammad Khalil, Brinkley Messick, and David S. Powers. *Islamic Legal Interpretation: Muftis and Their Fatwas.* Cambridge, MA: Harvard University Press, 1996.

Mattern, Susan P. *Rome and the Enemy: Imperial Strategy in the Principate.* Berkeley: University of California Press, 1999.

Meyer, Karl E. and Shareen Blair Brysac. *Tournament of Shadows: The Great Game and the Race for Empire in Central Asia.* Washington, D.C.: Counterpoint, 1999.

Miller, J. Maxwell, and John H. Hayes. *A History of Ancient Israel and Judah.* Philadelphia: The Westminster Press, 1986.

Mishal, Shaul and Avraham Sela. *The Palestinian Hamas: Vision, Violence and Coexistence.* New York: Columbia University Press, 2000.

Morris, Benny. *Righteous Victims: A History of the Zionist-Arab Conflict, 1881–2001.* New York: Vintage Books, 2001.

Munson, Jr., Henry. *Islam and Revolution in the Middle East.* New Haven: Yale University Press, 1988.

Murata, Sachiko and William C. Chittick. *The Vision of Islam.* New York: Paragon House, 1994.

Nakash, Yitzhak. *The Shi'is of Iraq.* Princeton: Princeton University Press, 1994.

Newby, P.H. *Saladin in His Time.* 2nd ed. London: Phoenix Press, 2001.

Palmer, Alan. *The Decline & Fall of the Ottoman Empire.* New York: Barnes & Noble Books, 1995.

Patai, Raphael. *The Arab Mind.* New York: Scribner, 1973.

Pillar, Paul R. *Terrorism and U.S. Foreign Policy.* Washington D.C.: The Brookings Institution, 2001.

Pipes, Daniel. *The Hidden Hand: Middle East Fears of Conspiracy.* New York: St. Martin's Press, 1996.

Piscatori, James, ed. *Islamic Fundamentalisms and the Gulf Crisis.* The Fundamentalism Project. Chicago: The American Academy of Arts and Sciences, 1991.

Rahman, Fazlur. *Islam.* 2nd ed. Chicago: University of Chicago Press, 1979.

———. *Major Themes of the Qur'an.* 2nd ed. Minneapolis: Bibliotheca Islamica, 1994.

Rashid, Ahmed. *Taliban: Militant Islam, Oil and Fundamentalism in Central Asia.* New Haven: Yale University Press, 2000.

Regan, Geoffrey. *Israel and the Arabs.* Cambridge: Cambridge University Press, 1990.

Robinson, Glenn E. *Building a Palestinian State: The Incomplete Revolution.* Bloomington, IN: Indiana University Press, 1997.

Roux, Georges. *Ancient Iraq.* London: Penguin Books, 1992.

Roy, Olivier. *The Failure of Political Islam.* Translated by Carol Volk. Cambridge, MA: Harvard University Press, 1994.

Rubin, Barry. *The Tragedy of the Middle East.* Cambridge: Cambridge University Press, 2002.

Said, Edward W. *The End of the Peace Process: Oslo and After.* 2nd ed. New York: Vintage Books, 2001.

———. *Orientalism.* New York: Vintage Books, 1978.

Schacht, Joseph. *An Introduction to Islamic Law.* New York: Oxford University Press, 1982.

Segev, Tom. *One Palestine, Complete: Jews and Arabs under the British Mandate*. Translated by Haim Watzman. New York: Metropolitan Books, 2000.

Shadid, Anthony. *Legacy of the Prophet: Despots, Democrats, and the New Politics of Islam*. Boulder, CO: Westview Press, 2001.

Shlaim, Avi. *The Iron Wall: Israel and the Arab World*. New York: W.W. Norton & Company, 2000.

Takeyh, Ray. "The Rogue Who Came in from the Cold." *Foreign Affairs*, May/June 2001): 62–72.

Tamimi, Azzam, ed. *Power-Sharing Islam?* London: Liberty for Muslim World Publications, 1993.

Telhami, Shibley and Michael Barnett, eds. *Identity and Foreign Policy in the Middle East*. Ithaca: Cornell University Press, 2002.

Thompson, Elizabeth. "The Climax and Crisis of the Colonial Welfare State in Syria and Lebanon during World War II." In *War, Institutions, and Social Change in the Modern Middle East*. Steven Heydemann, editor. Berkeley: University of California Press, 2000.

Tibi, Bassam. *The Challenge of Fundamentalism: Political Islam and the New World Disorder*. Berkeley: University of California Press, 1998.

Varisco, Daniel Martin. *Medieval Agriculture and Islamic Science: The Almanac of a Yemeni Sultan*. Seattle: University of Washington Press, 1994.

Voll, John Obert. *Islam: Continuity and Change in the Modern World*. Syracuse: Syracuse University Press, 1994.

Von Denffer, Ahmad. *'Ulum Al-Qur'an: An Introduction to the Sciences of the Qur'an*. 3rd ed. Liecester, UK: The Islamic Foundation, 1994.

Von Grunebaum, G.E. *Classical Islam: A History 600–1258*. Translated by Katherine Watson. New York: Barnes & Noble Books, 1970.

Watt, W. Montgomery and Richard Bell. *Introduction to the Qur'an*. 2nd ed. Edinburgh: Edinburgh University Press, 1977.

Weiss, Bernard G. *The Spirit of Islamic Law*. The Spirit of the Laws. Alan Watson, ed. Athens, GA: University of Georgia Press, 1998.

Williams, John Alden. *The Word of Islam.* Austin: University of
Texas Press, 1994.

Wistrich, Robert S. "The Old-New Anti-Semitism." *The National
Interest.* Number 72, Summer 2003.

Yergin, Daniel. *The Prize: The Epic Quest for Oil, Money & Power.*
New York: Simon & Schuster, 1991.

Zakaria, Fareed. *The Future of Freedom: Illiberal Democracy at
Home and Abroad.* New York: W.W. Norton & Company,
2003.

Zakaria, Rafiq. *The Struggle Within Islam: The Conflict Between
Religion and Politics.* Middlesex: Penguin Books, 1989.

Index

Ottoman-Rashidi alliance, 165
overcoat (*binish*), Egyptian, *159*

Palestine
    after World War I (1920–1947),
        181–185, 187
    early inhabitants, 13–14
    Hamas, 231
    intifada (1980s uprising), 215–216
    Islamic conquest, 35, 37
    Israeli-Palestinian conflict,
        201–202, 205–206, 208–209,
        211, 213, 215–216
    Jewish-Palestinian conflict,
        166–169
    struggle for peace, 250–253
Palestinian Arab Party, 184
Palestinian Authority (PA), 237, 252
Palestinian Liberation Organization
        (PLO), 208, 211, 213, 235, 237
Palmyerens, 10
Palmyra, 12–13
Pan Am Flight 103, 231
Pantelleria, 78
Paris Peace Accords, 174–175, 191
pastoralism, 5
Peel Commission Report, 185, 187
Pentagon, 238–239
people. *see also specific groups;*
        specific tribes
    ancient origins, 3–6
    Northern Arabia and Syria, 9–10,
        12–14
    South-Central Arabia, 7–9
persecution/discrimination
    Arab nationalists, 181
    Christians, 35, 52
    Jews, 35, 52, 80, 183
    Jews in Europe, 167
    Jews in Palestine, 181, 182
    Mu'atezila, 58
    Muslims, 79
    Shi'a, 55, 58
Persia, 35
Persian Barmakids, 56–57
Persian Buyids. *see* Buyid Empire

Persian Empire, 8–9, 13, 35, 60
Persian Gulf Emirates, 165–166, 229
Persian Gulf War, 234–235
Persian Shi'a Ziyarids, 60
Petra, 12
Philistines, 14
philosophy, 122–124
Pliny, 14
political parties, 184, 191, 193–194,
        208, 223
Popular Front for the Liberation of
        Palestine (PFLP), 211
population
    growth, 220
    Palestine in 1881, 166
Porte de Elvira in Granada, *87*
Portuguese fortress El-Jadida,
        144, 145
printing press, 150
prohibition on innovation, 150

Qader/Qaderite Arabs, 5–6
Qahtan tribe, 52
qanun (man-made law), 71
Qarmatians, 59
Qataban, 7
Qays tribe, 52, 53
Qibya, 202, 205
qiyas (analogy), 70
Quran, 41–42, 50, 57, 121, 122
Quraysh tribe, 23, 25, 26, 27, 29, 30
Qusta ibn Luqa al-Ba'labakki, 118
Qutb, Sayid, 226

Rabin, Yitzhak, 235, 237
Rashidi Emirate, 165, 166
Reagan, Ronald, 235
religion. *see also* Islam
    and Abdulmejid's Imperial
        Rescript, 163–164
    Byzantine influence, 66–67
    Christianity, 8, 18, 19, 79, 140
    hanifs, 18
    Judaism, 8, 18
    Manicheanism, 56
    Maronite Christians, 180

Suleyman I (Suleyman the
    Magnificent), 133, 135, 138
Sumerians, 3, 4
Sunna ("way of the Prophet"), 69–70
Sunnis, 55, 57, 59, 91
Sykes-Picot Agreement, 174
Syria, 35, 37, 193, 205, 208, 211, 213,
    215, 228. *see also* Palmyra
Syrian Arab Congress, 179
Syrians, 9

Tahir, 58
Talaat Bey, 171
Talha ibn Ubaydullah, 41, 42
Talib, Abu, 26
Taliban movement, 238, 239
Tanzimat Era, 163–164
Tarif, 80
Tariq ibn Ziyad, 80
Tawfiq Pasha, 160
Tayma, oasis of, 9
Tekish, Ala al-Din, 104
terrorism, 211, 231, 259, 260
Thabit ibn Qurra, 118
Thamud tribe, 10
"Third Universal Alternative,
    The," 231
Tiglath-pileser III, 5
Tigris-Euphrates region, 3
Tinmel Mosque, *141*
tomb of Sultan Hasan, *155*
tombs from the Mamluk period in
    Cairo, *107*
trade
    British, 161
    Buyid Empire, 92
    commodities, 112
    Dilmun, 4
    and economy, 219
    Egyptian, 161
    European, 149–150
    international, 149–150
    intra-Arabian, 19
    Nabataean, 12
    Ottoman Empire, 149–150

Sa'did, 140
Umayyad, 82–83
trade routes, 8, 14, 27, 115
Trajan, 14
Treaty of Amasya, 135
Treaty of Carlowitz, 147, 149
Treaty of Dara, 15
tribal confederations, 9–10
tribal customs, 15, 17–19
Tulun, 59
Tulunid dynasty, 59, 60
Tunisia, 196, 216, 226–227, *227*
Turkic military class, 97–98
Turki ibn Abdullah, 164

Ubayd Allah, 77
Umar al-Khayyam, 118
Umar ibn Abd al-Aziz. *see* Umar II
Umar ibn al-Khattab, 26, 32, 33, 35,
    40–41
Umar II, 50, 52
Umar Suhravardi, 104
Umayyad mosque, *46*
Umayyads, 45, 47–50, 52–53, 73,
    82–83
umma, 27, 29
United Arab Republic, 194
United Nations, 252
United States
    and al-Qaeda, 238–239
    in the Arab world, 253, 255, 257,
        259–260, 262
    Bush Administration (1st), 234, 235
    Bush Administration (2nd), 239,
        252, 262
    Camp David Peace Accords, 213
    Clinton Administration, 237
    commercial presence, 255
    and Egypt's War of Attrition, 211
    foreign policy, 211
    and Hizbullah, 215
    Iraqi invasion, 239, 257, 259
    Islamic monarchies, 229
    and Israeli-Palestinian conflict,
        206, 208

Illustrated Histories from Hippocrene Books

Each of these volumes depicts the entire history of a region or people, from earliest times to the present. Fifty handsome black-and-white illustrations, maps, and photographs complement each book. Written in an accessible, engaging style, they are ideal for students, inquisitive travelers, and anyone interested in the heritage of a particular nation or people!

CITIES

Cracow: An Illustrated History
Zdislaw Zygulski, Jr.
160 pages • 5 x 7 • 60 photos/illus./maps • ISBN 0-7818-0837-5 • $12.95pb • (154)

London: An Illustrated History
Robert Chester & Nicholas Awde
224 pages • 5 x 7 • 360 b/w photos/illus./maps • ISBN 0-7818-0908-8 • $12.95pb • (300)

Moscow: An Illustrated History
Kathleen Berton Murrell
250 pages • 5 x 7 • 50 b/w photos/illus./maps • ISBN 0-7818-0945-2 • $14.95pb • (419)

Paris: An Illustrated History
Elaine Mokhtefi
182 pages • 5 x 7 • 50 b/w photos/illus./maps • ISBN 0-7818-0838-3 • $12.95pb • (136)

CIVILIZATIONS

The Arab World: An Illustrated History
Kirk Sowell
200 pages • 5½ x 8½ • 50 b/w photos/illus./maps • ISBN 0-7818-0990-8 • $14.95pb • (465)

The Celtic World: An Illustrated History
Patrick Lavin
185 pages • 5 x 7 • 50 b/w photos/illus./maps • ISBN 0-7818-1005-1 • $12.95pb • (478)

COUNTRIES

China: An Illustrated History
Yong Ho
142 pages • 5 x 7 • 50 b/w photos/illus./maps • ISBN 0-7818-0821-9 • $14.95hc • (542)

Egypt: An Illustrated History
Fred James Hill
160 pages • 5 x 7 • 65 b/w photos/illus./maps • ISBN 0-7818-0911-8 • $12.95pb • (311)

England: An Illustrated History
Henry Weisser
166 pages • 5 x 7 • 50 b/w photos/illus./maps • ISBN 0-7818-0751-4 • $11.95hc • (446)

France: An Illustrated History
Lisa Neal
150 pages • 5 x 7 • 50 b/w photos/illus./maps • ISBN 0-7818-0835-9 • $14.95hc • (105)
150 pages • 5 x 7 • 50 b/w photos/illus./maps • ISBN 0-7818-0872-3 • $12.95pb • (340)

Greece: An Illustrated History
Tom Stone
180 pages • 5 x 7 • 50 b/w photos/illus./maps • ISBN 0-7818-0755-7 • $14.95hc • (557)

India: An Illustrated History
Prem Kishore & Anuradha Kishore Ganpati
224 pages • 5 x 7 • 50 b/w photos/illus./maps • ISBN 0-7818-0944-4 • $14.95pb • (424)

Ireland: An Illustrated History
Henry Weisser
166 pages • 5 x 7 • 50 b/w photos/illus./maps • ISBN 0-7818-0693-3 • $11.95hc • (782)

Israel: An Illustrated History
David C. Gross
160 pages • 5 x 7 • 50 b/w photos/illus./maps • ISBN 0-7818-0756-5 • $11.95hc • (24)

Italy: An Illustrated History
Joseph F. Privitera
142 pages • 5 x 7 • 50 b/w photos/illus./maps • ISBN 0-7818-0819-7 • $14.95hc • (436)

Japan: An Illustrated History
Shelton Woods
200 pages • 5 x 7 • 50 b/w photos/illus./maps • ISBN 0-7818-0989-4 • $14.95pb • (469)

Korea: An Illustrated History from Ancient Times to 1945
David Rees
154 pages • 5 x 7 • 50 b/w photos/illus./maps • ISBN 0-7818-0873-1 • $12.95pb • (354)

Mexico: An Illustrated History
Michael Burke
180 pages • 5 x 7 • 50 b/w photos/illus./maps • ISBN 0-7818-0690-9 • $11.95hc • (585)

Poland: An Illustrated History
Iwo Cyprian Pogonowski
272 pages • 5 x 7 • 50 b/w photos/illus./maps • ISBN 0-7818-0757-3 • $16.95hc • (404)

Poland in World War II: An Illustrated Military History
Andrew Hempel
120 pages • 5 x 7 • 50 b/w photos/illus./maps • ISBN 0-7818-0758-1 • $11.95hc • (541)
120 pages • 5 x 7 • 50 b/w photos/illus./maps • ISBN 0-7818-1004-3 • $9.95pb • (484)

Romania: An Illustrated History
Nicolae Klepper
298 pages • 5 x 7 • 50 b/w photos/illus./maps • ISBN 0-7818-0935-5 • $14.95pb • (366)

Russia: An Illustrated History
Joel Carmichael
252 pages • 5 x 7 • 50 b/w photos/illus./maps • ISBN 0-7818-0689-5 • $14.95hc • (781)

Sicily: An Illustrated History
Joseph F. Privitera
152 pages • 5 x 7 • 50 b/w photos/illus./maps • ISBN 0-7818-0909-6 • $12.95pb • (301)

Spain: An Illustrated History
Fred James Hill
176 pages • 5 x 7 • 50 b/w photos/illus./maps • ISBN 0-7818-0874-X • $12.95pb • (339)

Tikal: An Illustrated History of the Ancient Maya Capital
John Montgomery
274 pages • 6 x 9 • 50 b/w photos/illus./maps • ISBN 0-7818-0853-7 • $14.95pb • (101)

Vietnam: An Illustrated History
Shelton Woods
172 pages • 5 x 7 • 50 b/w photos/illus./maps • ISBN 0-7818-0910-X • $14.95pb • (302)

Wales: An Illustrated History
Henry Weisser
228 pages • 5 x 7 • 50 b/w photos/illus./maps • ISBN 0-7818-0936-3 • $12.95pb • (418)

STATES

Arizona: An Illustrated History
Patrick Lavin
250 pages • 5 x 7 • 65 b/w photos/illus./maps • ISBN 0-7818-0852-9 • $14.95pb • (102)

Also available from Hippocrene Books

A History of the Islamic World
Fred James Hill & Nicholas Awde

". . . a useful introduction to a complex and largely foreign
subject . . . each chapter eschews controversy for consensus, maintaining an even-handedness that quickly
earns the reader's trust."
—*Publisher's Weekly*

224 pages • 5½ x 8½ • 65 b/w photos/illus./maps • ISBN 0-7818-1015-9 • $22.50hc • (545)

Prices subject to change without prior notice.

To order **Hippocrene Books**, contact your local bookstore, call (718)
454-2366, or write to: Hippocrene Books, 171 Madison Avenue, New York,
NY 10016. Please enclose check or money order adding $5.00 shipping (UPS)
for the first book and $.50 for each additional title.